My Face Is Black
Is True

My Face Is Black Is True

Callie House and the Struggle for Ex-Slave Reparations

MARY FRANCES BERRY

Alfred A. Knopf   New York   2005

THIS IS A BORZOI BOOK
PUBLISHED BY ALFRED A. KNOPF

Copyright © 2005 by Mary Frances Berry
All rights reserved. Published in the United States
by Alfred A. Knopf, a division of Random House, Inc.,
New York, and in Canada by Random House
of Canada, Limited, Toronto.
www.aaknopf.com

Knopf, Borzoi Books, and the colophon are registered trademarks of
Random House, Inc.

Library of Congress Catalogue-in-Publication Data

Berry, Mary Frances.
My face is black is true : Callie House and the struggle for ex-slave
reparations / Mary Frances Berry.—1st ed.
p. cm.
Includes bibliographical references and index.
ISBN 1-4000-4003-5 (alk. paper)
1. House, Callie, 1861–1928.   2. African American women political
activists—Biography.   3. Women political activists—United
States—Biography.   4. African Americans—Reparations.   I. Title.

E185.97.H825B47 2005
323'.092—dc22
[B]   2004051330

Manufactured in the United States of America
Published September 8, 2005
Second Printing, October 2005

For Mindy

CONTENTS

Prologue 3

1 We Need a Movement 6

2 Organizing the National Ex-Slave Mutual Relief,
Bounty and Pension Association 50

3 The Association Under Attack 81

4 Voices of the Ex-Slaves 93

5 The Movement Fights Back 122

6 Avoiding Destruction 142

7 The Association Goes to Federal Court 171

8 Jailed for Justice 188

9 Passing the Torch 212

Epilogue: The Reparations Movement
Still Lives 230

Notes 253

ILLUSTRATIONS

9 Union soldiers with "contraband" *(Prints and
Photographs Department, Moorland-Spingarn
Research Center, Howard University)*

13 Sunday morning in the Virginia pines *(Prints
and Photographs Department, Moorland-Spingarn
Research Center, Howard University)*

16 Preparing for school *(Prints and Photographs
Department, Moorland-Spingarn Research Center,
Howard University)*

17 A New England ma'am holds primary classes in
Mississippi *(Prints and Photographs Department,
Moorland-Spingarn Research Center, Howard
University)*

23 Canvassing for votes *(Prints and Photographs
Department, Moorland-Spingarn Research Center,
Howard University)*

25 A political discussion *(Prints and Photographs
Department, Moorland-Spingarn Research Center,
Howard University)*

31 The Negro exodus *(Prints and Photographs Department, Moorland-Spingarn Research Center, Howard
University)*

35 Walter R. Vaughan *(Prints and Photographs Department, Moorland-Spingarn Research Center, Howard
University)*

Illustrations

36   Cover of the book Freedmen's Pension Bill: A Plea for American Freedman *(Prints and Photographs Department, Moorland-Spingarn Research Center, Howard University)*

38   Frederick Douglass *(Prints and Photographs Division, Library of Congress)*

40, 41   John Mercer Langston, Thomas E. Miller, and H. P. Cheatham *(Prints and Photographs Department, Moorland-Spingarn Research Center, Howard University)*

45   Isaiah Dickerson *(Department of the Interior, Bureau of Pensions, National Archives)*

53   Woman washing clothes *(Hargrett Rare Book & Manuscript Library, University of Georgia Libraries)*

57   African-American children and William Harding Jackson, Jr. *(The Collection of Carl and Otto Giers/Tennessee State Library and Archives)*

62, 63   Two signed ex-slave petitions *(Department of the Interior, Bureau of Pensions, National Archives)*

71   Notice of the Ex-Slave Association 1898 convention *(Department of the Interior, Bureau of Pensions, National Archives)*

74   Reverend Dudley McNairy *(Department of the Interior, Bureau of Pensions, National Archives)*

76   Early certificate of the Ex-Slave Association *(Department of the Interior, Bureau of Pensions, National Archives)*

77, 78   Legal documents from the Ex-Slave Association *(Department of the Interior, Bureau of Pensions, National Archives)*

Illustrations

99 Slaves driven South by the rebel officers *(Prints and Photographs Department, Moorland-Spingarn Research Center, Howard University)*

103 Freedpeople eating corn cake and soured milk *(Prints and Photographs Department, Moorland-Spingarn Research Center, Howard University)*

110 Old master and old man *(Prints and Photographs Department, Moorland-Spingarn Research Center, Howard University)*

112, 113 Squire Smith, Boone County ex-slave and an unidentified Boone County ex-slave *(Harris Family photographs, 1880s–1960s, Western Historical Manuscript Collection, Columbia, Missouri)*

114 Richard and Drucilla Martin *(WPA Slave Narratives, American Memory, Library of Congress)*

115 Ex-slaves *(Prints and Photographs Department, Moorland-Spingarn Research Center, Howard University)*

130 Senator Jacob Gallinger *(Prints and Photographs Division, Library of Congress)*

153 Henry Clay Evans *(Prints and Photographs Department, Moorland-Spingarn Research Center, Howard University)*

153 Ell Torrance *(Prints and Photographs Division, Library of Congress)*

160 James Tyner (The Story of Our Post Office *by Marshall Henry Cushing* [Boston: A.M. Thayer, 1893] *page 626*)

164 Certificate of mutual assistance work of the Association chapters *(Department of the Interior, Bureau of Pensions, National Archives)*

xi

Illustrations

175   Cornelius Jones *(Prints and Photographs Department, Moorland-Spingarn Research Center, Howard University)*

175   Calvin Chase (Men of Mark, Eminent, Progressive, Rising *by William Simmons [Cleveland: George M. Rewell & Co., 1887] page 120)*

177   Rolling cotton *(Prints and Photographs Department, Moorland-Spingarn Research Center, Howard University)*

193   The official badge of the Ex-Slave Association *(Cowan's Historic American Auctions)*

205   The Jefferson City, Missouri, Penitentiary Women's Wing *(Mark Schreiber, Associate Superintendent, Missouri State Penitentiary)*

207   Emma Goldman *(Prints and Photographs Division, Library of Congress)*

219-222   Sarah Graves, Edgar and Minerva Bendy, Tiney Shaw, and Molly Ammond *(WPA Slave Narratives, American Memory, Library of Congress)*

223   The Atlanta chapter that continued to work after House's jailing (The Constitution, *Atlanta, Georgia*)

232   Marcus Garvey *(Prints and Photographs Division, Library of Congress)*

238   Queen Mother Moore *(Brian Lanker, 1988)*

241   Christopher Alston and the organizers of a sit-down strike *(Walter Reuther Archives, Wayne State University)*

250   Flyer for Millions for Reparations march *(Dr. Conrad Worrill, cochairman of the march)*

ACKNOWLEDGMENTS

This book has existed in my mind since I first found some of the materials with the help of the late Detroit activist Christopher Alston and the late Sara Dunlap Jackson of the National Archives, who first taught me how to negotiate the collections. Walter Hill at the Archives began where Sara left off. Rodney Ross of the Archives Legislative Center and the entire staff in the Manuscript Division have tolerated more of my ever more detailed inquiries about the records of the Pension Bureau and the Post Office Department than anyone should have to bear. Also in Washington, at Howard University's Moorland-Spingarn Collection, Joellen Bashir and Donna Wells never tired of helping me track down a person or a photograph. Staff at the Postal Library and Archives in Washington, the National Archives Photographs and Films Division, and the Library of Congress Photographs and Film Division patiently helped me find what was available.

At the Historical Research Room at the Linebaugh Public Library in Murfreesboro, Tennessee, Donna Jordan, the overworked one-person staff member, let me wander freely through the records. Carol Kaplan at the Nashville Public Library, and Karina McDaniel and Marilyn Hughes at the Tennessee State Library and Archives aided in documenting the social context. Deborah O. Cox at the Nashville Metropolitan Government Archives assisted in tracking down materials in her collection and anywhere else she thought they might be found. Joe Daugherty McClure, law librarian for the Sixth Circuit Court of Appeals Nashville Library helped to confirm the composition of the jury in the absence of a trial transcript.

Tom Miller, Manuscript Specialist at the Western Historical Collection, Ellis Library, University of Missouri-Columbia, and Arvah Strickland Professor Emeritus of History at the University of Missouri-Columbia aided in deciphering the Boone county records. The staff at the New Orleans Public library, Louisiana Division, who have sustained me for years as I work on other projects, and at the New Orleans Notarial Archives helped track down several members of the New Orleans chapter.

Historians John Egerton, Genna Rae McNeil, Barbara Savage, Carroll Smith Rosenberg, Steven Hahn, and Rebecca Scott gave valuable advice. Melinda Chateauvert helped me think more critically about social movement theory. Deadria Farmer-Paellmann of the Restitution Study Group, and Attorney Willie Gary shared useful information concerning the present-day reparations movement. Jacqueline Ridly Jennings, Robert Natalini, and Luther Adams assisted with the research, and Maida Odom contributed a number of good ideas. John Hope Franklin assured me that the Ex-Slave Pension Movement was virtually unknown, even among historians, which led me to actually sit down and write the book.

My editor Victoria Wilson and my agent Charlotte Sheedy recognized the importance of this book to the history of the late-nineteenth-century United States. Thanks to Krishna Toolsie, who, as always, helped me find time to write, and Zachary Wagman, who kept us on track. Mindy graciously shared her ideas, companionship, and encouragement.

Mary Frances Berry
Washington, DC.

My Face Is Black
Is True

Prologue

WHEN I WAS TWELVE, I became an outlaw, a transgressor of racial boundaries. That summer I did the ironing while taking care of the Abbotts' infant boy. They lived in an all-white well-off Nashville neighborhood founded as a streetcar suburb in the late nineteenth century. On a July afternoon when Mrs. Abbott came home, I showed her a phonograph record I had taken from the shelf and played while I worked. Excitedly, I told her how I just loved the music, but the more I talked, the more agitated she became. Suddenly she snatched the record from my hands and practically exploded. "You had no business touching those records, and you shouldn't be listening to such music in the first place." I told her I was sorry, but she still seemed angry. I knew I had misbehaved terribly, but I did not understand how or why listening to that music was wrong.

I did not tell my mother, but when I finally told my Aunt Serriner, she worried aloud that I might become labeled a troublemaker. "Gal," she said, "don't be getting out of your place, stay out of those white folks' things." I stayed out of "white folks' things" thereafter, or at least kept silent when I did not. However, the episode forever clouded my pleasure upon discovering Beethoven and his Symphony Number Nine.

Callie House did not stay out of "white folks' things" either.

She was also a racial outlaw. An African-American laundress from Tennessee, she became the leader of a turn-of-the-twentieth-century poor people's movement that sought pensions from the federal government as compensation for slavery. Her movement, federal officials concluded, "is setting the negroes wild." They thought that if they did not stop her, when African Americans understood that the government would never grant pensions, the nation would "have some very serious questions to settle in connection with the control of the race." Consequently, the government harassed Callie House for exercising her constitutional right to petition the government and to mobilize others in the cause. When she would not relent, calling her "defiant," the Post Office Department and the Pension Bureau redoubled their efforts to smear and confine her. Her organization was the first mass reparations movement led by African Americans.[1]

Callie House and the ex-slave movement did not accept the preachments or adopt the meek attitudes that Booker T. Washington counseled at the time. Today, some people argue against reparations because those who experienced slavery are no longer among the living. It is worth remembering that thousands of ex-slaves devoted years to pressing the reparations cause. They organized support networks and helped one another through very difficult times. That they bore the marks of bondage, as living ex-slaves, did not help them. Whites and elite African Americans ridiculed their pleas for redress, and the government disrespected their claims.

The first homes I knew, the orphanage on Laurel Street and the house of my mother's eldest sister, Aunt Everleaner, where I lived in the 1940s, lay a few streets away from where Callie House resided until her death in 1928. There in South Nashville, down in the valley, looking up to the state capitol on the hill, we both became troublemakers. Commercial development has, for the most part, overtaken the neighborhood, erasing every vestige, every physical structure of that time and place. The address at which Callie House lived has long been occupied by a public housing unit. This book tells her story.

CHAPTER I

We Need a Movement

*We are organizing ourselves together as a race of people
who feels that they have been wronged.*

CALLIE HOUSE
(1899)

CALLIE HOUSE knew hard work. Born a slave, now a washerwoman and a widow with five children, she was at the bottom of America's social and economic ladder as she stood
proudly before a cheering crowd of African Americans. The
National Ex-Slave Mutual Relief, Bounty and Pension Association had just elected her its first and only female officer.
Addressing the convention delegates who had honored her
with their votes, she talked about the thousands of people she
had met on the road in the cause of compensation for slave
service. House spoke of organizing local branches and collecting petitions to submit to Congress. She told them of her long
hours spent "among strangers laboring to the best of my ability
for the rights which my race is justly entitled to." This woman
of modest means but great courage would soon become the
association's leader. For her work, she would be praised by poor
African Americans, ridiculed by the race's elites, and targeted

6

by high government officials, who feared her influence with the masses, and eventually land in jail. But on this November day in 1898, as she stood before supporters, newly elected assistant secretary of the nation's largest reparations movement, all things seemed possible.[1]

Callie House came to prominence in the period historian Rayford Logan labeled the nadir, the lowest point along the long, rough road African Americans had traveled since Emancipation. Women were legally barred from voting, and black men suffered disenfranchisement through subterfuge and violence. Booker T. Washington advised against political activism. But many like Mrs. House chose another course. By the early twentieth century, her organization, the National Ex-Slave Mutual Relief, Bounty and Pension Association, according to federal officials, would swell to about 300,000, determined black people petitioning a government that barely recognized their existence and demanding a law ordering reparations for slavery.[2]

Through cajoling and explaining, House inspired the old ex-slaves to exercise their rights as citizens to demand repayment for their long suffering. She urged them not to give up despite continued oppression and listened as they shared stories about their lives under slavery. Often in tears, aging and ailing men and women recalled being treated as less than human during their years of unpaid labor for masters who sexually abused slave women, broke families apart, and who had "the power to whip them to death."[3]

Although steeled for the effort to gain reparations, House and her cohorts were living in desperate times and still reeling from a bleak, awful past. House's life experiences made her intimately familiar with the plight of those she referred to as the "ignorant, bare footed and naked" among her fellow ex-slaves.

From family accounts, she was born into slavery in Rutherford County near Nashville, Tennessee, in 1861. (Her birth, like that of other slaves, was not officially recorded.) There, in a landscape of rolling hills, cereal and tobacco production, and horse farming, slave owners depended upon the labor of the approximately 13,000 blacks who constituted about 50 percent of the total population of the county.[4]

Whether slaves had masters who, as one Tennessee slave put it, "gave them rations and warm clothes to wear" or scraps and rags that did not cover their nakedness, their lives in bondage etched indelible memories of suffering and abuse. A collective consciousness born of brutal experience shaped the reactions of Callie's family and other slaves when freedom finally came. One Tennessee ex-slave remembered that on the plantation where she lived they could go to church, where they were admonished to obey their masters. She went to services "barefoot with a rag tied around her head and a dress that came up to her knees," which was all she had to wear. She also was "whipped with a bull whip" and was not ashamed to say, in old age, that she "still had scars on her back put there by the master." Another Tennessee ex-slave told of being sold away from her husband, whom she had never seen again. At the slave yard they told her to take off her clothes and roll down the hill so the prospective buyers "could see you had no bones broken or sores on you."[5]

The coming of the Civil War finally brought freedom but not an immediate response to the suffering. In 1862 and early 1863, when Callie House was a toddler, the Union Army swept through Tennessee, which had joined the Confederacy. In their wake the slaves made a mass move toward freedom. Her family was among the thousands of so-called contraband—slaves who either ran away or whose masters fled at the Union approach—

*When the Union soldiers came, slave men, women, and children,
called "contraband," followed along behind them. The women
did laundry and cooking for the soldiers; the men worked as
laborers, digging ditches and building fortifications. Congress
enacted a law in July 1861 endorsing their use. These men began
flooding into Fortress Monroe near Hampton, Virginia, when
the Union occupied it in May 1861. "Morning Mustering of
the 'Contrabands' at Fortress Monroe, on Their Way to
Their Day's Work,"* Harper's Weekly, *1861.*

in their wake. When the Union soldiers, whom the children
called "the Blue Men," came, slave men, women, and children
followed along behind them. The women did laundry and
cooking for the soldiers; the army gathered up the black men to
work as laborers, digging ditches and building fortifications.
Refugees slept where they could and ate what they could find.
Then the Union decided to recruit blacks as soldiers. Callie
House's father, Tom Guy, like many other freedmen, probably
joined the Union Army in the 29th U.S. Colored Infantry Reg-

iment. The unit served in the area at the Battle of Stones River at the end of 1862 and the beginning of 1863. In heavy fighting that the Union won, more than a third of the Union and Confederate troops were killed, wounded, or captured. In November and early December 1864, the 29th Regiment also helped repel the Confederate drive into Tennessee, ending at Franklin just south of Nashville. The fighting and the federal occupation devastated farms and communities in much of the surrounding area, including Rutherford County. The numbers of refugees—contraband—fleeing slavery increased to a torrent.[6]

House's family and other African Americans tried to gain and maintain their freedom without being demoralized by the uncertainty all around them. African-American mothers and fathers begged Union officials to help them regain their children and reunite their families. At the same time, some former slave owners tried to regain or retain African-American children as slaves, even after abolition had come, by taking them as apprentices without their parents' permission, or simply assaulting any parent who came to claim a child. A soldier stationed in Nashville in August 1865 begged his wife from Clarksville to join him. She did not want to leave before rescuing their daughter, who was still claimed by her former owner as a slave. The Freedmen's Bureau agent gave her an order for the child's release. The former slave owner complied, but as mother and child started down the road he overtook them and "beat her with a club and left her senseless on the ground after which he returned home with the child." The former slave owner was arrested by Bureau officials and fined $100 for having "maltreated" her. However, in the meantime her soldier husband thought she had forgotten him, and he "married" another woman. Bureau officials refused to help dissolve the new "marriage" because upon seeing that some of the children of his original wife were "mulattoes" and others were "black," they did not believe the soldier could have fathered all of them. The beleaguered mother was treated as a loose woman who could not be helped.[7]

The chaos and confusion, the elation over freedom, the struggle to survive, and the scars of their bondage shaped ex-slaves' thinking about the meaning of abolition. Freedom for Callie and other ex-slaves would have been very different if the Union had kept its promises to give them land confiscated from Confederate slaveholders. The reparations question could have been settled at once. For the ex-slaves, the promise of land was real, not just something they imagined or hoped for. General William Tecumseh Sherman made the promise when thousands of freed people followed the troops when he marched his army from Atlanta to the sea in 1864–1865, laying waste the Confederacy. Secretary of War Edwin Stanton heard reports that Sherman had been heartless and shown indifference to the poverty-stricken condition of the newly freed people. Stanton came to Savannah in January to meet with Sherman and talk to African-American leaders about their needs. Twenty blacks selected by Union authorities, deacons, and ministers, three quarters of whom had been slaves, came to the meeting and let national leaders know that land was their major priority. When asked how they could best support their families, their self-selected leader, sixty-seven-year-old Baptist minister Garrison Frazier from Granville, North Carolina, replied, "To have land and turn in and till it by our labor."[8]

With Stanton's support, Sherman approved the request. He issued Order Number 15 of January 16, 1865, designating the rich sea islands and plantation areas from Charleston to Jacksonville, thirty miles inland, for settlement by the freedmen. Each adult male could claim a forty-acre tract. The March 3,

1865, Freedmen's Bureau Act repeated the promise that each freedman would be assigned "not more than forty acres" of abandoned or confiscated land at rental for three years and an option to purchase at the end of that time with "such title thereto as the United States can convey." Word of the promise spread quickly among the ex-slaves.[9]

By June 1865, 40,000 freedmen had been settled on the coastal lands and were growing crops. The promise of forty acres and a mule seemed a reality. However, any hope that this policy would expand to the rest of the South proved to be an illusion. After President Abraham Lincoln was assassinated, President Andrew Johnson gutted the policy. He issued an amnesty proclamation on May 29, 1865, pardoning many rebels and restoring their lands to them. Abolitionists tried to stop the policy change, but to no avail. The government dashed the sea island freedmen's hopes after their hard work tilling land they thought was theirs. General Oliver Howard, who later founded Howard University, was ordered to either persuade or force blacks occupying the land under Sherman's orders to abandon their claims to their former owners and return to work for them as laborers. Incredulous, the freedmen cried out at the betrayal. The accusation: that the government would "make freedom a curse to us, for we have no home, no land, no oath, no vote, and consequently no country." Years later Wiley Childress and other aging ex-slaves recalled with still burning anger that "before Freedom the slaves were promised forty acres of land when freed but none ever got it." He had also never heard of anyone "getting money" for their labor from the government.[10]

Although the rumors of land distribution continued to spread among the freedpeople, the government failed to keep the promise in the sea islands, middle Tennessee, or anywhere

"Sunday Morning in the Virginia Pines," Harper's Weekly, *June
5, 1897. Freedpeople saw the ability to worship in their own way
as one of the essential differences between slavery and freedom.
The church was the meeting place for religious and social activities, including political action and the local ex-slave pension
chapters. These worshipers attended a rural church in Virginia.*

else in the South. House's family worked and scrimped to help
themselves with no government assistance. Members of Callie
House's family and other ex-slaves, such as ex-slave Ellis Ken
Hannon, "dun all kinds of jobs. Anything that came along," to
stay alive. By 1866, Reverend John Savary, an abolitionist trav-
eler in the South, reported the beginnings of the sharecropping
and crop lien system, which soon gained a stranglehold on the
freedpeople. He knew they would have great difficulty improv-
ing their status if they had no land and no capital: "They will
continue to work on from day to day, and from year to year,
without more than enough to keep soul and body together."[11]

In the confused, fluid atmosphere of war and Reconstruc-

tion, although poor and landless, the freedpeople in Rutherford County and elsewhere in the South worked together and
organized their own churches and schools. Before the war,
slaves had worshiped separately in white churches or independently in secret when they could escape the eyes of their masters. Free Negroes in the North had established the African
Methodist Episcopal (A.M.E.) Church. After the war, separate
black churches proliferated as African Americans sought to
exercise autonomy over their religious lives. They wanted to
have their own facilities and to hear from their own preachers,
who, though God had called them, had been prevented from
preaching freely during slavery. Now ex-slaves wanted to worship in their own way. They saw choice in the matter as one of
the essential differences between slavery and freedom. Beginning in contraband camps, in Rutherford County and elsewhere in the South, separate African-American denominations
soon appeared as southern and northern churches united. In
1867, Baptists organized the Consolidated American Baptist
Convention, which was absorbed by the National Baptist Convention in 1880. The representatives of three million members
met in Atlanta, Georgia, in 1895 and formed the National Baptist Convention of the United States. Southern Methodists
formed a new denomination in 1870, the Colored Methodist
Episcopal Church. As new denominations were formed, the
African Methodist Episcopal (A.M.E.) Church spread in the
South. Most of the congregations, especially rural ones, were
small and could rarely pay ministerial salaries. Consequently,
black ministers had to hold full-time nonministerial jobs, as
did House's brother and brother-in-law. Most also usually
served two or more churches.[12]

Despite their financial poverty, Callie and other freed children gained some primary school education. Northerners,

moved by the ex-slaves' plight, used private charitable resources to augment the freedpeople's own efforts to obtain an education, and philanthropic agencies sent "Yankee schoolmarms" to operate schools in the South. By 1869, seventy-nine northern aid societies supported African-American schools in the South. The Freedmen's Bureau, established in 1865, had spent more than $5 million on black education by 1871. By 1870, the bureau operated 4,239 schools with 9,300 teachers and almost a quarter-million pupils. By early 1865, there were eight teachers teaching five hundred black children in Murfreesboro, the Rutherford County seat, a pupil-teacher ratio of more than sixty to one.[13]

African Americans in House's community, like those elsewhere, so intensely desired education that they immediately began to teach one another. They believed there could be no real freedom without education. One Tennessee ex-slave recalled that "The white folks didn't want them to learn nothing." If they saw a slave pick up a piece of paper with writing on it, "they would yell put that down, you want to get into our business." Freedpeople built their own schools. Out of their meager resources, they purchased lots and raised money by subscription to pay for the materials to erect buildings, most of which had neither water nor lavatories on site. Blacks paid the salaries of northern white teachers, raised money for their board, boarded black teachers in their own homes, and paid tuition and fees at Freedmen's Bureau schools. The schools used a primer published by the American Tract Society that taught reading, Christian morality, and civic duty. In March 1867, the Tennessee legislature passed a public school law to support schools by a state property tax. The Freedmen's Bureau schools gradually came under the control of the state. But in 1869, the state repealed the law and left education to the counties.[14]

*The former slaves eagerly sought education. Women helped
establish schools and made sure children attended. Other children
are already on the way to school while these two are tardy.
"Preparing for School,"* Harper's Weekly, *November 2, 1872.*

Northern white teachers, like this one, took great risks to fill the gap when there were few black teachers to help educate the freed children and adults. By 1869, seventy-nine northern aid societies supported African-American schools in the South. "Primary School for Freedmen, in Charge of Mrs. Green, at Vicksburg, Mississippi, " Harper's Weekly, *June 23, 1866.*

Obtaining an education put Callie and other black students at considerable risk. While African Americans passionately desired education, some whites just as adamantly wanted to limit their opportunities. These whites understood that, for blacks, education could lead to empowerment. During the early years of Reconstruction, southern whites burned schools (thirty-seven in Tennessee in 1869) and insulted and abused white teachers of African Americans. Some southern whites feared that educated African Americans would undermine white supremacy and challenge entrenched beliefs about the genetic, physical, and mental superiority of whites over blacks. Education might also enable blacks to keep track of their wages, credits, and debts. In 1869, the Tennessee legislature decided that counties could, but did not have to, levy taxes to provide separate schools for blacks and whites. In 1872, the Freedmen's Bureau relinquished entire control and responsibility to the states and the counties. Education as a form of compensation for slavery was abandoned.[15]

Despite the state and county governments' neglect, until at least the early 1900s, African Americans in Rutherford County provided their own schools. They received little help from government at any level. African-American church congregations built structures to use for both education and religious services. During Callie's early years, the buildings were generally one room with a potbellied stove for heat. The teachers would sometimes cook a meal of soup or beans. In 1879, the state mandated a course in agriculture along with reading, writing, arithmetic, and civics. The school term was barely six months long. One teacher taught all grades using primers and large cards with simple religious wording. Students were of all ages, including adults who were learning to read and write for the first time.[16]

Because of the lack of resources and their poverty, African-American students often attended school for only short spurts between their hours of labor during the few months of the school term. The education they received was also problematic because of the skepticism of some northern teachers about the ability of their charges and the cultural differences between teachers and students. Local African-American teachers were always in short supply, if available at all. Many schools lacked room or teachers for the numbers of pupils who tried to attend. Churches established colleges to train African-American teachers, beginning with Fisk University in Nashville in the 1860s. Responding to the immediate need after the war, the Freedmen's Bureau created a number of short-term institutes to prepare basically trained teachers quickly. However, the state of Tennessee did not fund a college for African Americans until 1909.[17]

W. E. B. DuBois, born in 1868, taught in a rural Tennessee school in the early 1880s and described the schoolhouse as a log hut used to store corn, with a fireplace instead of a stove and benches made of rough planks without backs, no blackboards, and a great distance for the children to walk. But, he said, "I loved my school, and the fine faith the children had in the wisdom of their teacher was truly marvelous. We read and spelled together, wrote a little, picked flowers, and listened to stories of the world beyond the hill."[18]

When House became an advocate for pensions, she told ex-slaves that their right to ask for a compensation law was guaranteed by the government. She pointed out that "the Constitution of the United States grants to citizens the privilege of peaceably assembling themselves together and petition their grievance[s]." She had learned this lesson despite her very rudimentary schooling available in the Rutherford County schools. During Callie House's youth, African Americans in Tennessee wanted land, schooling, and religious freedom. But they also wanted to participate in electoral politics. Before the Civil War was over, blacks held conventions that pushed for abolition and the right to vote. The organizers were men who had been free before the war or freed in the military, some of whom were Baptist or A.M.E. ministers. In October 1864, 144 blacks from eighteen states, meeting in Syracuse, New York, in a National Convention of Colored Citizens of the United States, issued an address to the people of the United States, written by Frederick Douglass. They asserted, "We want the elective franchise in all the states now in the union, and the same in all such states as may come into the union hereafter. The position of that right is the keystone to the arch of human liberty; and without that the whole may at any moment fall to the ground; while, with it, that liberty may stand forever." The group also demanded abolition and lamented the abandonment of the promise of land to the freedpeople. They organized a National Equal Rights League to continue the work. Five delegates from Tennessee attended that convention.[19]

African Americans showed immediate interest in the right to vote and hold political office. In Louisiana, where the Union captured New Orleans in the summer of 1862, freedpeople of color organized early. By November 5, 1863, a meeting of free colored persons at Economy Hall demanded political rights for themselves but did not include the ex-slaves. Pinckney Benton Stewart Pinchback, a Union Army Louisiana Native Guard veteran, led the speakers.[20]

African-American conventions took place in most of the Confederate states during 1865. In January 1865, a Convention of Colored Men of Louisiana organized to discuss giving support to the National Equal Rights League. From a published attendance list of eighty-three names, some of the wealthiest and most prominent Afro-Creoles attended. Captain James Ingraham, a Louisiana Native Guard hero, was elected president. The local French-language newspaper that served the free colored community, *La Tribune,* trumpeted the solidarity between free and freed at the convention. However, the relationship between free people of color and new freedpeople remained uneasy. The New Orleans riots, along with the passage of Black Codes and Confederate resurgence in the other southern states, helped to elect the congressmen who passed the Reconstruction Act of March 1867, affirming African-American suffrage. Temporarily, at least the fissure between Afro-Creoles and freedmen seemed healed. In Louisiana, the Constitutional Convention established under the act, consisted of ninety-eight delegates, half white and half African American, six of whom were former Native Guards. They enshrined universal suffrage in the new Constitution.[21]

Since the Union defeat of the Confederacy came early in Tennessee in 1862, just as it had in New Orleans, blacks had some freedom to act politically before those elsewhere. Memphis and Nashville also had free Negro populations that could exercise leadership. In Nashville, beginning in 1863, demonstrations for freedom and political suffrage led by free-before-the-war literate blacks and ministers and veterans became common. In Nashville, these men, enacting the part of "political citizens," went to Union Party rallies. They campaigned for Lincoln in the 1864 campaign and cast their ballots at a mock polling place. In January 1865, on the same day that the Convention of Colored Men met in Louisiana, in Nashville sixty-two colored citizens petitioned the white Unionists meeting in a Constitutional Convention there at the time to abolish slavery in the state. Tennessee, because it was not in rebellion, had been exempted from the Emancipation Proclamation. Therefore, Callie, as well as the large population of refugees in the cities and slaves still in rural areas, remained legally in bondage in the state. Tennessee slaves were not formally freed by the state until March 1865.[22]

After a Nashville convention held in August 1865 attended by blacks from Rutherford County and surrounding areas, the Nashville *Colored Tennessean* reported how they defined their change from slaves and subordinates to persons with rights. African Americans expected whites to

Deal with us justly. Tell us not that we will not work, when it was our toil that enriched the South. Talk not to us of a war of races, for that is to say you intend commencing to butcher us, whenever you can do so with impunity. All we want is the rights of men. Give us that and we shall not molest you. We do not intend leaving this country. No land can be fairer in our eyes, than the sunny one beneath whose skies we have lived. We were born here. Most of us will die here. We are Americans and prouder of the fact than ever. Deal justly with us. That's all we want. That we mean to have, come what may![23]

The Reconstruction Act of March 1867 gave black males the political rights the conventions demanded. They could vote and run for office for the first time. The Union League and political clubs, mass meetings, and speakers, as well as the selection of black registrars designated by the Freedmen's Bureau, all added to the excitement of the era. At the local level in towns and cities, they learned how to organize local councils or branches. African Americans would listen to a speaker, learn the rituals, and adjourn to form a council. Those who were literate would also read newspapers and other materials aloud to the illiterate. As the meeting place of the local councils where African Americans discussed issues from politics to wages, the churches developed as political institutions. The churches were the community.[24]

Women, though they could not vote, also attended the political meetings and joined in the activism. E. Franklin Frazier described how African-American women asserted themselves politically under Reconstruction. During the election of 1868, "if a husband refused to wear a picture of Republican

African Americans wanted land, schooling, religious freedom, and pensions. They also understood that they needed to vote and hold political office. This man is urging another to vote. "Canvassing for Votes," Harper's Weekly, *November 2, 1872.*

presidential candidate, former Union General Ulysses S. Grant around the old plantation, in the presence of the old slave Master, and or the overseer, his wife would wear it. If he would not give it to her she would walk all the way to town to buy, beg, or borrow one to wear."[25]

Ex-slaves saw voting and the election of new conventions and legislatures with African-American members as defining events. Men, women, and children crowded the audiences in the state houses. They expected a new day of opportunity and empowerment. Each of the constitutional conventions called in the southern states had African-American members, but they were in a majority at the conventions in South Carolina and Louisiana. In most states, African Americans constituted a small minority. In six states, native whites were in the majority. Some African-American members were former slaves and others had been free before the war; some were emigrants from the North; and many were veterans of the Union Army. Those who spoke in the conventions took a moderate conciliatory position toward white Confederates, even supporting their enfranchisement. The state constitutions approved by the Reconstruction conventions were much more progressive than the constitutions of antebellum days. They abolished property qualifications for voting and holding office, and some ended imprisonment for debt. Slavery was formally abolished in all of the constitutions they adopted. In every constitution, universal male suffrage was enacted except for certain classes of former Confederates. William Whipper, an African American who emigrated from the North to serve in the Union Army and a delegate to the South Carolina convention, even proposed women's suffrage. Public school systems and modernized local government administrative provisions were also included. These constitutions were apparently so highly regarded that

*Black women and men eagerly made political decisions as
freedmen gained the vote for the first time. In towns and rural
areas men and women learned how to organize and eagerly
discussed issues and candidates. "A Political Discussion,"*
Harper's Weekly, *November 20, 1869.*

even when Reconstruction was overthrown by white suprema-
cists, the basic provisions of the constitutions were maintained.
The whites overthrew Reconstruction to regain power; they
had no problem with the advanced structures of government
the conventions established.[26]

Reconstruction unraveled all over the South as chaotically
as it began. In House's community, as elsewhere, whites used
personal intimidation, threats of dismissal from employment,
manipulation of ballots, and Klan violence to force blacks out

of the political arena while the national government acquiesced. C. C. Henderson, an early historian of Murfreesboro, Tennessee, wrote that when former masters and former slaves having the same surname sought the same office, election officials counted all of the votes cast for the freedmen in favor of the election to the former master.[27]

In 1869, Reconstruction ended in Tennessee and with it an almost complete exclusion of African-American men from politics. A few continued to vote and run for office, and a few received Republican patronage appointments. However, the poll tax, biased election officials, intimidation, and violence kept most African Americans from the polls. According to the Rutherford County historian Carlton Sims, "the better class of white people took over the government." In the 1870s, Callie's family, like the rest of the county's still large, mostly disenfranchised, black population, engaged in farming as tenants or sharecroppers, or employment as domestics or laborers. However, there were a few carpenters, blacksmiths, ministers, teachers, railroad engineers, shoemakers, boatmakers, and two physicians. Blacks had been able to experience political organizing and office holding. Some had even exercised real power for a time.[28]

African Americans in House's community and elsewhere in the South began to consider other routes for political action once Reconstruction ended and black voters were largely driven from electoral politics. With African Americans no longer a factor, white voters divided sharply along class lines. In the 1880s, depressed economic conditions for poor farmers led them to join radical agrarian organizations. The whites-only Southern Farmers' Alliance was joined by a Colored Farmers' National Alliance and Cooperation Union in 1886. Radical leaders such as Tom Watson in Georgia began preaching soli darity for poor black and white farmers. In 1892, the Populist Party tried to protect African Americans in the exercise of the franchise, to ensure equal application of voting procedures, and to gain the black vote. The Democrats retaliated first by trying and failing to make an alliance with the Populists and then by forcing African Americans who worked for them to vote Democratic. The Democrats also resorted to riots and murder to maintain political power.[29]

Soon, however, Democrats began to complain that even when they controlled black voters, they often had to use intimidation or threats of violence. The Populists feared that they would not always be able to control African Americans if they were permitted to behave as allies and not subordinates, and they also feared Democratic control of black voters and efforts to disfranchise poor whites. Poor whites, the planter class, and industrialists joined together in forcing African Americans out of the political arena in the 1890s. State after state formally disfranchised African Americans by the discriminatory use of "reading and understanding clauses," by writing rigid educational and property tests for voting into their constitutions, and by enacting "grandfather clauses" that enfranchised only those whose fathers and grandfathers had been qualified to vote on January 1, 1867, which automatically excluded blacks, most of whom had still been slaves on that date.[30]

Callie grew to adolescence during Reconstruction and the reaction that followed it. In 1880, she lived in Rutherford County with her widowed mother, Ann Guy, in the household of her sister, Sarah, and Sarah's husband, Charles House, a laborer and minister. Callie attended school, and her mother, who could not read or write, took in washing. In 1880, the black population of the county grew to 16,493, still about 50 percent of the total population.[31]

In 1881, Tennessee had the distinction of passing the first law in the South that officially mandated the segregation that already existed in fact. In 1883, at age eighteen, Callie left her sister's household, marrying William House, a laborer, who may have been related to her brother-in-law, Charles. Callie and William House had six children, five of whom, three girls and two boys, survived. Thomas, the eldest, was born in 1885 and Annie, the youngest, in 1893. Callie House's mother apparently died sometime before the 1900 Census was taken. She no longer lived in the household of any of the relatives, and she does not appear in the Census anywhere thereafter.[32]

In the years after Reconstruction, as African Americans considered alternative routes to empowerment, people in House's neighborhood joined in talking about emigration to the North or to Africa. The discussion was not new. One segment of white opinion in the early Republic believed that democracy and Christianity required the deportation of blacks to Africa. This philosophy, espoused by Thomas Jefferson and others, was the basis of the founding of the American Colonization Society (ACS) in December 1816–January 1817 and the establishment of Liberia on the west coast of Africa in 1822. By the beginning of the Civil War, the ACS had removed about 11,000 African Americans to Liberia.[33]

Although some historians insist that there was little real interest in emigration before the passage of the Fugitive Slave Act of 1850, the thousands of letters in the files of the ACS suggest another story. Slaves and free blacks continually wrote to the society after 1817, expressing their desire to emigrate to Liberia to escape discrimination, to establish a Christian outpost in Africa, to obtain the same kinds of opportunities in a new land as European immigrants had found in the United States, and to aid in crushing the African slave trade. Peter

Butler, a semiliterate free black from Petersburg, Virginia, expressed the typical view when he wrote in 1848, "I wish to Go to Liberia So as I may teach Sinners the way of Salvation and also Educate my children and enjoy the Right of a man[.] I have tried a great many places in these united state and I find that none of them is the home for the Culerd man and So I am Looking in my mind for a home and I find that Liberia is the onley place of injoyment for the Culerd man."[34]

Some African-American emigrationists saw efforts toward colonization in Africa of free Negroes and subsidization of the American Colonization Society by Congress as claims for redress. They consistently demanded that the U.S. government pay blacks for their sufferings and unrequited toil while in bondage. At the Emigration Convention of 1854, blacks insisted, "Nothing less than a national indemnity, indelibly fixed by virtue of our own sovereign potency, will satisfy us as a redress of our grievances for the unparalleled wrongs, undisguised impositions, and unmitigated oppression, which we have suffered at the hands of this American people. . . . For our own part, we spurn to treat for liberty on any other terms or conditions."[35]

The advent of the Civil War and the hope that it would bring complete liberation led to a decrease in interest in emigration. However, after the Civil War, in 1865, the ACS renewed its work. By 1868, the ACS had sent 2,232 blacks to Liberia from all over the South, including Nashville and the surrounding area in middle Tennessee. This was more than twice the annual average for the entire period from 1820 to 1861. In addition to educated blacks who wanted to become missionaries, poor African Americans, still seeking land, were attracted. Henry Adams, a former slave in Georgia and Louisiana, became one of the mass leaders. For three years he served in the Union Army, where he learned to read, write, and count. Faced with the mistreatment blacks experienced in the service, he and a few others began to organize. Adams traveled throughout the South, splitting rails, working and organizing, and observing the poor conditions of blacks everywhere. The violence attending the post-Reconstruction regaining of power by whites in Louisiana caused him and others to petition President Ulysses S. Grant to send blacks to Liberia. In 1874, they sent a similar petition to Rutherford B. Hayes. They noted that twelve years after the Civil War, African Americans in some ways were "in a worst condition . . . than they were before those constitutional guarantees were extended." They cited their disfranchisement, violence, landlessness, and inability to control their lives and protect their families. They had no hope that their prospects would improve.[36]

African-American political participation, starting in 1867 during Reconstruction in the deep South, reduced the interest in emigration, but the brutal white reaction against Reconstruction stimulated it again. Blacks participated in electoral politics when they could but then organized and kept the emigrationist idea before them. Information spread through the local political councils, benevolent associations, schools, black newspapers, and the ACS's *African Repository,* which was read aloud at church or local political meetings.[37]

Heightened interest in African emigration, in Tennessee and elsewhere, came in 1879 and 1880. At the same time the Exodus to Kansas Movement, started by the illiterate Benjamin "Pap" Singleton, a former Tennessee slave who had escaped to Canada before the Civil War, gathered momentum. Returning to middle Tennessee after the war, Singleton urged blacks to abandon politics because they were being swindled. As a result of the emphasis on politics during Reconstruction, Singleton

"The Negro Exodus—the Old Style and the New," Harper's
Weekly, *May 1, 1880. Unlike the runaway slave fleeing alone
through the swamp, these blacks moved in a group to Kansas
to form new communities as an escape from Jim Crow and
repression after Reconstruction ended.*

contended, "whites had the lands and the sense and the blacks
had nothing but their freedom." In order to make this freedom
real, Singleton organized a land company in 1869. After prices
in Tennessee proved too high, in 1871 he began urging African
Americans to acquire public lands in Kansas. Between 1873 and
1879, he took several groups of Tennessee and Kentucky blacks
there. Singleton and his cohorts wanted to create an independent, separate African-American enclave in Kansas.[38]

Southern blacks showed a feverish interest in emigration
between 1876 and 1881; thousands of Louisiana, Mississippi,
and Arkansas blacks moved into Kansas during this period. By
1879, they had purchased about 10,000 acres of public land.

The emigrants were generally so destitute, however, that initially they had to obtain relief from Kansas whites. As their numbers increased and discrimination and segregation arose in Kansas, Singleton began urging blacks to emigrate to Canada or Liberia, and in 1885 he formed the United Trans-Atlantic Society to foster African colonization. Despairing that they would ever achieve full citizenship in the United States, the society argued that only in an African state with a separate national existence could blacks survive.[39]

Henry Adams worked with Singleton for a time. His petition to Rutherford B. Hayes in 1874 insisted that "the exodus of our people to some other country" was "the only hope and preservation of our race." He supported the exodus north or emigration to Liberia as alternatives. He thought blacks needed to leave the South for someplace where they might have an opportunity for self-development and control over their own lives.[40]

Southern whites reacted negatively to the prospect that they might lose the use of exploited black labor. So concerned did the government become about the exodus and the Back to Africa emigration movement that in 1880 the U.S. Senate held an investigation into the "Causes of the Removal of the Negroes from the Southern States to the Northern States," producing three large volumes of testimony and assessment. No matter how much discontent African Americans expressed, probably no more than 25,000 blacks actually emigrated to Kansas in 1879–1880. Also, probably no more than about 4,000 managed to reach Liberia during the whole post–Civil War period.[41]

However, emigrationism as a political solution did not die. Segregation, lynching, poverty, and disfranchisement kept the idea alive among African Americans. In the late 1880s and thereafter, despite Booker T. Washington's opposition, the idea gathered steam. Washington thought blacks should stay in the South and accommodate themselves to conditions there. However, letters to the American Colonization Society came from blacks in Nashville and almost every other sizable city and the surrounding areas, inquiring about going to Liberia.[42]

In the 1890s, A.M.E. bishop Henry McNeal Turner, a former Union soldier and Georgia legislator, was the chief supporter of the back-to-Africa idea. Although Turner had no viable organizational base or economic means for sending blacks to Africa, some whites supported him. In 1894, with the backing of Alabama senator John Morgan, Turner formed the International Migration Society, and by 1896 he sent two boatloads of emigrants to Liberia.[43]

African-American ministers were divided on the subject of emigration because they could lose congregations. Further, politicians who had combined with Democrats to maintain some power, by pretending they had voting constituencies, would lose their posts. Therefore, although people met in churches and schools and made plans to leave, they often met with hostility from their leaders.

Some African Americans in House's community emigrated to Kansas, and others discussed the possibility of going there or to Africa. She remained in Rutherford County raising her children after the death of her husband, William. She became a washerwoman, taking in laundry like her mother and other women in similar circumstances. Soon a new idea for political action surfaced in Rutherford County and other communities all over the South and Midwest where ex-slaves lived. Agents came to the community selling a pamphlet entitled "Freedmen's Pension Bill: A Plea for American Freedmen." Ten thousand copies of the pamphlet, at one dollar each, were sold in 1891, and several editions were produced thereafter. Poor

African Americans bought such publications, usually jointly, and passed copies around and read them to one another since they often could not afford the purchase price. Just as they had done with newspapers and other literature in their churches and community organizations since slavery, those who could read the pamphlet read it to the others. This idea of pensions for ex-slaves captured House's imagination.[44]

From reading his pamphlet, she learned that the author Walter Vaughan, a former editor of the Omaha, Nebraska, *Daily Democrat*, a native of Selma, Alabama, and a white Democrat, had used political contacts to have an ex-slave pension bill patterned after the idea of the very popular Union veterans' pensions introduced in the Congress. Callie and other African Americans had Union veterans in their families, and they knew pensions were available, although widows and children had difficulty obtaining them because they lacked documentation of their marriages and births.

Vaughan had persuaded his Nebraska congressman, the Republican William J. Connell, to introduce the legislation in 1890, establishing a formula later used by the Ex-Slave Mutual Relief, Bounty and Pension Association. The measure called for providing for a pension of $15 per month and a bounty of $500 for each ex-slave seventy years old or older. Those under seventy would receive $300 as a bounty and $12 per month until they reached the age of seventy, when it would increase to $15. Those under sixty years old would receive a $100 bounty and $8 a month until they reached age sixty. Those less than fifty years of age would receive $4 per month and then, at age fifty, $8 per month. Ex-slaves and such persons as "may be charged by laws of consanguinity with the maintenance and support of freedmen who are unable by reason of age or disease to maintain themselves" were eligible. Relatives who cared for a freed-

*Walter R. Vaughan, former editor of the
Omaha, Nebraska,* Daily Democrat,
*native of Selma, Alabama, and white
Democrat who first proposed the idea of
ex-slave pensions. Wanting to indirectly
increase the financial resources of whites in
the South, he created a proposal that
was patterned after the idea of the popular
Union veterans' pensions of the period.*

man could, upon providing satisfactory proof to the secretary
of the interior, receive the pension. Ex-slaves under the bill
included only those freed by Lincoln's Emancipation Proclamation, by state constitutional amendment, or "by any law,
proclamation, decree or device." The plan appeared uncompli-
cated, requiring only that a claimant had been enslaved. Under
the law, any black person alive before 1861 was presumed to

VAUGHAN'S FREEDMEN'S PENSION BILL

BEING AN APPEAL IN BEHALF OF THEM RELEASED FROM SLAVERY

A PLEA FOR AMERICAN FREEDMEN

AND A RATIONAL PROPOSITION TO GRANT PENSIONS TO PERSONS OF COLOR EMANCIPATED FROM SLAVERY

W.R. VAUGHAN AUTHOR
CHICAGO, ILL.

Southern Products grown by stolen Negro Labor for over 100 years. The revenue made the Government friendly with other nations and enriched its treasury.

Cover of the book Freedmen's Pension Bill: A Plea for American Freedmen. *The cover of Vaughan's book shows his interest in remedying the harm done to the South and not necessarily the harm done to slaves. Vaughan hired agents and sold his pamphlet at one dollar each in 1891; several editions were produced.*

have been a slave in the South unless proof to the contrary was presented.[45]

Vaughan's explanation for his involvement in the issue did not impress House. He mixed concern for the freedpeople with disdain and economic opportunism. As he explained it, seeing groups of freedpeople in a "tattered condition" while on a trip through Mississippi in 1870, he had decided that the government should pension the ex-slaves, who, he asserted, had been well cared for until Emancipation had left them poverty-stricken. But he wanted to help blacks primarily in order to revive the southern economy. The ex-slaves would, through spending the pensions they received, pass along the financial benefit to whites. By adding to the region's meager resources for business and industrial development, the money provided to ex-slaves would relieve the devastation of the South caused by the Civil War. Vaughan's regrets that he had been too young to serve in the Confederacy, his sadness over the Confederate defeat, and his nostalgia for antebellum days were rejected by House. Like other Reunionists, Vaughan saw slavery as a benign institution that had benefited African Americans. His pro-slavery sentiments may have been in accord with the reigning pro-Confederate ethos among whites North and South, but it devalued blacks. At the time whites in both the North and the South were engaged in a great reconciliation movement in which they emphasized brotherhood. They also redefined the causes of the Civil War as totally about saving the Union. They lamented the unfortunate destruction of the southern way of life and left no place for a discussion of the war as focused on freedom and equality for African Americans.[46]

Despite her misgivings about Vaughan's motives, House paid careful attention to Vaughan's detailed description of how he had gained support for ex-slave pension legislation. Until

Frederick Douglass—an integrationist and the most important African-American leader until his death in 1895. He supported reparations even though most elite African Americans opposed the idea.

then, she had had no idea how the lobbying process worked. Vaughan explained in detail how he wrote to luminaries asking for "testimonial" letters that he could publish in his newspaper to aid in organizing and lobbying. Those he solicited included Frederick Douglass, the most important African-American human rights leader of his day, who had become increasingly disgusted with the public's fading memory of slavery and its impact on African Americans.

Initially, Douglass responded that he found the reparations idea impractical, but finally decided that the nation owed retribution to African Americans, for the nation had "robbed him of the rewards of his labor during more than 200 years." Furthermore, Douglass continued, the promise of land had been broken: "The Egyptian bondsmen went out with the spoils of his master, and the Russian serf was provided with farming tools and three acres of land with which to begin life, —but the Negro has neither spoils, implements nor lands, and today, he is practically a slave on the very plantation where formerly he was driven to toil under the lash." Douglass asserted that if land had been given as promised during the Civil War, "The [N]egro would not today be on his knees, as he is supplicating the old master class to give him leave to toil." In the absence of land, if a measure like the one proposed by Vaughan had been adopted earlier, "untold misery might have been prevented."[47]

Callie House and other African Americans had heard of how the African Americans in Congress were trying to obtain federal aid for education as compensation for slavery. They also knew that the same leaders demanded greater protection for the right to vote as a priority. House and other blacks understood, even though Vaughan did not, why black newspapers and the three African-American representatives still in Congress after Reconstruction refused to support the pension bill.[48]

Those leaders, instead, focused on education and voting rights. The congressmen were Republicans Henry P. Cheatham of North Carolina, Thomas E. Miller of South Carolina, and John Mercer Langston of Virginia. Representative Cheatham, born in 1857, had lived in the Big House, where his mother had

*John Mercer Langston, one of three African-American
congressmen when ex-slave pensions were first proposed.
He opposed the idea and worked instead, unsuccessfully,
for the passage of bills to support education
and protect the right to vote.*

worked as a house servant. He attended school and college and
became a school principal and later recorder of deeds in Vance
County. Described as a "distinguished looking mulatto," he
read law, ran successfully for Congress in 1888, and was
reelected in 1890. While in Congress, he introduced a number
of bills designed to help African Americans, including one to
reimburse the depositors of the bankrupt freedmen's bank, but
his major emphasis was on aid to black public schools.[49]

Miller, born in Ferrebeeville in 1849 to free Negro parents,

(Left) Thomas E. Miller, African-American representative in Congress from South Carolina. Miller, like Langston, opposed ex-slave pensions. Right: H. P. Cheatham, African-American representative in Congress from North Carolina. Cheatham joined Miller and Langston in opposing ex-slave pensions.

"could have passed for white but refused to do so." His parents paid for his education, and he attended college and law school. Admitted to practice in Beaufort, he became active in the Republican Party and won local offices. Elected to Congress in a dispute decided by the House of Representatives in 1888, he lost the election in 1890. He returned home, where he worked to establish South Carolina State College for Negroes and became its president. He, too, thought education and voting rights were the only routes to empowerment for African Americans.[50]

Langston, born in Louisa County, Virginia, in 1829, was the son of Captain Ralph Quarles, a white plantation owner, and Lucy Langston, of both "Indian and Negro descent." His white father educated and supported his African-American children and arranged for a friend to take care of them after his death. Educated at Oberlin in Ohio, he became a lawyer, theologian, and active participant in antislavery societies. During the Civil War, he helped recruit soldiers and worked for the Freedmen's Bureau. He also ran the law department and became acting president of Howard University. He held two diplomatic posts to which the Republican administration appointed African Americans at the time, minister to Haiti and chargé d'affaires to the Dominican Republic. In 1890, he won a contested election to the House of Representatives but left the Congress in 1891. Langston, too, insisted that instead of pensions and bounties for ex-slaves, "what we want is the means of obtaining knowledge and useful information, which will fit the rising generation for honorable and useful employment." Education and political rights were his priorities.[51]

These legislators also shared House's distrust of Vaughan's motives. They suspected that he and his cronies wanted to give a few dollars to blacks to spend quickly, consequently enriching southern business but not uplifting the African-American community. They also did not believe the pension bill would pass and that it, instead, distracted from the education and voting rights initiatives they had urged on the Republican Party to help African Americans. In 1890, the Republicans made two unsuccessful legislative efforts to gain their objectives. Senator Henry Blair of New Hampshire pushed an aid to public education bill that would indirectly help blacks to gain an education. First introduced in 1884, the bill provided federal assistance to public schools with the amount based on the number of illiterate persons in each state. States with segregated school systems would have to apportion the money to black and white schools based on the proportion of illiterates in each race between the ages of ten and twenty-one. The bill would have given a shot in the arm to the inadequate black public school systems and provided a form of reparations not seen since the Freedmen's Bureau efforts. The bill passed in the Senate in 1884, 1886, and 1888 but failed each time in the House of Representatives. In 1890, the Senate refused to pass it again. Opponents argued that it would weaken private schools or that taking funds out of the federal Treasury would support demands for a higher tariff. The other bill, introduced by Representative Henry Lodge, provided for federal supervision of elections. Supporters noted that each Congress spent thirty to sixty working days on contested elections and questions related to the black vote in the South as Republicans tried to overturn the election of Democrats. Sponsors of the Lodge bill thought they could pass it with President William Henry Harrison's support.[52]

The president, more worried about cracking the solid South to obtain votes for the high-tariff McKinley bill of 1890, gave only lukewarm support to the Lodge bill. In his first annual message, on December 3, 1889, Harrison praised "the Negro race" generally, and especially soldiers, veterans, and other African Americans who had remained in the South despite deprivation of their rights. The Lodge bill passed the House on a strict party-line vote but lost in the Senate after being held over until the next session to make way for a vote on the McKinley Tariff of 1890, which became law. The Blair education bill and the Lodge elections bill, although advocated by African-American leaders, had also been rejected. Nevertheless, House was not dissuaded from her interest in reparations.[53]

House understood the opposition to ex-slave pensions by African Americans in business and the professions, and congressional representatives. However, more bothersome was the opposition of influential white reformers, such as Albion Tourgee, who usually joined social justice causes. Tourgee, a

Massachusetts lawyer who had gone South to serve as a judge after the war, repeatedly expressed disgust with the national abandonment of the cause of justice for the freedpeople since Reconstruction. However, he thought the idea of pensions would draw even more attention away from the effort to protect the civil rights of blacks. In 1892, he published a pamphlet in which he argued, "The Colored Race does not demand reparation—thank Heaven for that—only justice, equality of civil privilege, political right and economic opportunity, properly guaranteed and secured for the future."[54]

Isaiah Dickerson, a Rutherford County African-American teacher and minister, had worked as a traveling agent for Vaughan. He left when they had a disagreement over management and the direction of Vaughan's organization. Dickerson, who prided himself on his appearance, was always "nattily but plainly dressed, in dark suit and cravat." Dickerson told audiences he had been drawn to the reparations movement when he saw "one morning in Memphis an old colored man being ordered by a policeman to leave a piece of meat he had taken from a swill barrel back of a hotel."[55]

Dickerson then "decided that the best way to help the old ex-slaves is to get some money in their pockets." For Union military veterans and their survivors, he said, "the pensions have increased so much since the War that anyone who's been anyplace near the army can get one for a lifetime." From where he stood, "there is no reason why the old ex-slaves who worked unpaid all their lives and then helped the Union digging ditches at the forts, washing the soldiers' clothes, cooking for them and nursing the injured" deserved less. This was especially true, Dickerson felt, given the government's generosity to white veterans.[56]

Dickerson told House that he thought the pension legisla-

Isaiah Dickerson. As a schoolteacher, minister, and former agent for Vaughan, he reinforced Callie House's belief that African Americans could successfully organize a movement for ex-slave pensions and mutual assistance.

tion could succeed. By April 1897, Vaughan had moved to Kentucky, where he described himself as engaged in the business of building electric street railways and other enterprises. Vaughan's involvement in ex-slave pension organizing languished, aside from supporting the introduction of legislation in connection with selling his pamphlet. He continued to express the view that caring for the ex-slaves had been a "burden" for southern white people too long, especially since they had been "deprived of their property without recompense." Not just Congressmen Cheatham, Miller, and Langston, but House and other African Americans who heard Vaughan speak, had been suspicious of his motivation and leadership. Vaughan's talk of the wonderful days of "moonlight and magnolias" during slavery and his autocratic style of operation repelled them.

In consultation with the federal Pension Bureau, Vaughan decided to denounce anyone as a scam artist who promoted the idea if they did not work for him. In September 1897, he distributed a letter to newspapers explaining that he was the "sole author" of the congressional legislation. Vaughan also selected a black Nashville man, P. F. Hill, "a reliable, educated gentleman, a 53rd degree mason" and head of several fraternal orders, to act as chief of the Vaughan ex-slave movement. Only Hill had Vaughan's "approval and authority in the work."[57]

Meanwhile, Vaughan continued to schedule lectures and to use his contacts to ask legislators to introduce or support the bill, in order to sell his pamphlet. The local newspaper reported his visit to Nashville, in the summer of 1897, at a meeting organized by Hill, his anointed successor. *The Nashville American* reported that about fifty people had paid the admission fee of twenty-five cents each at St. Paul's African Methodist Episcopal Church, after some people who refused to pay the fee had left.[58]

Despite problems and setbacks, the pension idea fascinated House. The information she gleaned from the pamphlet and talking to Dickerson reflected her own experience and that of her family and neighbors. Talk of pensions for ex-slave men and women reminded them of how even the black Civil War soldier, who had become a hero among African Americans, was ignored by whites, who wanted to forget the racial reasons for the war. Paul Laurence Dunbar, who wrote "The Colored Soldier" in 1896, reflected the views of African Americans that military service should guarantee the rights at least of those who had served:

> *They were good to stop a bullet*
> *And to front the fearful fray.*
> *They were citizens and soldiers,*
> *When rebellion raised its head;*
> *And the traits that made them worthy,—*
> *Ah! those virtues are not dead.*

House and other ex-slaves knew of the role black soldiers had played in the war and the difficulties they had in receiving the pension benefits that flowed freely to white veterans. The 1890 pension act had severed the link between pensions and service-related injuries. Any veteran who had honorably served ninety days in the military, even if never injured or a noncombatant, could apply for a pension if he could find a physician to affirm his unfitness for manual labor. In fact, old age became the only legal requirement for a pension. In 1906, Congress changed the law to say so explicitly. After the turn of the century, Congress also raised the benefit levels for veterans and dependents several times. By 1915, 93 percent of surviving veterans, as pensioners, received what had become, essentially, an old-age survivor's benefit. In addition, many veterans held federal jobs and collected a pension.[59]

Pension-eligible veterans constituted a privileged group. Mostly northern whites, the group included some 186,017

African Americans who had served in the Union forces, about three fourths of whom came from the southern states. A significantly lower percentage of blacks received veterans' pensions than white veterans. Racial hostility among Pension Bureau officials blocked blacks' access to pensions. Northern blacks probably fared better than the southern freedmen or their dependents, who often lacked documentary evidence of their service, their dates of birth, or their surnames. Widows of the men who had served in the ranks in southern black regiments suffered most severely from this problem. Unable to prove their relationships or to obtain service records for the deceased, they went without aid. For example, the widow Félicie Cailloux spent years trying to obtain back pay and a pension for the service of her late husband, André Cailloux. He was a much-publicized Louisiana Native Guard hero who died in 1863 leading a charge at Port Hudson. In 1871, destitute, she finally received a pension of $20 per month, three years before her death on October 19, 1874. Harriet Tubman, the "Moses of her people," who had escaped from slavery herself and ushered others to freedom on the "Underground Railroad," had served in the Union Army as a cook, nurse, scout, and spy but received no pension despite years of petitioning and the aid of the secretary of war and Union Army officers, who had observed her contributions. In 1888, the government awarded her a widow's pension upon the death of her second husband, Nelson Davis, who had served in the Union Army during the Civil War. She received $8 a month until 1899 and then $20 a month until her death in 1913. The $20 Harriet Tubman received was less than the $25 provided by law. In 2003, the protests of grade school children who visited her former home in Auburn, New York, led to a $11,750 congressional appropriation to make up the difference. However, Tubman's family has yet to receive a pension for her service.[60]

House, and the people she knew, experienced extremely low wages, hard work, illness, and disease in the days after slavery ended. But as the ex-slaves aged, their problems worsened. Families lacked resources for health care and had to scrape together money to pay for funerals. Neither land nor education as reparations for poor freedpeople had been achieved by African-American political leaders. And so, to Callie House, pensions for ex-slave women and men seemed a worthy cause.

CHAPTER 2

Organizing the National Ex-Slave Mutual Relief, Bounty and Pension Association

If the Government had the right to free us she had a right to make some provision for us and since she did not make it soon after Emancipation she ought to make it now.

CALLIE HOUSE
(1899)

CALLIE HOUSE'S LIFE was transformed when she stepped into public view as an activist working for the pension cause. Sociologist Alden Morris has described how the 1950s and 1960s civil rights movement found a base and leadership in the church, the only place where blacks could meet freely with a minimum of white control. This was not new. Throughout the period since Reconstruction, African Americans used the church as the center of community action, and the reparations movement found a home in church, too. House and Dickerson established their headquarters in Nashville, which had become the black church hub of the South, including the publishing operations of the two largest black religious denominations: the National Baptist Publishing Board and the African Methodist Episcopal Church Sunday School Union Publishers, both located there.[1]

The city of about 76,168 people in 1890, 40 percent of whom were African Americans, was just thirty miles from Murfreesboro, the Rutherford County seat. It may not have been the most obvious venue for a poor people's movement despite its attractiveness as a transportation hub and its history as the place where Pap Singleton's exodus had started. A sizable African-American middle class grew around Fisk University and two other local black private colleges and at Meharry Medical College and the publishing houses.[2]

Using the contacts Dickerson had established from his work with Vaughan, House and Isaiah Dickerson traveled throughout the former slaveholding states to enroll members and organize local chapters through the churches. In the years before his death in 1909, Dickerson's experience was invaluable to House. They went on the road, organizing the National Ex-Slave Mutual Relief, Bounty and Pension Association and receiving immediate and enthusiastic responses from African Americans. At the grassroots level, the ex-slaves, who were at the lowest economic level, embraced what was essentially a poor people's movement. Old and disabled by so many years of manual work, bad diet, and no medical care, these people understood and supported the association's demand for pensions to compensate for years of unpaid labor. The effort also was endorsed and supported by local preachers, and the association's membership grew rapidly. Part of the association's program included offering medical and burial assistance. It also offered a democratic structure in which local people had control and a voice, at a time when blacks were practically disfranchised or on the verge of becoming so throughout the South.

Soon after House began the Ex-Slave Association work, she and her children and her brother and his family moved to South Nashville, where she made her home for the remainder of her life. Despite organizing work, she still described herself as primarily a washerwoman and seamstress. House's sister Sarah and her family continued to live in Murfreesboro.[3]

Her brother, Charles Guy, worked as a porter and first boarded in South Nashville with House at 1003 Vernon Street, near Eighth Avenue between the reservoir and the capitol. Later he would move his family, consisting of his wife, Mandy, or Amanda, and daughter Annie Mary to Nashville. The homes in House's neighborhood were single or double tenant, with a living room, bedroom, and kitchen adjacent to each other in a row. Because it was possible to stand at either end and look straight through, such homes were named "shotgun" houses.[4]

In her work as a washwoman, House was like many African-American women of the time, either married or widowed with children, who took laundry-work into their homes. Generally, before she married, a woman would work as a maid or cook in a private home. After she had children she stayed home and took in wash. Washing machines did not appear for home use even for the wealthy until about 1914. Consequently, these women washed bedding, towels, and every item of clothing by hand; they also ironed for an entire family each week. The pay sometimes totaled about $2. At the time rents or mortgage payments in the neighborhood were $5 to $12 a month, thus such women had a difficult time earning enough to maintain even a meager existence. In addition, women who worked at home so they could care for their children did not receive the food

*African-American women washed their family's laundry and
took in washing from poor and well-off white families. This
woman had to boil the clothes and constantly bend to stir the
wash kettles and lift soaking wet, heavy bedding.*

scraps to take home that women working as domestics outside
the home used to help feed their families.[5]

About the time House moved to Nashville, gasoline washing machines became available, although clothes first had to be
soaked in kettles of water heated over a wood fire. However,
poor people could not afford the washing machines, and even
with the advent of commercial laundries, poor and well-off
white women continued sending their clothes to black
women's homes for laundering well into the twentieth century.
Race remained a significant issue even in getting clothes
washed, and Nashville commercial laundries thought it wise to

advertise on streetcars and on the sides of its delivery wagons "No Negro Washing Taken." Washerwomen purchased soap, if they could afford it, or made lye soap from pork grease saved from cooking. They scrubbed the clothes on washboards, used bluing for whitening, and made starch by boiling flour. They heated irons on the stove and removed excess starch from the clothes' surface by running the iron back and forth across salt poured on paper covering the ironing board. The women's hands were reddened from the harshness of the soap, and they worked with constant pain from bending over to stir the wash kettles and from lifting soaked, wet, heavy bedding. This method of doing laundry by hand remained unchanged from House's day until the 1950s for poor African Americans in Nashville, including my own family. In the 1940s, in Nashville, the mother in the family next door to us took in laundry and washed on a washboard, much as House had done but with the addition of a recently bought hand wringer.[6]

House and her brother, Charles, like their neighbors, were the first generation of African Americans to reach maturity after the abolition of slavery. Their parents were the first generation to experience old age in freedom, but their work conditions remained harsh. Although the 1890 Nashville City Directory listed four African-American women as managers and owners of boardinghouses, three as dressmakers, and nineteen as sick nurses; fifty-five were listed as laundresses—washerwomen. The 1910 and 1920 Censuses reported most women in the neighborhood as either domestic workers or laundresses. The men worked as live-in or live-out chauffeurs, laborers, porters in department stores and hotels, bootblacks in barbershops, packers in factories, and an occasional plumber in a plumbing store or a carpenter or plasterer working for a contractor. Some of the men, such as House's brother, Charles, also worked as itinerant Primitive Baptist preachers. They felt called to preach, although they had neither congregation nor church income.[7]

To a casual observer, Nashville after the Civil War appeared as a provincial, unpretentious southern city. Most of the city's area lay within a two-mile radius of the capitol. Poor people lived in the streets and lanes around Capitol Hill. The water-front and the railroad depots dominated their views. Among the dirty houses, trash-filled streets, taverns, and brothels, the *Republican Banner* cried, "Our city looks like a pig pen, and is profitable to the owners of the city scum, but it speaks badly for our notions of health and cleanliness."[8]

House's neighborhood evolved from Edgehill, one of five camps the Union Army had established for the freedpeople—called "contraband of war" until legal abolition—in Nashville. South and below the capitol on the hill, House's neighborhood bordered "Black Bottom," with Lafayette Street, a pathway cut through to give better access to Murfreesboro Pike (Eighth Avenue South), the northern boundary.[9]

The old city cemetery and Fort Negley, built by contraband to protect the city from the Confederates, the Louisville and Nashville railroad yards, and white residents between the tracks and Ninth Avenue South, served as the eastern boundary of Edgehill. Fort Negley is still standing. Near Eighth Avenue South, another pocket of blacks lived in Rocktown. The entire South Nashville black neighborhood was within walking distance—about a mile—from downtown.[10]

The freedpeople developed their neighborhoods from the camps, where they at first lived in shacks. Soon they built wooden shotgun houses. Nashville had gaslit streetlights after the Civil War, and electricity, waterworks, and a streetcar system came before 1900. However, working-poor African Americans usually had no plumbing, electricity, or gaslight until well after the turn of the century. As late as the 1940s, in that same South Nashville neighborhood, the utility services still did not come to our part of town. Our poverty and blackness made us easy to ignore. At night, we still depended on light from oil lamps or the burning fireplace that was the only source of heat. Sparks left telltale scars on the legs of anyone who sat or stood too close to the fire, indelibly marking a shared experience of need and deprivation. In this neighborhood, House and her family made their home and eked out a difficult existence.

In South Nashville, where House's family and other working-class blacks who had started their lives in the contraband camps lived, the new industries created a noxious environment. Their housing subsisted with the noise and pungent smells of four mills, breweries, and chemical processing plants near the rail yards.[11]

Nashville's overall cityscape changed fundamentally between the Civil War and the 1890s, when House moved to town, as a result of industrial and business transformations. Annexation, the acquisition of Edgefield in 1880 with a 65 percent white population, and streetcars to outlying regions shifted the population in the city, making it blacker, while the overall population of the legal metropolitan entity became less black. The process of annexation has led to continued dilution of the black population in the metropolitan Nashville area today. By the turn of the century, the city had become a major commercial center and wholesale marketplace in the South for industry, banking, and professional services. The rail, water, and turnpike facilities gave Nashville an advantage over most other southern cities. Once the home of the upper class, the city's uptown core became a more concentrated commercial district that pushed most residential uses outward as it expanded.[12]

A contrast between rich and poor in the 1890s. (Top) African-American children playing marbles. (Bottom) William Harding Jackson, Jr., a son of William H. Jackson of Belle Meade Plantation, in his pony carriage in front of the mansion.

The adult freedpeople in House's community continued to labor at the lowest-paying work as they aged or had to be cared for by their poor, hardworking children. Most rented their homes, though rent and mortgage payments ranged from $5 to $12 a month and absorbed most of their income. Callie House and other washerwomen, with the $2 a week they earned for their labors, struggled to make ends meet and keep a roof over their heads. Poor African Americans could not afford more than a diet of hoecake and greens, often without meat and similar to what they had eaten during slavery. Their diet, along with polluted water, outhouses, poor heating, and minimum medical care, continued to erode the quality of life for poor black Nashvillians. When the smallpox epidemic of 1895 killed large numbers of black children, the city quarantined the African-American neighborhoods. The city's health officer called repeatedly and unsuccessfully for attention to the acute need for medical services for black citizens. While white health conditions improved, high comparable death rates and infant mortality remained problems in the black community.[13]

Tennessee's segregation law of 1881, the first in the South, affirmed the racial subordination that already existed. By the 1890s, in Nashville as in Rutherford County, Callie House and other African Americans felt deeply the effects of Jim Crow. Men could still vote legally, but they faced powerful whites who enacted poll taxes and shifted polling places and registration lists to keep black men from the ballot box. Under Jim Crow, the city provided separate fairgrounds for blacks and whites, and the trolley cars and streetcars separated African Americans from whites. Railroad stations had separate waiting rooms, and saloons and brothels were separate or segregated. Amusement parks had separate areas within them for African Americans. Ostracized African Americans developed the habit early of organizing mutual aid when they established burial assistance associations that used the Mt. Ararat and Green-wood cemeteries to bury their dead next to, but segregated from, the white cemetery.[14]

Ex-slaves in other communities fared no better, which is why they, too, eagerly joined the Association. Mrs. House and her colleagues worked to establish chapters across the former slaveholding states, working separately from Vaughan. House and Dickerson encouraged members to sign petitions to Congress and held conventions culminating in the chartering of the association under the laws of Tennessee in Nashville in 1898. House and Dickerson identified members to apply for charters in each state where they organized. The state chapters recognized local lodges and councils.[15]

The five incorporators were apparently all Primitive Baptist ministers, although confirmation for one of them, W. H. Gosling, has not been found. Reverend Nathan Smith from Bransford, Tennessee, who according to the 1900 Census was a fifty-year-old farmer, lived with his wife and stepson. He owned their farm and worked the property with his stepson. Luke Mason, the fifty-year-old pastor of Lewis Street Baptist Church, who made his living as a painter, and Squire Mason, probably his brother, a sixty-two-year-old shoemaker who had operated a downtown shop catering to whites for almost twenty years, joined the group. Both their wives "kept house," which meant they stayed at home and did not, insofar as the Census taker could tell, take in laundry, and they each had five grown children.[16]

Callie House and the founders of the Ex-Slave Association echoed Samuel Cornish and John Russwurm when they published the first African-American newspaper in 1827 announcing "to Long Have other Spoken For us." House and the other leaders at the first convention, in Nashville in 1898, asserted that they could better advocate their own cause: "Thirty-three years of advantages of schooling has prepared the Negro to look out for the welfare of his race; and he can better foster the cause of his race—he has the brains to do so and race pride and manhood are needed at the front; race loving men and women too." House, believing that the development of disconnected small pension organizations would weaken the effort to gain legislation, declared unity as a goal of the association. She asserted, "Let us consolidate all ex-slave organizations and bring to bear upon the lawmakers of the country which we labored so long to develop every degree of influence within our power."[17]

House and the association officers explained to the membership that repeatedly introducing legislation, submitting petitions from old ex-slaves, and engaging lobbyists would someday gain a committee hearing and then perhaps a vote. Standing before the poor and working blacks who had elected her to office, Callie House expressed both the optimism of the moment and the practical view learned from years of black struggle. She told members that grassroots petitions and lobbying would someday gain victory in Congress for their efforts, but the bill would not pass soon. The struggle would be necessarily long and problematic, but the principle of debt owed should never be abandoned.

Unlike Vaughan's operation and other mutual assistance fraternities, the association opened its membership to all, emphasizing that their organization had no "secret grips or passwords." The association's simple goal was to put the name of every ex-slave on a petition asking Congress to pass a bill providing pensions. Surely the plight of these old African-American men and women, aging, ill, and impoverished from hard work and ill treatment during slavery—many of whom were the relatives of the white middle class—deserved recognition. These people's unpaid labor and service had continued during the Civil War as they had served as washerwomen, nurses, and laborers repairing levees, widening drainage ditches, and building fortifications. Their cause should compel sympathy and money when their status was compared to that of Union veterans, who, even if they had served for only ninety days far from the battlefield, could claim an inability to perform manual labor, whatever their occupation or income, and receive a government pension of $12 a month.[18]

The Association placed great emphasis on self-help. Local chapters were required to use part of the dues to pay for the burial of members and to provide mutual assistance in time of sickness and need. At the time such private aid organizations were the only help available for poor African Americans. These functions did not depend on the success of the pension legislation but would build solidarity in the group. In the meantime, the association would keep the reparations claim before the public, declaring it a matter of justice for African Americans.

The Ex-Slave Association was unusual in its origins and purposes. Sociologist Rebecca Ash and other scholars argue that movements have either radical change or service goals. The ex-slave movement had a dual mission from the beginning: the attainment of federal pension legislation and mutual aid to poor members. Although the controversial nature of the pension demand brought the association legal troubles, its mutual assistance activities accorded with the national self-help emphasis of the late nineteenth century.

African Americans had long been in the habit of forming mutual assistance associations, providing help when government refused to help. For African Americans, such mediating institutions historically provided the only available social assis-

PETITION TO CONGRESS.

To the Senators and Representatives of the Congress of the United States of America:

WHEREAS, Generation after generation of Colored people served this country as slaves for two hundred and forty-four years or more, and

WHEREAS, This government owes the unknown and deceased Colored Soldiers a large sum of money which is unclaimed, and

WHEREAS, Many of these soldiers have brothers, fathers, mothers and sisters among us, who are destitute and starving, and

WHEREAS, It is a precedent established by the patriots of this country to relieve its distressed citizens, both on land and sea, and millions of our deceased people, besides those who still survive, worked as slaves for the development of the great resources and wealth of this country, and

WHEREAS, We believe it is just and right to grant the ex-slave a pension :

Therefore, We, the undersigned, citizens of the United States of America, appeal to your Honorable Body to pass Senate Bill, No. 4718, introduced June 6, 1898, by Senator Mason, of Illinois, providing pension for Freedmen, etc.

NAME.	AGE.	NAME OF MASTER.	STATE AND COUNTY.	PRESENT POSTOFFICE.
Winnie Williams		Cornell Williams	Mo Boone Co	Columbia
Lucy Baily	25 50	Cornell Williams	Mo Boone Co	
Dan'l Taylor	25	Henry Keene	Mo Boone Co	
Alice Jacobs	25		Mo Boone Co	
Margrett Washington	45	William Robonette	Mo Boone Co	
Ellen Washington	48			
Gilbert Brown	45			Colored
Laura Davis	25 48	Pleasant Robonette		
Matalie Cook				
Peter Cook				
Susan Henderson				
Lizzie Clark				
David Watkins				
Warren Wilson				
Mary Ann Miller				
Lawrence Miller				
Pauline Hickman				
Ellen Warden				

22.

Thousands of ex-slaves signed petitions like this one to Congress asking for pensions for their forced labor during slavery. Those who could read and write made sure that those who could not were included.

PETITION TO CONGRESS

To the Senators and Representatives of the Congress of the United States of America:

WHEREAS, Generation after generation of Colored people served this country as slaves for two hundred and forty-four years or more, and

WHEREAS, This government owes the unknown and deceased Colored Soldiers a large sum of money which is unclaimed, and

WHEREAS, Many of these soldiers have brothers, fathers, mothers and sisters among us, who are destitute and starving, and

WHEREAS, It is a precedent established by the patriots of this country to relieve its distressed citizens, both on land and sea, and millions of our deceased people, besides those who still survive, worked as slaves for the development of the great resources and wealth of this country, and

WHEREAS, We believe it is just and right to grant the ex-slave a pension;

Therefore, We, the undersigned, citizens of the United States of America, appeal to your Honorable Body to pass Senate Bill, No. 4718, introduced June 6, 1898, by Senator Mason, of Illinois, providing pension for Freedmen, etc.

NAME.	AGE.	NAME OF MASTER.	STATE AND COUNTY.	PRESENT POSTOFFICE.
Henry Clay	79	Jefferson Garth	Kentucky Scott	Columbia Mo
Puly Clay	68	D W Knally	Alexander Papa	Columbia Mo
Sallie Woods	21	Budge Mauphin	Columbia Boone	Columbia Mo
Marion Thomas	47	Robert Garth	Columbia	
Caroline Wills	74	Gachinah King	Ken Winchester	Columbia Mo
Joseph Gosling	57	Sylvest Gosling	Columbia Boone Co	Columbia Mo
Edmond Cook		Shineal Vanhoun		Madalia McClain
Eliza E Miller	20	David Gordon	Columbia Boone	Columbia Mo
Lucy ann Marshall	84	Col Thomas Russ	Virginia Scott Co	Columbia Mo
Harriet Bledson	74 75	Robert Bledsoe	Georgia	Columbia Mo
Matilda Harris	54	John Bivion	Columbia Boone	Columbia Mo
Ned Harris	28	Dr Jacobs	Columbia Co	Columbia Mo
Scott Brashears	70	James Brashears	Howard Co	Columbia Mo
Amanda Brashears	68	Richard Robinson	Boone Co	Columbia Mo
Ruben Fields	67	Jack Cotton	Boone Co	Columbia Mo
Elizabeth Hueston	52	don't exactly know	Boone Co	Columbia Mo
Silas Hueston	56		Boone Co	Columbia Mo
Evaline Hueston	56		Boone Co	Columbia Mo
Sillie Payne	44	John Harris	Boone Co	Columbia Mo
Geo B Bryant	75	Richard Bryant	Virgenia	Columbia Mo
Sallie Bryant	64	Haven	Columbia	Columbia Mo
Maria Hedricke	70	Samuel Strawd	Jefferson City	Columbia Mo
Dead Harriet Thomas	64	Jefferson Garth	Scott Kentucky	to third daughter Marion D Jun Columbia Mo
Jennie Conaray	47	James Bellenger	Columbia Boone	Columbia Mo
Sandy Turner	74	Henderson Jackson	Scott County	Columbia Mo
Harriet Tune (23)	23	Captain Ship	Virgena	Columbia Mo
Mildred Redman	54	John Clarkson	Virgenia	Columbia Mo

tance. Government provision of social services to the African-American community is a relatively recent development.[19]

In 1787, in Philadelphia, blacks led by Richard Allen and Absalom Jones withdrew as a body from the prejudiced whites of St. George's Church and formed the Free African Society, the first African-American mutual-aid society. The members pledged to help one another in sickness and death and to provide for widows and children of the deceased. They also purchased a plot to use as a burial ground. Mutual-aid societies, often connected with a church, spread rapidly in northern urban communities and among free Negroes in New Orleans, Charleston, and other southern cities. In this period, long before the Social Security Act of 1935, the societies aided the elderly or disabled and provided a decent burial for the impecunious.[20]

With Emancipation, the concept of the benevolent association grew rapidly until it was employed by Mrs. House and the association. It was one component of the broad effort at community care among African Americans, which included secret societies, homes for children, old-age homes, and a flexible family system for individuals throughout the life cycle. At the end of the nineteenth century, when the Ex-Slave Association began, a freedman or -woman emancipated at age thirty would have been sixty-seven. Among the first generation of African Americans to enjoy freedom, large numbers were in their sixties, seventies, and eighties and unable to work at manual labor because they were suffering from a variety of ills, some stemming from the hardships endured during slavery. The rapidly aging members overwhelmed local benevolent societies. The crisis underscored the need for both parts of the Ex-Slave Association's agenda of mutual aid and pensions.[21]

In 1898, when the Ex-Slave Association sought its charter,

Nashville already had a number of benevolent institutions. The 1895 smallpox epidemic and the continuing admonitions of the public health officer caused the white Ladies' Relief Society to increase help to poor whites and to challenge black leaders to do the same for African Americans. Thirty leading African-American women formed the Colored Relief Society for this purpose. Other relief organizations, including the Nashville Provident Association, founded in 1865 to give firewood and soup to needy freedmen, still operated. Nashville's African-American churches, like those elsewhere, offered benevolent auxiliaries. The association's mutual aid filled a crucial gap in these disparate and generally underfinanced services for an aging and ill population. Suffering from poverty, bad diet, injuries from abuse during slavery, and hard work since, many ex-slaves over the age of seventy had a difficult time making their battered bodies continue to work at the hard-labor jobs available to them. Moreover, the poverty of the "first freedom" generation of African Americans meant they could not sustain both their older relatives and their own families.[22]

Nashville's better-off African Americans put some resources into helping the poor, but they showed more concern for civil rights and opportunities than for addressing poverty. As Jim Crow and disenfranchisement became law and the lynching of African Americans became common across the South, they also took their toll in Nashville. Indelibly etched in the minds of local ex-slaves was the 1892 lynching of Eph Gizzard, who had been accused of raping a white woman. On April 30, while the city was still in the grips of the seventeen-foot March snow-storm, the largest in history, Gizzard was hanged by a mob right downtown at 2:40 P.M. on the Woodland Street bridge.[23]

Most of Nashville's frustrated African-American leadership ignored pension seeking to spend their energy and political capital on other concerns where they believed they could make a difference. For example, the year before House and others met in the city to promote reparations, the elites worked hard to gain participation in the Centennial Exposition of 1897, held to mark Tennessee's one hundredth birthday. Preoccupied with their own image as an educated group, the elites thought it valuable to join the exposition even though they would have to accept segregation. Northern middle-class African Americans, far from the Jim Crow environment, objected to the strategy, earning the resentment of their Nashville counterparts. On February 27, 1897, the *Nashville American* criticized the only African American in the Massachusetts legislature for complaining that public funds should not be used to pay the expenses of Massachusetts officials visiting the Tennessee fair because of its segregation. In a period when House and most other African Americans lived in rental housing without light or heat except for a fireplace, and worked at low-wage, labor-intensive jobs with which they could barely make ends meet, the business and professional leadership fought for inclusion in the exposition and boasted that they'd achieved a Negro day at the fair. In the end, the emphasis on culture, sketches, oil paintings and drawings, musical compositions played daily by a pianist, and carvings by Negro sculptor G. R. Devans of horns and walking canes engraved with pictures of Civil War generals contrasted sharply with the real-life social and economic problems of poor African Americans. When the exposition was over their problems remained.[24]

But it was in 1895 in Atlanta, on precisely such an occasion of proud cultural displays, that Booker T. Washington gave his racial accommodationist speech:

"In all things that are purely social we can be as separate as the five fingers, yet one as the hand in all things essential to mutual progress." He continued, "To those of my race who depend upon bettering their condition in a foreign land or who underestimate the importance of cultivating friendly relations with the Southern white man . . . I would say 'Cast down your bucket where you are.' " His widely reported Atlanta Exposition speech essentially amounted to telling African Americans to stay in the South, work hard, and accept segregation to show they "deserved" citizenship rights someday. Washington's speech made him white America's favorite race leader and gave him control of African-Americans' access to money and power.[25]

In Nashville, the Tennessee Exposition officials followed the example set in Atlanta to establish a segregated "Negro Department" at the beginning. They appointed a committee chaired by the city's most prominent African-American Republican leader, James Napier, a former member of the city council who held various patronage posts and saw to it that his friends did so as well. As chief of the Negro Department, Napier's committee included fifteen of the most prominent African Americans.[26]

With this nod to Napier by the state's leading white businessmen, Nashville's African-American leadership determined to show its agreement with the philosophy of Booker T. Washington. It publicly accepted segregation as a road to equality and applauded the selection of Washington as a speaker. It also seized the opportunity to display the "progress" African Americans had made since emancipation. When Napier was later forced to resign because of ill health, he publicly underscored the value of this opportunity to the community. His resignation letter pointed out that since Emancipation "intelligent" blacks had "rapidly increased in numbers" and the "Negro Exhibition Hall" would prove their progress. Under the leadership of Richard Hill, a "Negro" schoolteacher and the son of

"Uncle John Hill"—a favorite fiddler for wealthy white parties, black Nashvillians designed and constructed the "Negro Building," which included a segregated first-aid station and other facilities for their use. Hill told African Americans that they were "on trial." He said, "The American people have spent no small amount and energy for our intellectual and moral training. Many are now asking 'What have they amounted to?'" If they failed to exhibit their accomplishments, "It will be our everlasting shame."[27]

Each college, university, and other acceptable African-American organization in the city enjoyed a special day for its segregated exhibits. The managers also set aside June 5, 1897, as "Negro Day" to enjoy the entire fair. From all over the state blacks came to Nashville to visit the site, and schools, churches, and civic organizations marched in the parade. Both races, kept segregated, attended affairs involving Republican president, William McKinley, the governors of some twenty states, and the Booker T. Washington speech on Emancipation Day, September 22, 1897. The white Nashville press usually restricted coverage of African Americans to reports of lynchings, vignettes and cartoons on the laziness and ignorance of blacks, or articles on the "misguided" efforts of African Americans who challenged the color line. For the exposition, the papers enthusiastically reported on the "Negro Building" and African-American activities. Leaders believed they had put their best foot forward at the fair and avoided "everlasting shame."[28]

Nashville's class of well-off African Americans concentrated on making gains in business and the professions within the segregated black community. Privately, like Booker T. Washington, they worked to remedy black exclusion from politics and were finally somewhat successful in 1911, when a black lawyer, Samuel P. Harris, was elected to the city council. He was the first African American elected since Napier's defeat in 1885. Poor and working-class African Americans such as Callie House and association members interacted with this group of blacks only in the course of business, such as in the incorporation of the organization.

The National Ex-Slave Mutual Relief, Bounty and Pension Association charter stated that the Association would work to unite African Americans and "friends" together in the cause. It made clear the dual mission of the organization. The association would collect petitions and lobby to pass the pension bill. However, mutual assistance was of equal importance. Local chapters would do "whatever is necessary in the way of charity and benevolence by aiding of its members in distress in sickness and in death and in looking after the interests of all."[29] Members contributed ten cents monthly to finance their ambitious goals.

Although chartered by Primitive Baptists, the church of working-class blacks, the first official association convention, at which Mrs. House was elected assistant secretary, took place at Gay Street Christian Church, a prominent Disciples of Christ congregation. The church, founded in 1824 as the "Negro congregation" of the white Vine Street Christian Church, trained and nurtured some of the most outstanding African-American church brotherhood leaders, including Preston Taylor, who became a nationally admired Disciples of Christ leader. Taylor was closely associated with James Napier and other well-off African-American Nashvillians. Taylor involved himself in every civic endeavor and enterprise in Nashville and the surrounding area and he introduced Booker T. Washington at the 1897 Centennial Exposition. He also served as parade marshal on "Negro Day." The Gay Street Church provided a quite respectable venue, giving the association credibility. The pastor serving the successor church today could find no records from this period but suggests that Gay Street became the venue for the association convention because of Preston Taylor's interest in every type of community involvement.[30]

Following the association's first postcharter convention, from November 28 through December 1, 1898, the newly elected assistant secretary, Callie House, reported to the membership that they had proudly thanked local Republican leader James C. Napier and Reverend Richard Henry Boyd for their attendance. Boyd's presence was important because he was the most successful Baptist minister, the founder of the National Baptist Publishing Board, and financier of the local black newspaper, *The Globe*. The association officers knew that the presence of Napier and Boyd at their first official convention could signal important political support for the pension cause. Napier's future father-in-law, for example, was John Mercer Langston, who had vocally opposed the pension idea while in Congress.[31]

In the materials she sent to the state and local chapters and after the convention, House reported that the convention had acknowledged, both at the meeting and in its literature, the role Vaughan had played by first suggesting pension legislation. She also candidly described a rift in the movement blamed on Vaughan's attempt to anoint Hill, who the association did not deem any more likely than Vaughan to garner grassroots support. Although "slanderous circulars" and competing efforts had ensued, the association now asked that any existing organization affiliate with it to "consolidate under one head."[32]

The delegates who went to Nashville for the meeting made clear their support of pension legislation and what they called the "Bodkin Bill," a measure introduced by Democratic congressman Jeremiah Botkin of Kansas in March 1898. The bill

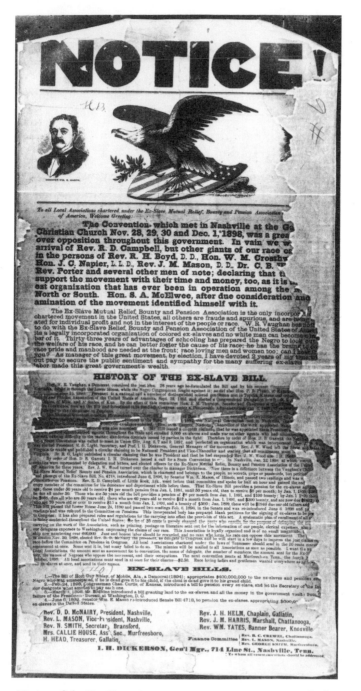

Notice of the Ex-Slave Association 1898 convention at which Callie House was elected assistant secretary.

gave ex-slaves homesteads of forty acres for individuals and 160 acres for a family. The families would also receive initial capital from a legacy or commissary fund that included uncollected deceased soldiers' pay and pensions. This bill, which did not pass, reiterated the original promise of land to the freedmen that had remained unfulfilled.[33]

The association announced opposition to a Senate bill designed to appropriate $100,000 for a National Home for Aged and Infirm Old Ex-Slaves in Washington as out of line with its objectives. The appropriation would come from funds in the Treasury, owed to deceased black soldiers but unpaid because wives and children were not aware they existed and did not apply or could not provide legal documentation of their relationship to the deceased. The bill's sponsor, Senator George Perkins, Republican of California and chairman of the Committee on Education and Labor, stated that as of July 27, 1895, the funds amounted to $230,018.84 even though the bill expressed a willingness to spend less than half that amount. A group of "the very best and most influential colored people in this country" had been asking senators and congressmen to introduce the bill since 1893. Their petition included leaders such as African Methodist Episcopal Church bishop Alexander Walters, chairman of the Afro-American Council, a civil rights protest and advocacy group; the four most prominent Washington, D.C., ministers, Francis Grimke of Fifteenth Street Baptist Church, Walter Brooks of Nineteenth Street Baptist Church, J. Albert Johnson of Metropolitan A.M.E. Church, and J. A. Taylor of Shiloh Baptist Church; and Calvin Chase, editor of *The Washington Bee*, one of the most important black newspapers. Those leaders had created a corporation and arranged to buy land to build the home. These men thought this appeal was more likely to receive support from Congress than any other proposals to help poor blacks.[34]

In the House debate on the bill, Congressman Ernest Roberts, Republican from Maine, stated, "There is no question that the aged and colored people who once were slaves are more subject to destitution and require charitable aid more than any other class of people in the United States." Since the government did not establish charitable institutions, it should assist those who would. He asserted that in the District of Columbia, the only available public facility, in the basement of the Children's Asylum on Eighth Street, could accommodate only ten persons at a time. Therefore, it made sense to help blacks care for the "needy and aged of their own race," using funds that belonged to African-American soldiers.[35]

Even though the convention liked the idea of the home, which to them seemed as unlikely to pass as the pension bill, it was opposed, according to Callie House's report to the members, because the small size of the proposed facility was grossly insufficient. In addition, members believed it would "block the passage" of reparations "for all time to come." Convention participants decided, instead, to continue their efforts to pass the Mason Ex-Slave Pension Bill.[36]

The tone of the congressional debate supported the ex-slave delegates' conclusion that the Home for Ex-Slaves Bill would not pass. Representative Joseph Cannon, Republican representative from Illinois and chairman of the House Appropriations Committee, explained that in reality no surplus funds existed from unclaimed pay and bounty for white or black soldiers because the Congress made appropriations only when needed. The bill therefore consisted of "mere leather and Brunella . . . mere deception, mere sticking in the bark-

*Reverend Dudley McNairy from Nashville, one
of the charter incorporators, was elected president
of the Ex-Slave Association at the 1898 convention.
The convention instructed him to go to
Washington to lobby for the Mason Bill.*

buncombe, so to speak. This bill would do the manly and
honest thing if it said, there is hereby appropriated $100,000
to build this home." Also, he saw no reason to cut off the possibility of claims by black soldiers' relatives in 1903 unless
claims were also ended for the relatives of white soldiers. They
might make claims later. He pointed out that "claims agents
are writing all over the country." They are "hunting up every-
body to whom we owe anything and three times as many bod-

ies to whom we do not owe anything. They are lively ducks." They might still identify claimants.[37]

Democratic representative John Gaines from Tennessee objected. He predicted that the home would attract the poor from different states to the District of Columbia and become a burden, making the U.S. government "a poor house." Georgia Democratic representative Charles Bartlett pointed out that the funds "did not come altogether—possibly in very small part—from colored soldiers of the District of Columbia." They came from "various parts of the union." But now the advocates wanted to use it "for the benefit exclusively of persons residing in or near the city of Washington." Roberts answered that it would be located there but for the "people of the whole United States." Committees in both houses of Congress reported out the Home Bill, but it did not pass.[38]

Most of the convention time was spent on deciding how to move the pension legislation forward. In addition to electing Mrs. House assistant secretary, the convention delegates named Reverend Dudley M. McNairy, one of the charter incorporators, president, and Isaiah H. Dickerson general manager, "to whom all communications should be addressed." At the end of the meeting, the delegates instructed McNairy to go to Washington to lobby for the bill, which they persuaded Senator Edmund Pettus, Democrat of Alabama, to reintroduce. It repeated the provision of earlier bills: a pension of $15 per month and a bounty of $500 for each ex-slave seventy years and older. Those under seventy would receive $300 as a bounty and $12 per month until they reached the age of seventy. Those less than sixty years old would receive a $100 bounty and $8 a month until they reached age sixty. Those less than fifty years of age would receive $4 per month and then, at age fifty, $8 per month. Ex-slaves and those legally obligated to take care of

*This early certificate of the Ex-Slave Association
does not mention mutual assistance.*

those who could not care for themselves were eligible for the pensions. McNairy expressed the hope that the "many ex-slave organizations striving to secure the enactment of the Vaughan Bill [Mason Bill]" would affiliate with the association so as to "consolidate under one head."[39]

The constitution and by-laws and the report of the convention included photographs of the officers, including Callie House. The membership certificates boasted a picture of Senator Mason of Illinois and, in one corner, the words "$500.00 bounty," the amount immediately payable, in addition to $15 per month, to those seventy or older if the bill passed. The cer-

CONSTITUTION AND BY=LAWS

NATIONAL EX-SLAVE

Mutual Relief, Bounty and Pension

ASSOCIATION

OF THE

UNITED STATES OF AMERICA,

SENATE BILL NO. 4718, HOUSE OF REPRESENTATIVES BILL
No. 8849, ETC., ETC.

[Headquarters, 708 Gay Street, Nashville, Tenn.]

46

NASHVILLE, TENN.:
NATIONAL BAPTIST PUBLISHING BOARD.
1899.

*The 1898 national convention approved the issuance of these
formal legal documents of the Association, including
photographs of House and the other officers.*

MRS. CALLIE HOUSE.
Assistant Secretary, National Ex-Slave Mutual
Relief, Bounty and Pension Association.

DEAR FRIENDS:

I have been a promoter of the Ex-Slave Bill and an advocate of the National Ex-Slave Mutual Relief, Bounty and Pension Association. For the past twenty-five months I have been among strangers laboring to the best of my ability for the rights which my race is justly entitled to. It is my firm belief that honest labor should be rewarded, regardless of the color of the man or woman who performs that labor. I am in favor of the principles embodied in the so-called Mason Bill because they are just, and should the Bill receive the consideration it richly merits, it will, in my opinion, be but a question of time when those of our race who have borne the burden and heat of the day, will receive some recompense for honest labor performed during the dark and bitter days of slavery.

Let us consolidate all ex-slave organizations and bring to bear upon the law makers of the country which we labored so long and well to develop, every degree of influence within our power.

Very truly,

CALLIE HOUSE.

*House's first letter to the membership, printed in the convention
proceedings after her election as assistant secretary.*

tificate did not explicitly reiterate the language in the charter concerning the mutual benefit mission but spoke only of efforts to aid "the ex-slave movement and raise funds to promote the passage of the bill."[40]

National African-American newspapers and leading politicians and activists did not change their views concerning pensions just because the effort became black-led and successful. While the white press derided the movement as ridiculous and fraudulent, these leading African Americans either ignored it or criticized it as a distraction from the struggle for political rights and a hopeless cause. House often expressed outrage at their refusal to provide publicity that would help to organize the movement. These leaders' efforts to gain land and education aid and even election protection in the Congress had failed miserably. Yet they would not even try another avenue for relief for poor black people. From her perspective, "The most learned negroes have less interest in their race than any other negro as many of them are fighting against the welfare of their race."[41]

Despite these divisions between better-off, better-educated African Americans and the poor freedpeople who supported pensions, the association had organized successfully and was rapidly growing. The fees it collected, House explained, paid "expenses of the movement in printing literature and postage on literature sent out to notify our conventions and meeting for speaking and to pay traveling expences [expenses] and support of men and women who are giving their whole time to the movement." The association also spent the funds to "send men to Congress as delegates to present our petition when Congress meet[s] the first Monday in December."

In addition, the local chapters used the ten cents' monthly dues they collected to pay for "places to meet at and to help old and decrepit members to render mutual assistance any way they see fit." Callie House expressed pride in the convention's work as she circulated the minutes to the membership. She was especially honored that she had been "elected by the people as an officer in this organization which belongs to the people and not to the officers." She was proud that old ex-slaves were helping one another locally. She also was excited that ex-slaves were exercising their citizenship rights to gain a new law at a time when disenfranchisement had closed other avenues for political action. The association was off to a promising start.[42]

CHAPTER 3

The Association
Under Attack

The ex-slave pension movement "is setting the negroes wild, . . . making anarchists of them."

PENSION BUREAU INSPECTOR W. L. REID
(1899)

ECSTATIC OVER HER ELECTION as assistant secretary, Callie House left the convention determined to continue the rapid expansion of the ex-slave pension movement. In the midst of her joy she received a letter from Harrison Barrett, acting assistant attorney general of the Post Office Department in Washington, D.C. Reading the letter, House sensed danger to the very existence of the movement. Barrett notified her that he was issuing an order denying the association the use of the mails because it supposedly engaged in fraud. The Association, like other organizations, was almost absolutely dependent on using the post office to correspond with members and to transact financial affairs. The people's commitment was the lifeblood of the organization, but the mails were a crucial means of communication and support. House and the other officers traveled constantly, but they could not be everywhere at once. They traveled by train and by horse and carriage, sometimes walking for miles in the country. Besides, travel was costly, arduous, and slow, especially in rural communities where many of the chapters developed. She did not know it at the time, but Barrett had sent the same letter to the other association officers and to Dickerson, the general manager.[1]

House knew from Dickerson that the Pension Bureau had investigated Vaughan's clubs at the behest of whites who wrote in to complain about the idea. She also knew that Vaughan had denounced others in the movement and stopped organizing. But she did not know the extent of the interest the Association's activities had aroused within the federal government. When House and Dickerson began organizing the Association, federal inspectors continued their monitoring of ex-slave pension advocates. Inspectors consistently wrote in their reports that they found nothing illegal in organizing a lobbying group and the government could not prosecute the pension-seeking leaders unless they claimed to be federal officials, and no evidence had been found of that. The Bureau sent Special Examiner William Baird to a local pension meeting in Chattanooga, and he reported seeing nothing misleading. The organizer, to whom he spoke, explained that the membership fee of twenty-five cents paid "expenses of agitation" for the legislation. The ten-cents-a-month dues paid for a hall, lights, maintenance, and publications.[2]

The Association enrolled at least 34,000 members between July 1897 and April 1899, and thousands thereafter. House had no idea that Bureau officials had stepped up their surveillance because of the Association's rapid growth. The Bureau sent letters to ministers and others who acted as association agents warning them of complaints of fraud. The letters told of individuals who collected small amounts of money from the ex-slave "dupes" to put their names on a pension list. The letters asked that they report anyone who traveled "throughout the southern states representing that the [pension] bill had become law, that various sums had been appropriated to pay the pensions thereunder, and that they were officers of the Government of the United States fully authorized and empowered to cause the names of these ex-slaves to be inscribed upon the pension rolls." The letters heavy-handedly warned that those who engaged in such representations could suffer punishment of a fine of not more than $1,000 and imprisonment for no longer than three years or both. The letters routinely pointed out that the government did not mean to interfere with the right to seek pensions since citizens had an "unquestioned right" to associate to lobby for legislation. But this disclaimer did not lessen the intentionally chilling effect the notices had on the organizers.[3]

After the Ex-Slave Association's charter convention in 1898 and the continued development of local chapters, the suspicion of their operations grew. House saw African Americans as victims and the federal government as an accomplice in their subordination and impoverishment. Now, in contrast, Barrett's letter indicated that government officials defined blacks as ignorant victims of the ex-slave pension movement. Moreover, the "ignorant" were also seen by the government as capable of dangerous rebellion. In May 1899, Pension Bureau Inspector W. L. Reid told his superiors that the ex-slave pension movement "is setting the negroes wild, robbing them of their money and making anarchists of them." If this continues, the government "will have some very serious questions to settle in connection with the control of the race."[4]

House was totally oblivious to the possibility that the Post Office Department would interfere with their efforts to gain pensions. If she had known about the evolution of postal authority and enforcement activities, Barrett's letter would not have been such a surprise. Essentially, Pension Bureau officials had decided to have the postmaster general use his antifraud powers to suppress the association. They assumed that cutting off the mails would strike a death blow to the movement. The federal government targeted the ex-slave pension cause as threatening enough for deployment of law enforcement resources, while at this same time the same federal government remained generally unreceptive to blacks' complaints of disenfranchisement, racially motivated assault, and even lynching, carried out with the cooperation of local and state authorities. In this general attitude of neglect of black concerns about safety and eroding citizenship rights, political officials in three agencies, the Justice Department and the Post Office Department, at the behest of the Pension Bureau, decided to declare war on the Association. Acting Assistant Attorney General Harrison Barrett rationalized their actions by explaining that House and her colleagues knew that there had "never been the remotest prospect" that Congress would appropriate pensions for African Americans. Of course, pension legislation had repeatedly been introduced in Congress. Further, often in the legislative process, proposals are made for years before public education and circumstances make passage possible. The income tax followed a similar path successfully until legislation, and then a constitutional amendment was enacted. The impoverished ex-slaves might presumably take longer and need more tenacity to achieve an objective than better-endowed groups.[5]

Barrett and the other officials registered their distaste at the temerity of Callie House and the others in acting, uncontrolled by whites, and asserting their independence and commitment. Federal officials feared the association's successful membership campaigns. Mobilizing so many freedpeople heightened the danger of rebellion by "wild" African Americans when freedom's first generation discovered that there would be no pensions or other compensation for slavery. As a result, federal officials kept close surveillance on the association's rapidly growing membership and put politically appointed local postmasters on the front lines of attack. The commitment of A. W. Wills, the postmaster in Nashville, where the association maintained its headquarters, was key. Arriving in Nashville from Philadelphia after the Civil War, he practiced law and was a claims agent before obtaining a political appointment as postmaster in 1890. A loyal Republican, he served as a delegate to the national convention in 1900 that selected the William McKinley–Theodore Roosevelt ticket. He was eager to implement the harassment policy ordered against the association.[6]

House and the association had become targets of a law enforcement process that had been developed for reasons totally unrelated to black activism. Fraudulent use of the U.S. mails to promote sin and commercial scams became a matter of great concern in the nation toward the end of the nineteenth century, leading to the exercise of extraordinary power by the postmaster general in controlling the use of the mails. This power had developed only gradually, but eventually the postmaster had the ability to suppress valid freedom of expression such as the lobbying and petitioning exercised by the Ex-Slave Association. The Constitution permits Congress to regulate post offices and the mails. Before the Civil War, Congress excluded from handling only matter that weighed more than three or four pounds. During the Civil War, the postmaster general exercised the power to ban material that might be considered treasonable or might give aid to the enemy. Congress had upheld the postmaster's actions while recognizing that they had the right to instruct him to declare certain matter unmailable. Extending the principle after the war, Congress established categories of unmailable matter.[7]

The gradual expansion of the postmaster's powers continued as Congress first focused on making obscenity unmailable in an 1865 law that excluded from the mails any "obscene book, pamphlet, picture, print, or other publication of a vulgar and indecent character." Congress repeated this provision in an 1872 codification of the postal laws, and extended it in the 1873 Comstock Law, passed at the behest of the New York Young Men's Christian Association's Committee for the Suppression of Vice, which had begun campaigning against obscene literature. The YMCA hired Anthony Comstock to fight the traffic in obscene literature. Comstock, an impecunious dry-goods salesman, said that religious fervor and the loss of a friend who had succumbed to sexual excess, supposedly caused by reading erotic publications, stimulated his interest in the issue. The Comstock Law expanded the obscenity category to include birth control information, appliances, and masturbatory materials, and permitted search and seizure. Comstock served until his death in 1915 as both a special agent of the post office and secretary of the Society for the Suppression of Vice in New York. Working under New York state and federal law that the New York YMCA had sponsored, he had the power to arrest violators and seize their materials.[8]

In addition to the campaign against obscenity, the Post Office Department gained increased powers when "gift enterprises" and lotteries that supposedly gulled citizens became a matter of public concern. Congress responded by enacting provisions against using the mails for fraudulent purposes. They gave the postmaster general the power to issue fraud orders to forbid payment on money orders and to return letters after marking them "Fraudulent" on the outside. However, he was not supposed to open letters but to base their exclusion on whatever appeared on the envelope.[9]

Lottery companies challenged the law unsuccessfully. By the 1880s, the postmaster general's enormous powers, including the protection of the public from matter that might impair their morals, including obscene literature, lottery tickets, contraceptive devices, and information about them, had been upheld by the courts. Almost every Congress in the 1890s discussed even greater extension of the postmaster's powers. The 1895 reenactment of the postal fraud laws made clear the power to exclude letters directed to any person obtaining money through the mails by false pretenses or promises. Having disrupted the dissemination of so-called obscene matter, Congress and the post office spent increasingly less time on obscenity and more time on fraudulent schemes involving counterfeit money and lotteries.[10]

Postmasters assumed powers that were virtually unreviewable by the courts to deny the use of the mails when they determined that an enterprise was using the mails to defraud. The Congress funded postal inspectors, who zealously enforced the law, and the courts upheld the postmasters' actions. By the end of the century, lotteries practically disappeared. The Post Office Department, however, tried to end practices targeted by Congress. The ex-slave pension movement's exercise of the right to petition the government became a target of the Post Office Department's expanded power. The postmaster's unconstrained power became abusive, and it unnecessarily interfered with civil liberties.[11]

When Barrett sent House the fraud order notice, he had no evidence of illegal activity. And federal officials knew they didn't because Pension Bureau officials in President William McKinley's administration had watched the growth of the Ex-Slave Association across the South. The inspectors had collected no evidence of fraud. Furthermore, the association's growth was unimpeded by pension inspectors' surveillance and also what they reported as efforts by authorities to "run" organizers out of town. Barrett's "evidence" of "frequent complaints" to the Post Office Department consisted of letters complaining that whites believed the movement was crooked and how it excited the old "negroes." The files also contain a much larger number of letters from ex-slaves and their family members. These letters express curiosity about the legislation and ask if anything had passed and, if so, how to apply. One ex-slave asked, "Is there anything to it?" and "When can I get a payment?" Others described their poverty and ill health since slavery and asked, "Is it true the government might help us?" Instead of recommending an analysis of the feasibility of ex-slave pensions, Barrett attacked with a fraud order prohibiting officers of the Ex-Slave Association from sending or receiving correspondence of any kind.[12]

When Callie House received Barrett's letter, her shock quickly turned to anger. Although her official title was only assistant secretary, House indicated in a long handwritten reply that the association acted on behalf of "four & half million slave[s] who was [were] turn[ed] loose ignorant bare footed and naked without a dollar in their pockets without a shelter to go under out of the falling rain but was force[d] to look the man in the face for something to eat who once had the power to whip them to death but now have the power to starve them to death. We the ex-slave [sic] feel that if the government had a right to free us she had a right to make some provision for us as she did not make it soon after our Emancipation she ought to make it now."

House insisted that a pension would remedy "wrongs this Government allowed to be suffered by us without redress." During slavery masters worked blacks as chattels, "in violation of the Declaration of Independence." Officials, under the auspices of the government, denied slaves liberty and equal rights.[13]

House's defiant response offered a sharp contrast to the nonthreatening demeanor whites expected from blacks, no matter what their economic circumstances. As Benjamin Mays, longtime president of Morehouse College in Atlanta, later reflected: "the more a Negro owned the more humble he had to act in order to keep, in the good graces of the white people." A Mississippi farm owner explained that he had made it through "hard work, slow saving, and staying in our place, acting humble, that's how I did it." African-American men who avoided trouble were required to be "always respectful, never disposed to fudge on the rights of the white people." African-American women were to behave as "simple and silly-minded" and as generally lacking any semblance of serious thought.[14]

Naturally, House's impassioned, thoughtful, unapologetic defense did not deter the Post Office from attacking the association. With the approval of Postmaster General Charles Emory Smith and Assistant Attorney General James Tyner, his supervisor and uncle, Barrett distributed the promised fraud order to local post offices and the press. The order instructed all post offices to deny payment on money orders made out to the National Ex-Slave Mutual Relief, Bounty and Pension Association or to any of its officers in their official capacity. It also excluded from the mails any literature of the organization or letters addressed to the association or any of its officers. The basis of the order was noted as "It having been made to appear to the Postmaster General, upon evidence satisfactory to him" that they were receiving money through the mails through fraudulent activity.[15]

The order was accompanied by Barrett's letter including the usual boilerplate that the post office did not interfere with citizens' constitutional right to petition the government. Instead, the department dishonestly claimed a paternalistic responsibility to protect "ex-slaves from the rapacity principally of unscrupulous members of their own race, who in the benevolent garb of ministers of religion or other (often assumed) Professors, endeavor to and do prey upon the credulity and inexperience of their unfortunate brethren." According to Barrett, the National Ex-Slave Movement existed only to provide "salaries, expenses, etc. for their personal use." These are "flagrant frauds" and can be of "no possible benefit to the colored race." Therefore, any mail for the association or its officers would be returned to a sender marked "Fraudulent."[16]

To Mrs. House's consternation, black newspapers published the post office's fraud order as the government requested, usually without comment. For the most part, they ignored the pension issue advanced by a poor people's movement with no notable leaders, and focused on the priorities advanced by well-known African-American leaders. For example, Calvin Chase's *Washington Bee,* perhaps the most important African-American newspaper, ignored House, the association, and their legislative efforts, even refusing to publish notices of meetings or information they were sent. Black newspapers used most of their space to cover social engagements and local religious services. They also focused on the need for vocational education and occasionally discussed the rapidly accelerating disenfranchisement of black voters.[17]

White newspapers denounced the members of the association, House, and other leaders as misguided. The papers blamed Vaughan because as a white man he should have known that his idea would excite the "negroes" unnecessarily and make them less tractable. The *Washington Evening Star,* on September 21, 1899, reported that Vaughan had offered to help the post office to suppress the other organizations. They noted that he had long since given up his own efforts to gain a pension as a fruitless cause. However, the paper laid the blame for the continuation of the movement not on African Americans but on "base white men." As the Washington edition of the *Nashville Banner* put it, some white members of Congress "might be brought to support it to bring money to their own districts." These men bought Vaughan's political argument of local benefit to the depressed southern economy or to northern locales to which blacks had migrated from the South, such as the "Exodusters" who had gone to Kansas. The *Star* concluded that these white men knew that pensions would never pass. It was "sickening and ludicrous" to stir up the "negroes" by supporting the cause.[18]

Certainly, real swindlers who used the pension idea bilked some unsuspecting ex-slaves. Rainey Badger of Blythe DeSoto County, Mississippi, sixty-five years old and a midwife, complained that a white man calling himself Woodruff had swindled her. He had come to her house in October 1899 and identified himself as a pension agent working for the government, telling her that she would receive $600 on October 28 and $12 a month thereafter. He had charged her $5 to "pay the men in Washington who handled the papers." She had only $4.50

saved for her house rent and store account. She gave it to him, and he said he would collect the additional fifty cents when she received her pension. She remembered that he mentioned President McKinley, but he "talked like a mocking-bird in the morning," so fast that she could "only recollect what he said in spots." She reported that he "staid there one night and got one meal but never paid her. Word got out that he was there and during the next day before he left several people came by and paid him." That day he left with "a good handful of silver." Local officials caught some swindlers; others remained free, while the federal government focused on House and the association.[19]

The government's priorities showed in the stark contrast between the hands-off attitude toward Vaughan and the pursuit of House and the Ex-Slave Association. It demonstrated the selective use of governmental power. Barrett charged that the ex-slave pension movement organizers enriched themselves and their families from the movement but offered nothing to support his assertion. At the same time the Pension Bureau and Post Office Department tracked funds Vaughan received and concluded that he had pocketed substantial profits. In 1899, the commissioner of pensions estimated that Vaughan had collected at least $100,000, although he reported spending no more than a total of $20,000 on lobbying and publications.[20]

Whatever Vaughan's motives, unlike Callie House, he had profited from the cause before abandoning it. However, the government began an almost twenty-year campaign to end the pension movement, and it targeted House, a thirty-three-year-old seamstress and laundress with no right to vote but the capacity to become the de facto leader of a movement strong enough to pose a threat to powerful national officials. Despite the government's threats, she was determined to organize the ex-slaves.[21]

CHAPTER 4

Voices of the Ex-Slaves

*To render assistance to its members in good standing and
to devise ways and means for the caring and establishment of decrepit ex-slaves, their widows and orphans,
and to unite all friends in securing pension legislation in
favor of the ex-slaves.*

CHARTER OF NEW ORLEANS CHAPTER
(JUNE 1899)

THE LOCAL COLUMBIA, Boone County, Missouri, National
Ex-Slave Mutual Relief, Bounty and Pension Association Lodge
Number 4 convened its monthly meeting in the basement of
Wheeler Chapel Church one evening in the fall of 1899. Luvenia Fields, the secretary for "the insuing year," carefully took the
minutes, and she also read aloud materials sent by the association headquarters to her husband, Reuben, and other members, some of whom could not read or write. The oldest
member present was 101 years old; the youngest, thirty-nine.[1]

It was a sadly impoverished group that the federal government had declared war on: small sects like those at the Boone
County meeting. But the power of the idea of reparations and
the growing number of supporters scared government officials,

even though they had the groups under surveillance and knew that they were nothing more than ex-slaves and their families meeting to commiserate and work peaceably to achieve economic justice.

The Boone County, Columbia, Missouri, Lodge was one of many branches and very typical of the groups Mrs. House and Dickerson had organized. The Association had continued to grow like wildfire after the 1898 convention. Mrs. House and Dickerson had enrolled at least 34,000 members by the middle of 1899 and thousands thereafter. Local association affiliates were organized in Atlanta, New Orleans, Vicksburg, Kansas City, and small rural and urban communities all across the South and Midwest. Like the veterans' pension lobbyists and land agents and Vaughan's example, they started a newspaper, the *National Industrial Advocate*. The paper's name reflected the ex-slaves' workers' consciousness in a period when attempts by blacks in some communities to demand pay for their work had led to violence.[2]

As they recruited members, Mrs. House and Dickerson distributed literature, arranged annual national meetings, collected petitions from ex-slaves, and supported lobbyists in Washington for the passage of pension bills. Along the way they also strongly emphasized the need for local mutual benefit activities as the linchpin of their solidarity. Membership, open to all ex-slaves and anyone who wanted to support the cause, required the payment of an initial fee of twenty-five cents and then ten cents' monthly dues. Local organizations paid $2.50 for a charter. The association's rules also permitted the possibility of "extraordinary" collections of five cents per member to defray unusual expenses. House traveled extensively even after they had identified agents among the preachers in communities to mobilize for the association. She spoke at public meetings constantly "to both white and black" people about the cause. Besides local ministers, Mrs. House and Dickerson recruited other leaders as agents of the national organization in the field to collect petitions and keep the membership informed.[3]

House's travels took her to all of the ex-slave states, including those on the border. She went to Kansas, to which ex-slaves had migrated as part of the 1879 exodus and to Oklahoma, where African Americans had developed black towns. Statewide chapters incorporated, and branches and lodges grew everywhere she went. At meetings like the one on that September evening in Columbia, Boone County, Missouri, where Luvenia and Reuben Fields and others met in a church basement, members told sad stories that were so much like Mrs. House's own personal history. In the telling and retelling of their slavery, hard work, poverty, and the condition of their relatives, neighbors, and friends, association members reinforced the commitment that kept the organization together and growing.

Everywhere Mrs. House went, the story was familiar. Boone County's ex-slaves lived among a population about the size of Callie House's birthplace in Rutherford County, Tennessee. The county lay in the middle of the state of Missouri, at the confluence of the nation's mightiest rivers, the Missouri, the Ohio, and the Mississippi. Its topography includes gentle prairies, water-fed plains, and Ozark uplands. Boone County farmers raised livestock and corn, oats, wheat, rye, barley, tobacco, and fruit. The county had few large slave owners; only 13 percent of slaveholders owned more than ten slaves and only 1 percent had more than twenty. On even the large plantations, the staple crop for-profit system of the South remained largely unknown. Slaves did general farmwork for farmers who raised diversified crops. Many of the male ex-slaves who joined the association continued as farm laborers, and the women worked as laundresses and domestic servants. Most of them were dark-skinned, heavyset, and of medium height, and Callie House resembled most of the other women at this meeting and others. She often visited local councils like this one during what she described as her travels "among strangers," organizing for the cause.[4]

Ex-slaves at the lodge meetings talked of how far they had come since slavery and yet in recent years they had a sense of skidding backward to destitution. Some had stories of harsh masters and slave patrols. They talked of how their actions were controlled by their masters and limited by the slave codes, and the risks they were willing to take to exercise some freedom. Almost everyone at the meetings had been part of trying to develop community with other slaves and had been whipped for their trouble. They had slipped away to dance with slaves at another plantation or chatted among themselves on market days or during trips to town or gathered to have prayer meetings despite the ban against having a religious meeting without a white person present.[5]

The ex-slaves had almost uniform recollections of constant deprivation. They talked of wearing clothes until they were worn out and going barefoot even in winter. Food consisted of an unvarying routine of water and cornmeal either fried into hoecake or boiled into grits. Even for slaves owned by wealthy whites who had smokehouses bulging with meat, meals did not vary much. Some ate buttermilk with cornbread crumbled into it. Less stingy owners permitted slaves to have biscuits made from "shorts" on Sundays, the "stuff dat they feed cows," and sorghum, a syrup made from grass. At Christmas, which "meant no more to us dan any other day," some were given sorghum and shorts to make gingersnaps.[6]

Beyond the poverty and persistent entrapment, the deepest wounds persisted from seeing other slaves sold away and families torn asunder. Done for whatever purpose, the separation of families was a painful memory for every ex-slave. They talked of mothers taken from their babies and being whipped for crying out in their pain. Some remembered being separated from their parents even when they had forgotten almost everything else about the slave experience. There was H. Wheeler, a local slave owner, who had sold his slaves so he could go to join the California gold rush. He had sold thirty-year-old Milly and her children and three other youngsters, all under ten years of age. At the sale of H. B. Hulett's estate in 1858, one buyer bought Henry, Caroline, and her two-year-old daughter. Three years later to settle business debts the family was sold again. John Bruton's widow inherited three men and two women. The remaining heirs divided up the ten children among his slaves, ranging in ages from two to ten years. Sometimes one member of the family would be manumitted but not others. William Jewell provided for the emancipation of a mother but not her children. John Tuttle freed George and left his wife the right to emancipate any slave. When she died, she freed George's wife, Eliza, but none of their children.[7]

The ex-slaves told of constantly praying and of hearing secret prayers for freedom all of their lives in bondage. They saw the coming of the Civil War as answering their prayers. Missouri was the state where the Compromise of 1820 had been a catalyst for fights over slavery along geographical divisions and the Dred Scott case, which reinforced slavery. The state's people, economy, and political interests had long been divided along sectional lines. Antislavery and foreign-born immigrants in St. Louis had defeated attempts to secede from the Union. But in the border states like Delaware, Maryland,

and Kentucky slavery remained even though they did not join the Confederacy. In 1860, there were 5,034 slaves, 53 free Negroes, and 14,399 white citizens in Boone County, Missouri.[8]

Some owners took their slaves farther south, hoping to keep them in servitude. Some blacks ran away to free territory; others followed the Union troops that passed through; and some joined the Union Army. Those who stayed behind heard about what happened to some who left. Seven men who ran away in 1863 enlisted in a regiment of Massachusetts troops and were sent to Morris Island, South Carolina; within six months only one survived. In Boone County so many slaves ran away that their flight became an exodus. In the whole state there were 114,931 slaves in 1860 but only 73,811 in 1863. In Boone County the numbers of slaves decreased from 5,034 to 2,265 between 1860 and 1864. Lincoln's Civil War policy included the payment of compensation to owners who freed their slaves for service in the border slave states, including Missouri. Slavery was abolished by the state legislature in January 1865.[9]

The ex-slaves in the association had vivid memories of the joy of emancipation and the confusion in its aftermath. Missouri was in chaos throughout the war and calm was not easily restored. Although the Union maintained political control, it had to endure several skirmishes and battles between U.S. soldiers and troops organized by the governor, Claiborne Fox Jackson, a secessionist, and Sterling Price, whom the governor appointed as commander of the pro-Southern militia. The state became a no-man's-land of hit-and-run raids, arson, ambushes, and murder. Confederate guerrillas became notorious "bushwhackers." Their followers after the war were people like the outlaws Jesse and Frank James and Cole and Jim Younger. The guerrillas tended to be sons of farmers or planters

"Negroes Driven South by the Rebel Officers," Harper's Weekly, *November 8, 1862. Slaves were driven to the deep South in the hope of keeping them in bondage. Some slaves ran away to free territory, others followed the Union troops who passed through, and some joined the Union Army.*

of Southern heritage, three times more likely to own slaves, and with twice as much wealth as the average Missourian. On the Union side, "jayhawker" counterinsurgency forces from Kansas matched the bushwhackers with similar tactics. In addition, Price, who retreated to the southwest corner of the state, continued to harass soldiers while claiming and losing territory during the war.[10]

The ex-slaves in the association told of the danger and constant uncertainty of the guerrilla warfare and the risks run by those who had run away. Some masters tried to avoid trouble by treating any soldiers or guerrillas who showed up, whether rebels or "blue jakets," with equal hospitality.[11]

The ex-slaves remembered how soldiers and guerrillas would suddenly appear, looking for food. They would pick apples from the orchards, raid smokehouses and granaries, and make the slaves kill and cook chickens for them. The owners would warn the slave children not to go off with the soldiers because marauders would sell them south, never to return again.[12]

The ex-slaves recalled that the bushwhackers had shot and killed two Boone County blacks working near the village of Stonesport. They also had to be wary of guerrillas who pretended to be Union soldiers, whom the slaves saw as bringing freedom. For example, a woman who had fled her slave master and established herself near Sturgeon went back to bring another woman and four children to live with her. Bushwhackers disguised in federal uniforms shot and killed all of them except two small children. Slaves and masters were caught between a rock and a hard place. If they helped bushwhackers, the Union Army would harass them and if they helped the "blue jakets," the bushwhackers would terrorize them.[13]

Even after January 1865, when slavery officially ended, the danger persisted. Ex-slaves told of the confusion and violence. The Jim Jackson gang of bushwhackers, several of whom were Boone County residents, terrorized the area's blacks. In February 1865, the gang posted a notice saying that freedpeople must leave the county by February 15 or be killed. They also warned that any farmers who hired the freedpeople would be killed. When the deadline passed, the bushwhackers murdered a freedman working for his former master. They also hanged two blacks and threatened the white man who had hired them. Such terrorism continued in the county until bushwhackers were suppressed by the Union military in June 1865.[14]

The ex-slaves bitterly described how their poverty and deprivation worsened immediately after emancipation. Within two months of the Missouri legislature's antislavery ordinance of January 1865, more than thirty men, women, and children died. On some days as many as three burials took place. The ex-slaves lacked food, fuel, and homes. They recalled that when they had been told they were free, it was hard to figure out what to do. Some owners asked them to stay but would not pay them. Some hired themselves out for food and clothing. Others left to try to find their mothers and fathers, searching the faces of any African Americans they met to see if they saw a resemblance. Others whose fathers and mothers were on the same farm told of how the families lived practically out of doors until they could build a log cabin. Others traveled around doing whatever work they could find. Some remembered being disappointed because they thought the slave owners' farms would be divided and land given to them. Some ex-slaves recalled how their masters had "turned them out of doors," to walk down the road in January 1865 in the snow. They were so angry at them for being free that they got rid of them as quickly as possible. Others had tried to keep the slaves in bondage, claiming their children as apprentices. Some ex-slaves had to leave secretly in the night because their masters were watching and would not let them leave in the daylight hours.[15]

The ex-slaves rejoiced when brighter days seemed to appear on the horizon. Whatever anger they had about emancipation, whites needed workers and signed labor contracts with the freedpeople. Freedpeople could work and get paid. George Jacob, following the usual local pattern, hired two women for $5 a week to do general housework and yard work. He also hired a black man to work his plantation for $12.50 per month. Businesses that had hired slaves from their masters now hired and paid the slaves. Christian College paid men $15 to $20 per month and women $8 to $10 to work as cooks, janitors, or fire lighters or to run the laundry. Those African Americans who had trades worked as blacksmiths or painters. Most of the men in the Boone County chapter took jobs as farm laborers; the women worked as laundresses and domestics.[16]

The Boone County ex-slaves' lives improved in the next few years after Emancipation, when the community quickly regrouped, as African Americans did throughout the slave states. They sought to pool their resources and work together. The free Negroes who had managed to gain their freedom before the Civil War provided the only economic base in Boone County afterward. There were fifty-three free blacks in the county in 1860, only twelve of whom owned property. Their total personal estate was worth $5,220, including the property of Cinthia Boyce, a washerwoman who had $100. Gilbert Akers, the largest landowner, bought his freedom, then purchased some town lots, which he resold. By 1864, he had enough money to buy his fourteen children and grandchildren. By 1880, the Census identified blacks as making up 18.4 percent of the county population; their occupation was farming, as owners, renters, or sharecroppers. The largest landowners were persons who had been free before the war. However, some of the ex-slaves had been able to make a living as farmers since emancipation.

The Boone County ex-slaves recalled with pride the glorious day when they had achieved a major goal: to have their own churches where they could worship freely and listen to their own preachers. Another sign of their progress in freedom could be seen in marriage data. After slavery the Missouri legislature made marriage mandatory for former slaves living as husband and wife. Three hundred marriages took place in

These impoverished freedpeople's diet consists of cooked corn cake crumbled in soured "clabbered" milk. "Hoecake and Clabber," Harper's Weekly, November 10, 1885.

Boone County between 1865 and 1866, most of which were performed by white ministers. There were only two black preachers in the county at first, the former slaves Henry Warfield and Armstead Estes, an African Methodist Episcopal Church minister, who began to perform marriages. By 1890, almost all marriages among blacks were conducted by African-American ministers, one sign of the growth of the black church and clergy.

Boone County African Americans made churches their most important community political, religious, and social institutions, and many of Mrs. House's meetings were held on church property. Most of the ex-slaves who attended church were either Baptists or Methodists. At first black churches met in homes until they were able to afford houses of worship. St. Paul's African Methodist Episcopal Church in Columbia, which had 206 members in 1900, had become the largest black Methodist church in the county. Second Baptist Church, founded in July 1866, had sixteen original members, with James Hudson, licensed by the local white Columbia Baptist Church, as the minister. With a $3,000 loan in 1894 from the pianist and successful entertainer "Blind Boone," the congregation completed a new brick church. John William "Blind" Boone became the most famous local black of the period. Boone, along with his manager, John Lang, Jr., traveled throughout the country exhibiting his extraordinary talent as a pianist; he could make the piano simulate violins, guitars, banjos, and tambourines. Boone was a great resource for the community and occasionally gave concerts specifically to help the poor. By the time the association was founded, about 23 percent of the 4,500 local blacks belonged to churches. The Baptists were the largest denomination, followed closely by the Methodists. Black churchgoers raised funds from cakewalks and picnics and even solicited contributions from white coreligionists.

When interested blacks organized in the Boone County Lodge of the Ex-Slave Association, they already had experiences with fraternal and benevolent societies in the county. These organizations fulfilled a need for social activity, provided relief for members in need, and acted as burial associations and insurance companies for members. In 1867, blacks established the First African Benevolent Society of Columbia to aid the infirm, destitute, and aged. Membership cost a $2 initiation fee and monthly dues of fifty cents. By June 1867, there were fifty-seven members. By 1869, the Masons organized a lodge, and in 1879, the United Brothers of Friendship was organized. Both provided burial benefits for members and some monetary assistance for families when a member died. The members of both fraternal groups were generally under fifty and in their prime working years. Sanford Estes, a laborer and preacher who joined the Ex-Slave Association lodge, was a member of both the United Brothers of Friendship and the Masonic Lodge.

The children of Ex-Slave Association members had some literacy, primarily because African Americans in the county founded schools. In the summer of 1865, a committee of African-American church members held a mass meeting to raise funds for a church and school dual-purpose building. They raised $149 and bought a lot for $20; the Baptists then pulled out and started their own school. In 1867, St. Paul's A.M.E. Church asked the state legislature for funds to support their school, but, instead, the legislature gave funds to the Baptist church and school. Consequently, by 1867 there were two schools in churches led by black men. The Baptist school, conducted by Charles Cummings, continued to receive state funding and was named the public school for blacks in 1868. Funds from the state, the community dinners, picnics, festivals, and the Freedmen's Bureau made it possible to erect a building, known as Cummings School until 1898, when, upon a petition by African Americans, the Columbia School Board renamed it Frederick Douglass Academy. By 1898, the school had begun a high school program.

Between 1875 and 1900, education was not ideal for either African Americans or whites; however, blacks' schools had worse conditions. The black schools were overcrowded, and the teachers were paid less than the white teachers. Missouri's schools were segregated by law in 1889, but segregated education had always existed in Boone County. In 1900, only 14 percent of the black population over age sixty was literate, as were 19 percent of those fifty-one to sixty, 34.6 percent of those forty-one to fifty, and 50.8 percent of those thirty-one to forty. However, 71 percent of those between twenty-one and thirty were literate. Most of the ex-slaves in the local branch of the association were illiterate, but most of their children and grandchildren could read and write.[17]

Gains notwithstanding, the old ex-slaves at the lodge meeting talked about their despair in recent years as the meager gains they had made since Emancipation had stagnated or evaporated in the 1890s. They not only suffered from the same poverty and discrimination experienced by blacks elsewhere, but they endured the same class divisions within the community. Their circumstances made them good candidates for Callie House's organizing efforts.

From the members, she heard how the county's always-present racial tension seemed to worsen. Ex-slaves recalled how a group of white men had shot into the African Methodist Episcopal Church during a festival in 1868. In 1878, a white man had shot a black cook for not preparing his breakfast quickly enough. In 1894, when a Boone County black woman ignored the vulgar remarks of a white man, he shot her. He was jailed, but not before he shot a black man. At least two riots occurred, one in 1878 in Ashland and another in 1882 in Rocheport, both with overly liquored participants, black and white, involved. In the second riot, six black men were jailed for two to seven years for shooting into a crowd of white men, injuring some after an intoxicated black man insulted a white man who drew his pistol and knocked him down. In 1895, Willie Eaton, the sister of one of the rioters, shot and killed Thomas J. White, the marshal responsible for arresting the black men. Convicted of manslaughter, she received a two-year sentence after a change of venue to Jefferson City. Clearly, African Americans in the county were prepared to try to protect themselves.[18]

After the enactment of the Fifteenth Amendment in 1870, male ex-slaves could legally vote. However, not all of the ex-slaves understood how voting would improve their lives since elected officials ignored their black people's pleas. In 1896, the year they organized the association lodge, Columbia blacks protested a legal decision directing four black women arrested as prostitutes to work on the city streets and a rock pile. Black citizens, led by Reverend R. L. Beal of the A.M.E. Church, opposed prostitution but thought this was an extreme punishment. They publicly asked the city council to eliminate the practice, but the council refused, replying that it needed to rid the city of disreputable women.

In the ex-slaves view, the relatively small amount of progress freedpeople had made by the late 1890s had come to a halt. The depressed agriculture of the country took a toll. Many blacks who owned land lost it. By the 1900 Census, only 69 percent of blacks who farmed in 1880 were still doing so. African-

American property ownership and taxpaying declined. Whites controlled blacks through segregation, lynchings, and a vagrancy law that provided for "selling away" anyone adjudged a vagrant by the local court for four years to an employer to work out his term. The law made no distinction based on race but targeted blacks.

For Boone County ex-slaves, their troubles had made it difficult to gather the resources to function after they organized the lodge. The national agricultural depression affected all Missourians but hit African Americans especially hard. They had become poorer in recent years, when in the 1880s they had thought they were just beginning to prosper. Increasingly after the Civil War black wives had to work, though, emulating the pattern of whites, the freedmen wanted to have their wives remain at home. Between 1870 and 1900, the number of households with only one worker decreased and the number of families with two or three workers grew. Also, relatives moved in together, so that nonnuclear households grew by 1900. In 1870, most wives did not work and only three women in the county worked as laundresses and one as a seamstress. In 1880, 129 worked as washerwomen and 3 as seamstresses. In 1900, 187 women washed clothes and 13 made a living sewing.

In 1900, Boone County had 39 African-American professionals: 13 ministers, 22 teachers, 2 physicians, 1 lawyer, and 1 musician. In Columbia, blacks owned one blacksmith shop, one barbershop, one grocery store, and a lunchroom. However, most African-American men worked as unskilled laborers earning seventy-five cents to a dollar a day. The women worked mostly as washerwomen, earning a weekly income of two to three dollars. Their economic status was only slightly improved since 1870, five years after Emancipation. In 1900, 186 black farmers operated 178 of the county's farms, only 5 percent of the total. The farms were mostly small landholdings of which blacks owned 52.8 percent. The largest African-American taxpayers, except for "Blind Boone," had lived in the county and had been free before the war. Even when blacks owned their homes, they were mostly mortgaged; but most owned no property at all. The city council enacted a poll tax of one dollar for every male citizen between twenty-one and fifty in 1895. These taxpayers numbered 812, and 31.2 percent of them paid no other tax. Among those assessed, 30.7 percent were black; of these, 225 paid no other tax or were delinquent in payment of their real and personal taxes. They were 88.5 percent of those paying a poll tax and were delinquent in other city tax payments. Less than 50 percent of those assessed paid the tax, and it was repealed two years later. The poor obviously had no resources with which to pay.[19]

Occasionally some African-American veteran or widow succeeded in obtaining a military pension, which became big news. Peter Hadan, a blacksmith, received a pension of $6 a month beginning in October 1885 for his injuries during the war. In 1880, Dorcas Williams, a fifty-year-old woman, received $2,074 in past due benefits. Her slave husband had been killed in the war in 1864. She was owed $8 a month since that date and $2 per month since 1866 for each of her four children. She would receive the pension until her children came of age or until her death. Insurance benefits payable at death also relieved pressure for some.

The economic distress in Columbia at the time the Ex-Slave Association was founded stemmed from many causes. Columbia failed to obtain a mainline railroad, which lowered land prices already depressed by agricultural depression. The steamboat declined as a result of competition with the railroads, and the river towns of Boone County lost their importance. Popu-

The world has changed for master and slave. "Old Master and Old Man, a New Year's Talk over Old Years Gone," Harper's Weekly, *January 11, 1890.*

lation losses abounded in the county. Everyone suffered, but African Americans suffered worse. The university, where some blacks worked as janitors and maids, remained a stable employer, but for only a small number of workers. Ironically, as literacy increased among blacks, the number and percentage of laborers and domestic servants increased. By 1897, most African Americans were either servants and laborers for white citizens or professionals serving their own community.

The ex-slaves lamented that because of their poverty, after the lodge was founded, dues payments were often hard to come by. Their carefully kept ledgers showed that some members paid in installments of five cents until they reached the requirement of twenty-five cents and ten cents for local dues. Most of the members were elderly. Henry Clay, born in Kentucky, had been the slave of Jefferson Garth, a prominent Boone County slave owner. Clay was seventy-nine and his wife, July, was sixty-eight. Auderine Wills, age seventy-four, had been born into slavery in Winchester, Kentucky, while Joseph Gosling had been the slave of local slaveholder Sylvester Gosling in Columbia. Squire Smith, who was sixty, worked on a farm. His wife was fifty-four; they had four children, three of whom were grown and the youngest of whom was sixteen. His two sons also worked on the farm. Allen Woods, who was fifty-nine, also did farmwork. His wife was fifty and his four children—three girls and a boy—were all grown; the youngest, a boy, was seventeen. Edward Lawson did farmwork. He was fifty-four, his wife was thirty, and four of his children—two boys and two girls—were grown; his youngest son was seventeen. Sandy Turner was a farmer. He was seventy-two; his wife, Harriet, was fifty-six and his five children, two boys and three girls, were grown. The youngest, Phoebe, was eighteen. Scott Brashears and his wife, Amanda, both in their sixties, lived with their

Squire Smith, Boone County ex-slave. Squire Smith
was a member of the Ex-Slave Association.

Unidentified Boone County ex-slave. African Americans like this man joined the Ex-Slave Association.

*Missouri ex-slaves Richard and Drucilla Martin. Many of the
ex-slaves who joined the movement were poor, and many
tried to work although they were old and frail.*

grandson Oliver Woods, born in 1892, and granddaughter Lillie Eaton, born in 1896.[20]

The ex-slaves were so poor that many of the old and infirm continued to work. Creasy Mack, who was about eighty and widowed, still did live-in household work for her employer, Jake Straun, a merchant. Despite their hardships, the local branch of the association was very important to the members. At the May 3, 1897, meeting, they planned to host a state convention on April 20 and set aside $5 to pay for the rent of Wheeler Chapel, "above and [below] the basement for 5.00 day and night."[21]

At one meeting only five people showed up, but by the end of 1899, the association was on its way with 125 members and

"*Rent Day,*" Harper's Weekly, *April 28, 1888. Many ex-slaves had miserable housing and few resources to pay for it. When they could work, the wages were too low. This old couple mull over whether they have enough to pay the rent collector.*

enough funds to pay the fifty cents' rent for each meeting in the church basement. It could also begin amassing a "treasure" for the local mutual benefit, medical care, and burial assistance for the members. It had also collected dozens of petitions and sent them off to headquarters. This was at a time when the entire black population of Boone County consisted of just about 4,500 people in the rural areas and surrounding towns, including Columbia. At this point only about 21 percent of the black population nationally had been born into slavery. In Boone County, only 676 persons were thirty-one years old or above and therefore could have been born in slavery and eligible for a pension. The membership of the lodge consisted of at least 20 percent of those African Americans who were eligible for a pension. With Callie House's encouragement, the Boone County lodge continued to send in petitions to the national office and to provide what relief they could to impoverished members.[22]

Although blacks' struggles were similar across the country and House encountered similar concerns everywhere she went, each community had its unique qualities and situations. The ex-slaves in New Orleans, for instance, lived in a community that had long had a sizable free Negro population and where Reconstruction had come early, but their post-Emancipation poverty differed little from that of the freedpeople in Boone County. When Mrs. House traveled to New Orleans in September 1899 to visit the local association council, she touched base with and provided inspiration to the members. She stayed in the home of a member, Lillie Brown, on Basin Street. While in the city, she spent hours with the local members collecting petitions and listening to their stories of slavery and the days since emancipation. They told her of their problems making ends meet, exacerbated by economic depression against the backdrop of the worsening inequality in that city and state. Racial turmoil erupted repeatedly among workingmen on the docks. In 1890, Louisiana legislators enacted bills to forbid equal accommodations on railroads and other conveyances. New Orleans' African Americans persistently agitated against segregation in the 1890s, although they repeatedly lost. In 1895, the Catholic Church announced the segregation of all services. *Plessy v. Ferguson,* in 1895, closed the final curtain. In 1898, the state took away African Americans' right to vote. At a state constitutional convention, delegates laid down the legal blueprint for white supremacy. The chair of the Judiciary Committee declared, "Our mission was to establish the supremacy of the white race." More than 120,000 African-American men were disenfranchised, and the Louisiana Democratic Party declared itself a whites-only organization.[23]

None of the ex-slave council charter members' relatives had joined local African-American men who had gone to Cuba, serving in one of four African-American "immune" regiments, as a result of the Spanish-American War. However, they described how the entire African-American community was upset at the insult, embarrassment, and unequal treatment the black soldiers suffered in the service. The troops were organized because, during the war, Washington officials from President McKinley on down had an almost superstitious dread of Cuba's yellow fever and malaria. Secretary of War Russel Alger advanced the idea that those who had come from semitropical or tropical climates had probably had the disease and were immune to it. Many of the soldiers became ill and some died, but the remainder spent their time as an occupying force engaged in guard and patrol duty.[24]

Many of the New Orleans council members, like those in Boone County and elsewhere, were old and experiencing great difficulties doing the manual labor that had always been their only occupation. Further adding to their problems, the economy remained depressed, which reduced employment opportunity for the younger generation. The members told House that the harsh conditions they faced made them anxious to join the association. Their chapter was incorporated on June 22, 1899, just a few days after the local African-American soldiers returned from Cuba. There were already a number of mutual aid societies still existing in the city. New Orleans' African Americans, like those elsewhere, had long organized mutual aid societies. Between 1880 and 1900, nineteen operated in the city, although not at the same time. A quite common way for the poor in a church or other organization to join together for mutual aid in time of illness or death, they developed because of habit and poverty. The local Ex-Slave Association's chapter had a somewhat different focus: "to devise ways and means for the caring and establishment of decrepit ex-slaves, their widows and orphans" and "to unite the efforts of all friends in securing pension legislation in favor of the ex-slaves, particularly by petitioning Congress" to pass the pension legislation reintroduced by Senator Mason. In working to gain pensions, they would "work under the advice and guidance of and cooperate with the National Ex-Slave Mutual Relief, Bounty and Pension Association of the United States of America."[25]

They engaged pension notary Louis Martinet to prepare and record their charter. He had been a major player in the progress of and reaction against people of color that had taken place in the city. He was a member of the class of the more educated African Americans who had executed the anti–Jim Crow litigation. A widely respected Afro-Creole lawyer, Martinet and other African-American graduates of Straight University Law School became organizers of a citizens' committee to attack the law that segregated transportation in the city. They organized one test case in which the local court defeated their efforts by releasing Daniel Desdunes after local police arrested him for violating the law on a city streetcar. They chose Homer Plessy next and succeeded in having him arrested and charged for refusing to vacate his seat on a passenger train. Martinet decided to ask Albion Tourgee to represent the cause. He explained that local black lawyers mainly practiced in police court. He also wanted an experienced appellate lawyer to take the case all the way to the Supreme Court. Martinet, who organized the effort, developed the litigation strategy, and picked the lawyers, remained a hero to the African-American community despite the eventual loss of *Plessy v. Ferguson* in the Supreme Court.[26]

The eight incorporators of the New Orleans Ex-Slave Association chapter included six men and two women. The participation of one of the women, Lottie L. Boyd, wife of Henry Boyd, as a married woman, required his personal authorization. The other woman, Lillie J. Bell, was single. They named as original officers Frederick S. Diamond, president; "Mistress" Lea Cavender, vice president; James T. Jones, manager; George A. Green, secretary; Lillie J. Bell, assistant secretary; William D. Brown, chaplain; Phillip S. Burton, lecturer; and Ervard (Edward) Barnes, inspector. Samuel A. Jackson was the other charter member. George A. Green served on the executive committee of the national organization. The founders set a convention of delegates to elect officers on the second Monday of August 1902. In the interim the board would manage the affairs and the founding officers would represent the association. Lottie L. Boyd, Henry Boyd, and Marcellin Zephilin, because of their illiteracy, signed with an X.[27]

Marcellin Zephilin's story, so similar to many House had heard, explained why even Civil War veterans eagerly joined the pension movement. Born a slave of Alexandre Mouton, of French origin but Arcadian "Cajun, not Creole," on the Ile Copal Plantation in Vermillionville, Lafayette, a prairie and bayou sugarcane region, he said he did not know why his master had named him Marcellin Zephilin. Mouton held Zephilin's father, Tom, and mother, Jennie, among the slaves on his plantation. Mouton, a Jacksonian Democrat, served in the legislature as a U.S. senator and as governor of Louisiana after his election to a term beginning in January 1843. He retired to life as a sugar planter and railroad promoter and then led a delegation to the Democratic National Convention in 1860 and chaired the Louisiana secession convention. During the war, when Union troops captured his plantation and used it as a headquarters, he had to flee. They burned the sugar mill and other works buildings and freed his 120 slaves, including Marcellin Zephilin.[28]

General Nathaniel Banks's Corps d'Afrique swept him up, along with thousands of other freedmen, into the Union Army, recording his enlistment at five feet, seven inches, black hair, black complexion, and brown eyes, at the Touro Building in New Orleans in May 1863. He served in the 97th Infantry Regiment of the U.S. Colored Troops until the end of the war. Wounded by a gunshot in the left leg below the knee at Fort Blakeley and hospitalized at Mobile, he also suffered a partial hearing loss. After his discharge he took the name of his slave father, Tom Jones, instead of Zephilin. He became a Primitive Baptist minister under the name Tom Jones, but when he applied for a pension the Bureau denied his claim. They found no Tom Jones on the rolls of the 97th U.S. Colored Troops.

Mrs. House knew from her own experience, and from what she heard everywhere she traveled, that many African-American soldiers and their widows had similar difficulties because they lacked documents to prove their names or dates of birth. He then filed as Zephilin and was at first rebuffed. After his continued complaints and a long investigation, he finally received a pension. However, the bureau agent told him he must call himself Zephilin and not Jones. He continued to identify himself as Jones except when dealing with the government and answered to both names. Sometimes others hearing his name spelled it Dephilin or Zephirin. By the time he responded to House's plea to organize and helped to charter the Ex-Slave Association, Jones had developed rheumatism, asthma, and shortness of breath and could no longer preach or perform manual labor. He had come to rely on his pension and friends and family for his livelihood.[29]

But his anger was reinforced when he applied for an increase in his pension under a provision covering veterans who reached age seventy-five and the bureau rejected him again. He could not prove his age. The bureau first asked why he did not simply submit his birth certificate or family Bible entry, which he, of course, had never had. When he obtained an affidavit from a grandson of his former owner, bureau officials refused to accept its validity since it reflected only his recollection. Widows and veterans who experienced such harassment from the Pension Bureau were naturally inclined to seek relief by joining the ex-slave pension movement.[30]

During House's travels, what she saw and heard from the old ex-slaves strengthened her commitment to the movement. However, the growth of the association had attracted the attention of the Pension Bureau. While she was still reveling in the progress of the chapters, the government was accelerating its attack on the association. She was successfully doing the work the members had elected her to do. But her resolve would be sorely tested.

CHAPTER 5

The Movement
Fights Back

*My face is black is true but its not my fault but I love my
name and my honesty in dealing with my fellow man.*

CALLIE HOUSE
(1899)

CALLIE HOUSE had a major problem after the Post Office
Department denied the Association the use of the mails. The
pension movement workers were left with Wells Fargo, Adams,
or American Express to distribute materials. However, having
to use commercial delivery services and to travel more often to
keep in touch took time and the Association's scarce resources.
Mrs. House needed to provide the inspiration that would keep
agents organizing and collecting petitions, and local chapters
providing mutual assistance to their members. She had to do
this in the wake of ongoing federal harassment, and avoid permitting the harassment from becoming a major distraction
from the Association's real work. Mrs. House remained optimistic and the work continued so successfully that soon their

press critics complained that the association had branches "in almost every little hamlet and village throughout the south."[1]

When Mrs. House received the September 1899 notice of the fraud order from Barrett, she had no idea how committed the federal officials were to stopping her and the movement. Responding as if she had some citizenship rights the federal government was required to respect, Mrs. House made no apologies for her work. She provided a detailed explanation of the movement's mission and actions. This, she thought, would allay Barrett's concerns. She explained, "1st we are organizing ourselves together as a race of people who feels that they have been wronged." She rejected his charge that they had misled members. On the contrary,

> We tell them we don't know whether they will ever get anything or not but there is something due them and if they are willing to risk their money in defraying the expenses of getting up the petition to Congress they are at liberty to do so.[2]

Her explanation, in keeping with her education in civics in Rutherford County's primary schools, insisted that "the Constitution of the United States grants to citizens the privilege of peaceably assembling themselves together and petition their grievance." Objecting to the government's disrespect of the movement, she continued that African Americans had

> a perfect right as ex-slaves to gather and organize ourselves and elect men and women to organize our race together to petition the government for a compensation to alleviate our old decrepit men and women who are

bent up with rheumatism from the exposure they undergone [underwent] in the dark days of slavery.

Furthermore, Callie House told Barrett:

Common horse sence [*sic*] will teach anybody that the officers of this organization are powerless to get a pension from the government for each ex-slave for 25 cts when ever there is no law on the statute books to pension them.

Proudly, she told him "My whole soul and body are for this-slave movement and are [am] willing to sacrifices [sacrifice] for it."[3]

Callie House's forceful and coherent response to Barrett angered federal officials. They also began to understand that she was the de facto head of the Association. From that day on, intent on breaking the ex-slave movement, postal officials focused on throttling her to silence. Nashville postmaster A. Wills explained to Acting Assistant Attorney General Barrett, "She is defiant in her actions, and seems to think that the negroes have the right to do what they please in this country."[4]

After the post office issued the fraud order on October 2, 1899, Postmaster Wills told headquarters that he had delivered the letters to Reverend H. Smith, the national secretary in Bransford, Tennessee, in addition to Callie House in New Orleans, through that city's postmaster. He also quickly disseminated it to newspapers all over the South, asking that they publish it immediately. He stopped twenty-two money orders amounting in total to $53.84 sent to the Association and had them returned to the senders.[5]

House and the Association continued to organize while

attending to the federal surveillance. She traveled more than ever, "lecturing to both white and colored people on this movement." This was a distinct hardship. Her brother and his wife, who lived next door, helped to care for her children; the oldest, Thomas, was fifteen and the youngest, Annie, was six. Mrs. House had worked all of her life but as a washerwoman and seamstress; this was the work that most black women with children did. But widowed and now working outside the home, Mrs. House had departed from the usual role.

When House traveled to meet with members or prospective members, she encouraged them to believe that pension legislation would eventually pass. However, she "always stated clearly and distinctly that the Bill was not a law but we wanted to petition to Congress to pass the Mason bill or some other." She explained to members and to the government officials that the dues and contributions paid for representatives in Washington "to look after the interest of the movement to work for passage." McNairy "went sometime in Jan 1899 and remains in Washington till the last of March," supported by the organization. As far as she knew, he was lobbying aggressively for the bill.[6]

The Association leaders had difficulty staying in touch with agents and chapters and members of their families. On November 9, 1899, after the issuance of the mail fraud order, Isaiah Dickerson politely wrote to Postmaster Wills, pointing out that since his mail had been stopped two of his children had become ill without his knowledge. He had found out about the order from "a white friend visiting our city."[7]

Feeling the pressure of her poor economic circumstances, House was particularly stung by Barrett's assertion that association officers had used membership money inappropriately for themselves or to hire members of their families. The Association's board of directors set a salary of $50 a month for Mrs. House, but actual payment depended on whether the organization could afford it. There was no reason not to hire members of her family, but in fact none worked for the Association. Records from the period show that in 1899 and her early years in the ex-slave pension cause, her daughters were still in school and too young to work. When her boys who were teenagers took jobs, they worked as clothes pressers, car cleaners, and other unskilled low-wage occupations completely unrelated to the organization. When her daughters became old enough, they became washerwomen or seamstresses, except for Mattie, who, as an adult, long after House's involvement in the pension movement, became a teacher. House's brother, Charles Guy, worked as a laborer and then a packer in a factory. His wife also took in washing. The Census reported their occupations, and the annual City Directory recorded each member of her family at their workplaces.[8]

Also unaware of the extent of the federal government's hostility, Dickerson responded to the fraud order, echoing House's concerns. He told Barrett that he failed to understand why pension legislation should not have the support "of all true American citizens, regardless of politics." He thought it "very wrong for any attorney to suppress our rights to petition to better our condition in life." They were legally incorporated by the "grand old state of Tennessee," which would certainly intervene if "we overstep our bounds." He questioned why the federal government should take an interest and hoped the order would be rescinded. This round of communication between the association and the government ended with House telling Barrett that she had done this work for two years and she "did not work for what I got out of it but I believe the movement to be right."[9]

Not knowing about the statements in the government's files expressing disinterest in local chapters and mutual-aid work, House tried to direct federal officials' attention to the branches. She regarded their activities as key to the work of organizing and sustaining the movement. The association gave the Justice Department a list of local agents and addresses so that they could track their work. The government used this information only to help prove that House was acknowledged as an official of the association. They ignored the proof that the association was more than an empty shell.[10]

Still not understanding the federal government's perspective, the association decided to seek revocation of the fraud order against its president, Reverend McNairy, so that he could communicate with the membership and officers as he lobbied in Washington. When their Washington lawyer, William C. Lawson, wrote to the post office asking for the revocation, postal officials refused. On December 9, 1899, Barrett responded that since letters and contributions had been sent to McNairy and he took an "active part" in the association's activities, he would remain subject to the order.[11]

After newspapers published Barrett's notice of the fraud order at the Post Office Department's request, House made herself even more objectionable to Pension Bureau and postal officials. She upbraided him for libeling her across the nation. Readers across the country read that she had fraudulently collected money from "ignorant ex-slave[s], when Barrett had no evidence to support his claims. She wrote to him:

> I am an American born woman and was born in the proud old state of Tennessee and I am considered a law abiding citizen of that state anyone that work honestly and earnestly for the upbuilding of their own race would

like for it to be recognize that way let it be a white man
or white woman are a black man or a black woman.

Although her face was "black," she valued her good name, and
believed in "honesty in dealing with my fellow man," Mrs.
House wrote. Since her election as assistant secretary of the
Association, she had worked hard to organize African Americans so they could "render assistance to all members in good
standing." She had also asked Congress to pass the pension bill
introduced by Senator Mason or "some measure as good."[12]

She reminded Barrett again that the ex-slave pension movement sought simply to exercise their constitutional right to
"gather and petition there [their] grievances." When she lectured to African Americans, she explained the right to petition
but "told them it would take some money to defray the
expences in getting up the petition or conducting the work."
She had been "honest in my dealing with my fellow man."[13]

Immune to criticism, complaints, and pleas for fairness
from the ex-slave pension movement, the postal officials assid-
uously refused to process mail sent to the organization or to
House and the other officers individually. Association organizers tried to evade the order by having postal express orders sent
from the chapters or by having mail sent through others. They
kept lobbying, mobilizing, and obtaining signatures on petitions, despite the obstacles. They also kept up the introduction
of bills in Congress. On December 11, 1899, when Senator
Edmund Pettus, Democrat of Alabama, reintroduced the legislation, instead of the serene reception experienced in the past a
tumult erupted. Senator Jacob Gallinger, Republican of New
Hampshire and chairman of the Pensions Committee, hur-
riedly denounced the idea as fraudulent. Senator William

Mason, a Republican from Illinois, explained that he had introduced the bill before and he had received letters saying "it was used for a bad purpose" by swindlers. Senator John Thurston, Republican of Nebraska, who introduced the bill in the Fifty-fourth Congress, said a Confederate veteran had urged him to introduce it but it had been misused. Senator George Hoar, Republican of Maine, thought the bill should at least be treated with respect because of the British discussion of old-age pensions, and if anyone deserved such consideration, certainly "those whose lives were spent in slavery and whose earnings and labor were given for the benefit of others" did also. Senator Gallinger, after reading letters from H. Clay Evans, commissioner of pensions, alleging "the fraudulent nature of the ex-pension organizations," referred the bill to his Pensions Committee.[14]

The negative attitude of the Pensions Committee arose from a consultation with the Pension Bureau, which asked Gallinger in January 1900 to issue an adverse report on the legislation. The Bureau requested that the committee dispose of the bill in a way that would advertise to members the "improper purposes" used with the various bills. Ignoring the mutual assistance purposes of the Ex-Slave Association, the Senate committee complied with the Pension Bureau's request; its report consisted mainly of a letter from H. Clay Evans alleging "the fraudulent nature of the ex-slave pension organizations" but included no evidence or facts to support the conclusion. The committee denounced the ex-slave pension movement as a means to "dupe the colored people" and said the measure was not even "deserving of serious consideration by Congress." The report concluded that no one should expect the Congress ever to enact pensions for the ex-slaves. This same committee over-

*Senator Jacob Gallinger (served 1891–1918), in an effort to
stop the petitions and the movement, colluded with the
commissioner of pensions to issue a report saying that
Congress would never pass a pension bill.*

looked its own evidence to the contrary, however, that at least 35,710 people had been issued membership certificates by April 17, 1899.[15]

Not knowing of the collusion among the government branches working against the Association and their fear of its successful mobilization, Mrs. House and her colleagues puzzled over why they were facing such racial paternalism and hostility from the Pensions Committee. After all, they did not challenge racial segregation or white supremacy and these fraud concerns had not been raised during earlier pension-seeking efforts. Despite their leaders' disappointment, they felt that giving up was not an alternative and they decided to continue working. They continued to collect petitions and to hold Ex-Slave Mutual Relief, Bounty and Pension Association conventions. They passed resolutions to send to Congress and state legislatures, and they continued to meet and organize local chapters to provide mutual assistance throughout the South and Midwest.[16]

While Callie House and the Association struggled against the postal authorities, Edward Cooper's Washington, D.C., *Colored American,* on April 21, 1900, summed up the attitude of many well-off African Americans toward the association and the pensions cause:

Despite the widespread warnings of the press both white and colored, there are still some people foolish enough to pay over their hard cash to sundry confidence sharks who run up and down the country pretending that Congress is about to grant pensions to the ex-slaves. No such thing will be done in this or any other generation and whoever asserts to the contrary is a knave, a humbug or worse.[17]

From Cooper's perspective, because Congress was unlikely to enact a pension, merely mobilizing to demand legislation constituted fraud.

The government's effort to suppress the movement continued and accelerated. In April 1900, Callie House received another notice reiterating the broad scope of the fraud order and reminding her that letters sent to individual officers, or to the organization and any postal money orders would be voided as fraudulent. She vented her fury to Barrett, telling him that she wanted to promote "mutual assistance" to members and continue to press Congress to pass pension legislation. She and the other officers had "not promised nothing to nobody." She denounced the charges as "not true and I believed they are made against us simply because we are negroes and helpless." To deflect the harassment, House hired a white attorney, H. Perry Stephens of Nashville. At that time sixteen black attorneys had offices in Nashville, but they practiced mainly in the local criminal courts. Further, some African Americans hired white attorneys, knowing how disdainfully white officials and the courts treated blacks.[18]

Mrs. House felt increasingly isolated and embattled. On April 30, 1900, Stephens asked Barrett for a review and revocation of the order, at least as it applied to her as an individual. He told him that she had been traveling on March 28, 1900, when the notice had come saying that she must immediately produce contrary evidence or otherwise another fraud order would be issued, and had not returned to Nashville until April 1. "It worked a great hardship," especially in case of the "illness of her children," if she could not receive mail. If the Post Office Department would not revoke the order, he wanted information on how to obtain judicial review.[19]

Mrs. House was further disappointed when the Post Office

Department rejected Stephens's appeal. Assistant Attorney General James Tyner replied that House had had ample time to make any defenses and could still do so, but no matter what she submitted, the order would remain in force. Further, Stephens needed to understand that "the issuance [of a fraud order] is solely determined by the department and there is no place to appeal." The courts had left the matter entirely up to the discretion of post office officials. Because taxpayers and citizens had no constitutional right to use the post office, a service provided on terms set by the department, then a denial for any reason raised no due process concerns. Still believing he might change their minds, Stephens submitted association materials and affidavits to the officials, but to no avail. Today, federal agency actions are reviewable in the courts under the Administrative Procedure Act. However, the act was not passed until 1946. If it had been in place in 1899, Callie House and the Ex-Slave Association could have at least asked for court review of the fraud orders issued against them. In 1899, association officials had no place to seek redress.[20]

The Post Office Department, at the behest of the Pension Bureau, continued to attack all ex-slave pension groups whether they were suspected swindlers or sincere promoters of the cause. They also made no effort to ascertain whether the Ex-Slave Association officers actually owned property or bank accounts or to determine the costs of their travel and petitioning or in any way to document their accusations. Instead they simply labeled pensions for ex-slaves a hopeless cause and held that anyone who promoted such pensions, by any means, had ulterior motives.

In February, Postmaster Wills in Nashville reminded his superintendents that they should continue to enforce the fraud order. Their focus should be on Callie House and anyone associated with her. On February 26, 1901, the Post Office Department charged that House and G. T. Abrams were "carrying on their ex-slave pension swindle" by publishing the *National Industrial Advocate* to promote the movement. Veteran pensions and other lobbyists routinely published newsletters or newspapers in this period. The post office, continuing its policy of assuming the existence of illegality, issued another fraud order forbidding the delivery of any mail personally addressed to Callie House or to G. T Abrams, manager of the *National Industrial Advocate.*[21]

On March 5, 1901, J. B. Mullins, who had been elected president of the Ex-Slave Association, decided to try appeasement and deference to gain revocation of the fraud order. In good faith, he naively wrote to the Post Office Department that after President McNairy's death, he had been unanimously elected president at the Montgomery, Alabama, convention on October 29–30, 1900. He immediately investigated whether any fraud existed. He found "many fraudulent acts of this nature being practiced upon the people by bogus agents who were not connected with the organization in any way." He assured them that if at the local level "unprincipled officers and agents" had been elected, it was without the knowledge of the association. But the government's labeling the organization a fraud meant that the "innocent must suffer with the guilty."[22]

Mullins described various impostors who had been reported to him and recalled that the organization had previously reported one imposter to the federal government who, he understood, had been arrested. He knew of a swindler who had "gulled" some people in Kentucky by claiming that he had been "appointed to preach McNairy's funeral and needed money to defray the expenses." They had tried to find this "so-called minister," but to no avail. In view of his cooperation,

Mullins hoped the department would reconsider the fraud order. The association, he wrote, had many honest agents and "did a lot of good for the poor old decrepit and worn out ex-slaves, who direly needed mutual aid and burial assistance." He proudly told them that there was "one local association at Greenville, Ala., that buried eleven members last year." The federal officials ignored his plea.[23]

On March 15, 1901, Mullins wrote to President McKinley expressing the same concerns as in his earlier letter to the Post Office Department. He cited the right to petition the government and wrote that the members wanted equal rights and equal protection under the laws; however, following the leadership of Booker T. Washington, "they do not ask for social equality." If he could obtain removal of the fraud order against the association, he would not even complain of "action taken upon" officers, including the dead President McNairy and the living Dickerson and House. Whether justified or not, an order against them should not have been extended to the organization. He asserted that the organization had nearly a million members. "They have always been loyal to the flag of this country and have no idea of revolting. It would be foolish." He asked, "If the South continues to disfranchise our people and resort to the mob violence instead of giving a right of trial by jury, what will be our position ten years hence?"[24]

Mullins's deferential letters had no effect. Having no access to the records now available, he did not know that official suspicion fell on anyone who worked on ex-slave pensions. He also did not understand that it was the Ex-Slave Association's success that frightened the bureau and not whether House and Dickerson were honest advocates. The postmaster in Nashville "had long suspicioned him" and requested a fraud order to stop Mullins's mail in the same month as he sent his letters to the bureau and to the president. The federal officials had no interest in burials paid for by the Greenville chapter or any other. Also, they regarded the large number of association members as evidence of the ignorance and susceptibility of African Americans, rather than as an affirmation of the support for the cause. They wanted the old ex-slaves to remain bereft of even the hope of ever receiving any form of reparations from the federal government. For the government to succeed, it had to demonize all pension advocates as venal agitators.[25]

Reporting on his pursuit of House, Nashville postmaster Wills wrote to George Christiancy, the assistant attorney general of the Post Office Department, bragging that "in order to effectually wipe out the whole thing, I feel justified at times to resorting to extreme measures." In his office they inspected all mail of African Americans to see if they had any involvement in the ex-slave pension "business" and then withheld it when they could find any "pretext" at all. "These fellows connected with this association are all slick customers."[26]

Federal officials who earnestly hoped that local law enforcement would join in the effort to stop the movement, rejoiced at what they regarded as a bit of good news from Wills: he gleefully reported that "the General Manager Dickerson is in jail in Atlanta" and hoped he would implicate Callie House. Dickerson had appealed but was "simply playing for time in order to pay his fine of $1,000.00 and continue his rascally proceedings." Wills forwarded to Washington headquarters clippings from the *Atlanta Constitution* and the *Nashville American and Banner,* containing inflammatory invective about the case from the local judge, who had said it was "such a succinct history of the life and possible death of I. H. Dickerson, General Manager, and the death of the Association." Wills thought they should "congratulate" themselves.[27]

The press clippings claimed that Dickerson had "deluded darkies" in thirty-four states and the Atlanta chapter sued and had him jailed for nonpayment of $800 bail. He allegedly owned considerable real estate in Nashville, dressed like a bishop, and appeared as a "thoroughly poised negro of the straight strain." At a time when secretaries and clerks were men, he traveled with "a female secretary named Callie House." The press also reported falsely that hundreds of witnesses had appeared in court. A story in the *Nashville Banner* of March 5, 1901, erroneously reported the filing of twenty-two cases against Dickerson already and that he and House had "reaped a rich harvest." In a March 6, 1901, article the *Banner* inadvertently affirmed the grassroots support for the Association by complaining about the proliferation of chapters "in almost every little hamlet and village throughout the south."

The Georgia State Supreme Court summarized the case very differently from the news stories: a local court had convicted Dickerson of "swindling" for his organizational activities in March 5, 1901. The judge had sentenced him to a fine of $1,000 and twelve months on the chain gang. However, the prosecution introduced only one witness, who accused Dickerson of selling three membership certificates for seventy-five cents each, promising to send the money to Vaughan's group in Washington and failing to send the funds. Dickerson testified that he had had no dealings with Vaughan and had never said he did. A local mutual assistance fund for burying the dead and caring for the sick controlled the funds in question. The State Supreme Court overturned Dickerson's conviction on July 22, 1901. At a time when most cases went no further than the local courts, the Association used its limited funds to pay for the appeal.[28]

The Georgia State Supreme Court, removed from the local

judge's rhetorical battering of the ex-slave pension cause, treated the case as a routine fraud charge. They announced that in order to swindle, Dickerson needed to state that pensions had been passed, and not that he wanted legislation enacted, a perfectly legal organizing goal. In August, two weeks after the State Supreme Court decision, Wills told his superiors that, unfortunately, Dickerson's conviction had been reversed but that he "had a good time for thought, having been confined in jail for a number of months" for not posting bond. However, Dickerson remained a "bad fellow, and I should to wonder if his confinement has given him an opportunity to invent new ideas to start in the work again." They would "watch and wait," he told his superiors in Washington.[29]

The prey the federal officials were determined to ensnare was Callie House. The production of the single witness against Dickerson and his prosecution seemed tied to the efforts of A. Wills and others in the Post Office Department and the Pension Bureau to make a case against her. Secretary of the Interior Ethan A. Hitchcock wrote to the postmaster general on March 18, 1901, forwarding a letter from Commissioner of Pensions Evans about Dickerson's conviction. The forwarded letter stated, "Callie House (Dickerson's Private Secretary) was charged with being implicated with Dickerson in this matter but could not be located and arrested." Meanwhile, Wills insisted that the department should have House prosecuted in Atlanta. He made it clear that he regarded her "as being as bad, if not worse than Dickerson."[30]

The postmaster general's office passed along the false information that Dickerson had been convicted and House charged to its legal department to include in a review of whether to grant the Association's request to lift the fraud order. The post office cited the Dickerson "conviction" and the implication of

House as a reason to refuse the revocation of the fraud order. Federal officials made the most of Dickerson's "conviction" in attacking House.[31]

Struggling to stay afloat, House and the local chapters repeatedly used not only the more expensive railway express but the names and addresses of various other individuals as mail recipients. However, House's name on anything raised suspicion. On September 25, 1901, the post office issued a fraud order against Delphia House, Callie's middle name and the name of her daughter, and A. W. Washington of Arcola, Mississippi, when Washington sent Delphia a money order for $1.80. The Arcola postmaster, on the alert for anyone involved in the movement and seeing the name House, stopped the letter, claiming that it had been "mailed open," which gave him an excuse to read it. The quite innocent letter asked for twelve membership certificates at fifteen cents each, stating, "I wants them so I can Collected National annual Dues from each member." Washington said she had received their notice about trying to have the fraud order revoked to "give us a clear speech with each other and our Governments." She had had extra meetings and would send $5 "on that fraud order to help have it revoke pass." Her local chapter "wants to hear Prof. I. H. Dickerson very bad." If he would come, they would "take care of him and pay his way down and back home from Nashville." The correspondence indicated strong local support for the movement, which only increased the federal officials' anxiety over the impact of the ex-slave pension cause.[32]

Mrs. House complained repeatedly about the denial of their First Amendment right to petition and the unfair lack of due process involved in the government's harassment of the association. She insisted that the unreviewable powers of the government could lend themselves to abuse. As if to validate her concerns, in 1904 the Justice Department indicted Harrison Barrett and Assistant Attorney General James Tyner, nephew and uncle, as well as the two principal Justice Department officials who harassed Mrs. House and the association, for collusion to profit by abusing their discretion under the fraud laws. Tyner, age seventy-seven, who had served as postmaster general under President Hayes, was planning to close out his career as assistant attorney general for the Post Office Department.

However, first, Barrett left for private practice. Then he and Tyner colluded to influence businesses to retain his services for protection against the possibility of a fraud order. Since Tyner remained in the government, he could ostensibly have decided to target any business he chose. Upon entering office, the Roosevelt administration found the Post Office Department filled with corruption and began an investigation. As a result, Tyner was accused of bribe taking. His wife and her sister, apparently Barrett's mother, went to his office and secretly took all the documents from the safe. When Postmaster General Payne learned they had been there, he chased them through the streets of Washington in his carriage, ending up at their house. They refused to admit him. Tyner and Barrett admitted that the charges were valid. However, based on a legal technicality they were acquitted.[33]

Needless to say, Barrett and Tyner did not offer the Ex-Slave Association the same insulation from fraud orders they dangled before businessmen to collect bribes. They knew the association of impecunious freedpeople could not afford the prices they charged. Their crimes, however, only underscored the unfairness in the Post Office Department's use of fraud orders.[34]

After Dickerson's conviction and the continued harassment and denial of personal mail, Mrs. House began to fathom the deep-seated hostility of the Post Office and the Pension Bureau toward their cause. The association could do little about scam artists and impostors except to report them. However, the officers continued to try to respond to the government's concerns. As she continued her work in the cause, House did not yet accept the reality that federal officials would remain unsatisfied until the association completely abandoned the pursuit of pensions.

CHAPTER 6

Avoiding Destruction

*More real harm is probably done by . . . regular
agents . . . arousing, as they do, false hopes concerning a
supposedly overdue restitution of Freedmen's Bureau
funds, or reparation for historical wrongs, to be followed
by inevitable disappointment, and probably distrust of
the dominant race and of the Government.*

COMMISSIONER OF PENSIONS H. CLAY EVANS
(1902)

BETWEEN 1901 AND 1915, Mrs. House and the harassed
and beleaguered Ex-Slave Association continued to organize
local chapters to deliver medical and burial aid to aged members and their families. Association members also continued to
collect petitions, believing that recording as many ex-slaves as
possible and petitioning the government was not only right but
might eventually succeed, although they became increasingly
embittered about federal harassment of the movement. Government officials continued to treat them as second-class citizens, unentitled to behave as political agents or free Americans.
However, Mrs. House's persistence kept the movement alive.

House felt little joy at the celebrations of the new century.

The expositions and fairs and the widespread expressions of hope that human aspirations would be realized through the wonders of technology and quickened social awareness held little meaning for her. Mrs. House's cause to help the poor ex-slaves would seem to have been attractive to progressives, who worked to cure social ills ranging from impure food and drugs to housing for urban immigrants, but wider support remained elusive. A few white progressives helped to found the NAACP and the National Urban League, but nationally whites paid little attention to solving the race problem or to the claims of ex-slaves. The Republican Party platforms of 1900, 1904, and 1908 had planks insisting upon the protection of black voters. Twelve more years of Republican control only saw the problem grow in magnitude. Equal protection under the law remained unenforced and the plight of blacks ignored. Between 1901 and 1910, newspapers reported the lynching of at least 846 persons in the United States. Of this number, 754 were African Americans. Ninety percent of the lynchings took place in the South. The largely unresponsive state and federal governments did little or nothing to remedy the abuse.[1]

While Mrs. House and other African Americans mobilized mutual assistance associations and civil rights organizations, mainstream newspapers' race coverage was largely devoted to stories about the threat of supposed "black-beast rapists." The papers also reported such sensational stories as a white woman in Chicago explaining that she had lived with a "Negro" for twelve years because he had held her "captive" in his apartment, too afraid to leave even when he went to work. Such limited documentation of the black experience was augmented by an occasional piece on the professional interests or leisure pursuits of the local African-American business and professional class. Meanwhile, African-American newspapers focused on social engagements, self-help activities toward progress for the race that made no demands on whites and did not upset the established order, and articles on Jim Crow and the absence of civil rights. These papers continued to ignore the embattled pension movement, the loyalty of its members, or its potential for the working class, barely educated nobodies and the poor.[2]

Also, in Nashville, the home base of House and the Ex-Slave Association, African-American business and professional leaders totally ignored House and the ex-slave pension cause. For these African Americans, the major stories of the early years of the twentieth century included an unsuccessful boycott of Jim Crow streetcars in 1905. It also included the founding of the *Globe* by Richard H. Boyd to support the boycott. The newspaper lasted into the 1960s as a voice of middle-class activities and aspirations. Black leaders also pointed proudly to the opening of a segregated public university for blacks, in 1912, the Tennessee Agricultural and Industrial (A&I) College, in a period when such colleges were being established by state governments throughout the South. Because of the presence of Meharry Medical College, the black private colleges, the National Baptist Publishing Board, and then Tennessee A&I, Nashville's professional class of lawyers, physicians, and dentists grew. The city also had a middle class of barbers, ministers, teachers, and semiskilled laborers. These groups were of sufficient size to support Greenwood Amusement Park, the *Globe*, and a number of civic and social organizations. African-American shoemakers, liquor dealers, blacksmiths, and barbers started to lose to white immigrant competition in 1900–1910. But the businesses that primarily served blacks continued to prosper by serving a segregated "captive" population.[3]

African Americans probably thought the Jim Crow chill in the early-twentieth-century air would diminish when, in office only a month, President Theodore Roosevelt not only invited Booker T. Washington to the White House but dined with him during their discussions. The incident outraged white southerners, but blacks hoped this social interaction would lead to a new commitment to punish lynching, ensure access to the ballot, and overturn Jim Crow. Mrs. House and the Ex-Slave Association thought it might lead to an end to their exclusion from the mail service; however, beyond the affirmation of Booker T. Washington's control of patronage, little of substance resulted.[4]

By the fall of 1901, Mrs. House and the other Association officers desperately needed the fraud order lifted. Their struggle to keep in touch with agents, the membership, and their families required a great deal of money, time, and energy. Members paid twenty-five cents, collected as an initiation fee, of which ten cents went to the territorial or state council; ten cents to the national; and five cents to the organizers and agents for each new member recruited. The ten cents paid monthly remained in a local fund for use as decided by the chapter for the mutual benefit of members. The national office utilized its funds to prepare and distribute literature, hold conventions and meetings, and to maintain the membership rolls and petitions. Special contributions paid for lobbying. General Manager Isaiah Dickerson's clerks kept the books and gave receipts to state agents. Callie House lectured and organized chapters and petition signing throughout the South. The association had to pay W. C. Lawson, its first attorney, hired to lobby in Washington when it decided it needed a professional to work on the association's behalf. In 1899, they paid him $204 for his work. The Association made a few changes in administration in order to restrict the impact of the government's campaign. In addition to using railway express services, Mrs.

House and the agents had to collect funds and distribute materials personally rather than through the mails after the issuance of the fraud order. Also, the board of directors increased the initiation fee. It became "so much harder to obtain enough money to travel from place to place that they raised the amount to fifty cents, including twenty-five cents for the agent."[5]

In addition to the changes in operation, the Association decided, in November 1901, to hire an experienced white Washington lawyer, Robert Abraham Lincoln Dick, to seek repeal of the fraud order. Dick specialized in pension matters and had been a law partner of Walter Vaughan at one time. He could see that the government was engaging in selective enforcement. He knew that the Post Office Department had not issued a fraud order or otherwise harassed Vaughan despite his profit seeking in selling his pamphlet and organizing his clubs. Dick believed that

> The condition of the colored people in this country today and especially in the south brings forward a number of *grave* and *serious* questions, commercial and social as well as political, and the ablest statesmen as well as accomplished scholars and big-hearted philanthropists differ as to a solution of or a remedy for those conditions. The trend of opinion, however, seems in the direction that a national government response is required. A dozen different propositions have been advanced and the pensions idea to some people appeals with as great force as does the colonization idea to others.

He also knew that "the luxury of today becomes the necessity of tomorrow." And that "a few years ago was generally regarded as a dream or an absurdity is today existing fact." He also saw that Callie House and her colleagues "believe that by education and agitation and with a strong organization appealing to Congress that eventually their appeal shall be listened [to] and they [are] earnest and honest in their belief and are acting in good faith."[6]

At this time social reformers in the United States routinely sought inspiration, approval, and support from their British counterparts to influence American public opinion. Ida B. Wells had successfully persuaded the British to condemn lynching. Jane Addams modeled the Settlement House movement on private British social welfare programs. Dick knew that the British idea of giving pensions to needy subjects sixty-five years of age or older was under serious consideration. Previously the idea, he surmised, "would have been laughed out of the Parliament with ridicule and contempt." However, having so many "feeble and decrepit people to support and the method of providing for them raises a serious question this as a matter of analogy."

Dick also thought that if President Lincoln had lived the southern slave owners might have been paid a million dollars for their slaves as one of the conditions of Reconstruction; also that the "poor unfortunate ex-slaves would have been helped other than merely being told 'you have your freedom like the animals and the birds,' now be thankful and fend for yourself." He also could not understand why the officers of the Ex-Slave Association could not "advocate these positions and not be guilty of any fraud."

Dick met with Post Office Department and Justice Department officials and explained that members joined the association for a perfectly valid reason: they received mutual assistance for burial or medical costs. But in promoting pensions they gained "the influence and power of organization and association, exchanges of opinion and ideas. The pieces of literature books etc., the attendance upon lectures, debates etc are all potent factors in benefitting mankind in general and especially those who attend such things with proper, lawful and moral motives." He also carefully outlined how the association handled its financial affairs in the usual pattern of such organizations.

The officials asked him why the mutual benefit features were not mentioned prominently in the association's national literature. He explained that "as in some other fraternal organizations" these benefits were controlled by the local councils. House and the other national officers and board "had nothing to do with the benefit fund, which remained in local hands." In order for them to be able to check his responses, he provided the names and addresses of local council heads, who could provide the names of members who had received a death or sick benefit or funeral expenses, in New Orleans; Vicksburg, Mississippi; Atlanta; Kansas City, Missouri; and other cities. Postal and Justice Department files indicate no effort to investigate the work of the local chapters or even to make inquiries of them.

The officials also asked Dick whether House and Dickerson had attempted to recruit African Americans by leading them to believe they could collect pensions only by joining the Association, if and when legislation passed. He responded that he had heard rumors but found no evidence to support the charge and that none of the literature contained such inducements. Finally, departmental officials asked whether the association had any credibility at all since, surely, Dick knew that Congress would not enact pensions for the ex-slaves. By their calculations, at least 7 million possible recipients would receive $10 per month, which would amount to more than $210 million annually. No rational person could believe Congress would ever appropriate such amounts or even a quarter of the total.

The officials exaggerated the costs since only persons who had actually been held in servitude would have been eligible, not the entire black population. In 1900, only 21 percent of the African-American population, or about 1.9 million persons, had been born in slavery. Their numbers, like those of the veterans under the lucrative Union pensions provisions, were slowly diminishing due to deaths.[7]

House and the officers decided to invite more federal scrutiny of their activities by holding their sixth national convention in Washington, D.C., on October 29–November 1, 1901. The board also acted on Attorney Dick's advice that the association reincorporate in Washington, D.C., in February 1902. It also issued new literature and membership certificates explicitly mentioning aiding the sick and burying the dead as local chapter functions. The Association also persuaded Republican congressman Edmond Spencer Blackburn of North Carolina to reintroduce the pension legislation in the House of Representatives, despite their experience with the Senate committee's 1900 negative report.[8]

Their efforts seemed to have borne fruit when Dick reported to the Association board that all signals from the officials at the Post Office Department indicated that he had succeeded in lifting the fraud order. The department "had decided to let the organization have the use of the mails & that there would be no further interruption so long as the organization and its officers complied with the strict observances of the law. So I trust that the organization & its officers will bear this in mind and strive to obey the law in all its requirements." He told them that the local chapters must strictly "act in compliance with the Constitution of the Supreme National Organization." If they failed to do so, they would "impair their usefulness to the general cause for which the association is in existence."[9]

House and the Association rejoiced at Dick's good news, but he had been misled. Without telling him, government officials had not only continued the fraud order, they had enlisted the aid of a private organization to help destroy the ex-slave movement. The Grand Army of the Republic, founded in 1866 as an organization of veterans of the Union military during the Civil War, had become a powerful influence in electoral politics and had great success in increasing veterans' pensions. Callie House and her association colleagues had no way of knowing that the commissioner of pensions, H. Clay Evans, had written to Eliakam "Ell." Torrance, commander in chief, Grand Army of the Republic, on February 7, 1902, asking him to help squelch the movement. Torrance, a veteran of the Union Army's Ninth Pennsylvania Reserve Corps, played a major role in reconciliation and reunion activities between white Union and Confederate veterans of the period. He served as chairman of the Gettysburg Fiftieth Reunion Committee. Commissioner Evans explained to Torrance that pension organizers had been too successful. The bureau knew of "ninety organizations . . . in a single southern state." Each local chapter was constituted of at least twenty-five members. Some of the organizers were "impostors," he told Torrance, and at least two white men who had taken advantage of the situation had been convicted and sent to prison. But "More real harm is probably done by . . . regular agents . . . arousing, as they do, false hopes concerning a supposedly overdue restitution . . . or reparation for historical wrongs, to be followed by inevitable disappointment, and probably distrust of the dominant race and of the Government." He wanted Torrance to have department commanders in the South "protect members of the order and others associated with them by advising post commanders as to wherein the movement has been used by designing persons to live at the expense of the colored people through grossly fraudulent representations," and warned that members should have nothing to do with the idea. Since there would be no reparations, suppressing the movement served the interest of the government and the ex-slaves.[10]

Now aided by the Grand Army of the Republic, the government continued to deny the organization the use of the mails. Dick told House and the other Association officers about a new third party to promote pensions. Some white former pension allies of Vaughan had "hit upon" the idea of organizing such a party, and when it was announced in Washington, Vaughan christened it "Vaughan's Justice Party." Vaughan had decided that "existing parties will never do justice to the south" by relieving them of the burden of ex-slaves by pensioning them. Dick thought that a party to support their cause was a bad idea. He sent the association's board and the Pension Bureau a copy of his letter of March 21, 1902, to Hadley Boyd, a Vaughan supporter, of Washington, D.C., who had asked for his help, saying that while he supported pensions, he thought the idea counterproductive. "History and experience teach me that but two substantial, permanent political parties can successfully exist under our form of government contemporaneously, and the more equally and evenly divided these two parties are in numbers, influence etc. the safer stands the government and its institutions." He believed that if people energized themselves emphatically, they could get the existing parties to respond to their concerns. Parties spasmodically come into existence, but like "a meteor they flash across the political sky and then fall dead into the arms of mother earth." Although there had been third-party challenges, including the Populists and Eugene Debs, none had been successful.[11]

Dick agreed with House and the other leaders of the association that they should regard President Roosevelt's dinner with Booker T. Washington as a good omen. Emboldened, he sent Roosevelt press clippings, a petition, and a description of the association's objectives and asked for his endorsement of the cause. He hoped Roosevelt would instruct the federal officials to tolerate the movement. He also insisted that the Association cooperate by forwarding to the Post Office Department any rumor of impostors. They apparently received no response from the White House, and no improvement occurred in official behavior toward the Association.[12]

As part of their strategy, still believing a lifting of the order imminent, on April 6, 1902, Callie House and the board accepted Dick's advice to select new officers in the hope that this might please the government. Because she appeared to have become a specific target, House agreed to continue as an organization leader, traveling, lecturing, and enrolling members, but to no longer appear on the list of officers and board members. They also gave Dickerson the title of national lecturer and elected A. W. Rogers general manager, Reverend J. W. Clift president, and Robert E. Gilchrist of Washington, D.C., financial secretary. One month later Dick responded to the government's request by taking Dickerson to a deposition at the Pension Bureau to show their willingness to help with the investigation of alleged imposters. He answered every question, but bureau officials seemed more interested in the association than in pursuing anyone else.[13]

In response to a question, Dickerson answered that he had originally managed Vaughan's organization when he had con-

Commissioner of pensions Henry Clay Evans (served April 1897–May 13, 1902), Union veteran, businessman, and former member of Congress, believed that the movement should be stopped as a danger to public order whether its leaders were honest or not. "Men Recently Chosen for Diplomatic and Other Public Service," Harper's Weekly, *1897.*

Ell Torrance, Minnesota judge who was commander of the veterans' organization the Grand Army of the Republic, was asked by Evans to aid in crushing the movement.

ceived the pension idea. However, Vaughan was not involved with the association. Dickerson told the officials that before he became a pension advocate he had taught school throughout Tennessee. When asked whether he had "collected thousands of dollars from these old ex-slaves all though the south," he answered no. "The association have [has] collected it and a great deal was paid for publication and railroad fare." He allowed that some of the money might have been embezzled by dishonest agents. In response to a query, he said he did not know whether any of the funds had gone to members of Congress to encourage their support of the legislation.[14]

Despite the complete cooperation and openness of the Ex-Slave Mutual Relief, Bounty and Pension Association, federal officials continued to enforce the fraud order. Withstanding the obstacles and strains, Mrs. House and her colleagues continued their work. On February 9, 1903, Nashville postmaster Wills wrote to the assistant attorney general at the Post Office Department that an enclosed news clipping from a local paper, *The Nashville Tenn Daily News* of February 6, 1903, showed the continuation of the "same old steal." It appeared that "Dickerson, Callie House and others are still interested in the matter." The news clipping gave Wills credit that the Association's activities "were finally driven from here through the action of your department." The article reported the arrest of B. F. Crosby in Montgomery, Alabama. Wills claimed he worked for the association. Furthermore, the paper stated that a newspaper published by the association at that time, the *Freedmen's Headlight,* had promised the payment of pensions by a specific time.[15]

Upon inquiries from the Post Office Department, attorney Dick gave officials copies of the newspaper to review. Each edition of the *Freedmen's Headlight* clearly stated that the pension bill had not passed. In one issue a front-page article by George

Green, one of the founders of the New Orleans chapter, reported that the association continued to work despite the federal fraud order. As a result of its efforts, "there have been bills introduced six different times in the Louisiana Assembly on the subject." He also went with a delegation of "southern colored gentlemen" lodge members from the Southwest, who presented a petition on behalf of those who wanted pensions to President Roosevelt. The president promised he would give the matter his "careful consideration." The article went on to extol the work of Mrs. House and Dickerson but stated, "If we fail in our efforts it will be no more than other great moves have done, and the people of this great nation will give those who worked in good faith credit for asking the government for something for what we thought was just and right. We will be like the South. They fought for what they thought was right, hence our position in this matter." The statements included no intimation that the legislation had passed.[16]

Crosby said he had been an Ex-Slave Association agent for four years. He had been arrested, according to *The Nashville Tenn Daily News* clipping of February 6, 1903, when some local citizens complained that pensions did not arrive in January. However, in their eagerness to find criminal activity, neither Wills nor the other postal officials examined the Nashville newspaper very carefully. The same paper indicated that the language of the certificate included the following language:

This is to certify that Mrs. Linda White is a member of the Association, having paid the membership dues of fifty cents to aid the movement in securing the passage of the ex-slave bounty and pension bill. . . . The holder of this certificate agrees to pay ten cents per month to the local association to aid the sick and bury the dead.[17]

Neither the certificate nor the *Freedmen's Headlight* asserted that the pension bill had passed. It also specifically affirmed the importance of the mutual-aid function of the association that so attracted members.

The association held a mass meeting in Washington, D.C., at Samaritan Temple between Second and Third on I Street, on February 12, 1903, to gather support for the pension bill, which had been reintroduced for the new session of Congress by Congressman Spencer Blackburn of North Carolina. According to *The Washington Post,* the meeting was attended by "a large gathering of colored citizens of both sexes." Dickerson told the group, "If the government don't pay us a cent it will always owe us. The ex-slave bill is not a fraud." The meeting passed a resolution thanking all those who supported the effort to pass the bill.[18]

As House continued her Association work, her disappearance from the list of officers confused postal officials. Inspector J. H. Wilson of the Washington, D.C., post office was assigned to solve the mystery. He expressed agreement with his bosses' suspicions but found nothing illegal. Inspector Wilson wrote to Captain W. B. Smith, inspector in charge, that two ex-slave pension organizations operated in Washington, the Ex-Slave Association and S. P. Mitchell's Industrial Council, a small ex-pension organization. Wilson thought perhaps House had become active in the council since she was no longer an officer of the association. However, he had no evidence that she was. Whatever her role in the association, everyone knew she spent her time working in the southern states. He read the literature of the Industrial Council and the Association and saw nothing illegal. There simply was no information that would lead to extension of the fraud order against the association or its application to the Industrial Council. The government had no information on mailings or any possible House connection that supported legal action. But they continued to exclude the association from the mails anyway and kept watch on the Industrial Council for any signs of connections with House. The assistant attorney general promised to keep the case open, as "something might develop later."[19]

The assistant attorney general and Post Office Department officials continued to reach conclusions about the movement without investigating the association's local chapters or their activities in local communities. Government officials did not follow up on the names and addresses and other information provided by the association. Instead, the government investigated only to determine whether Callie House, Dickerson, or some individual possibly connected to them was continuing their organizing work. Following a policy of harassment and disdain for the organization's existence and despite the lack of evidence of illegality and Dick's assurances, the Post Office Department issued another fraud order against the Ex-Slave Association on October 28, 1903. The order prohibited the payment of money orders or the delivery of letters to the association or to Dickerson, Gilchrist, or any other officers. The 1899 order against House personally still stood. The reorganizations, the full disclosures, and the absence of Mrs. House from the official leadership had no positive effect with regard to relieving the government harassment.[20]

Then the U.S. Supreme Court strengthened the Post Office Department's hand in dealing with alleged fraud. The high court had only once before reversed a postmaster's decision and in no case did the Court deny the power of Congress to give unfettered authority to the Post Office Department. In the first test case under the 1895 amendments to the fraud section, *American School of Magnetic Healing v. J. M. McAnnulty,*

(1902), the Supreme Court affirmed the postmaster general's full and absolute authority over the mails. However, the high court did not agree that magnetic mind healing necessarily constituted fraud. Justice Rufus Peckham stated that the postmaster had no facts that proved that such healing did not work.[21]

Two years later in the *Public Clearing House* case, the Court denied a request for an injunction to prevent enforcement after the Post Office issued an order. Public Clearing House acted as the fiscal agent for a voluntary association for unmarried people; each person paid $3 as an enrollment fee and $1 a month for sixty months. If the individual had not married in a year, he or she received a certificate worth $500. The Post Office Department decided that this was a lottery and the organization could not use the mails. Justice Henry Brown, with Justices David Brewer, Edward White, and Oliver Wendell Holmes, concurred in an opinion that had far-reaching consequences: "The postal service is by no means an indispensable adjunct to a civil government." In other words, no one had the *right* to use the mails, and therefore matters concerning the post office were not subject to government rules of due process. This body of law gave no recourse to Mrs. House in her effort to have ex-slaves organize to use mail service as they expressed their citizenship rights to petition the government.[22]

While Callie House tried to keep the ex-slave pension cause alive, she hoped for some support from leaders in the Nashville African-American community, but they had other priorities. They were focused on the boycott of 1905, blacks' response to a new state law specifically reinforcing segregation on streetcars, except for "nurses attending or helpless persons of the other race." Blacks walked instead of riding public transportation until Preston Taylor and others organized their own transportation company. The company ultimately failed, in part because of a $42-a-car privilege tax on cars the white city government promptly enacted. Thereafter, the protestors settled into accommodating themselves to segregation, while poverty and racism still hampered the ex-slaves and their progeny in the poor black neighborhoods.[23]

The Association was in deep financial difficulty, and the legislative effort seemed stalled. Federal harassment of the Ex-Slave Association slowed the receipt of membership dues to a trickle. The chapters continued to provide mutual assistance but national political action came almost to a halt. Each time the association sought revocation of the fraud order, the assistant attorney general requested another supposed "investigation" of their current affairs. After the usual lack of investigation, government officials always reached the same conclusion: that Mrs. House and the others were "colored agitators and crooks." This time inspector G. B. Keene reported that the national office of the association had not actually carried on any activities in two years since the fraud order "choked off" their resources. He calculated that since June 1905, based on intercepted mail, $95.53 had been collected and $62.93 disbursed, but a "considerable bill" for office rent had gone unpaid. Also, according to Keene, the secretary's salary of $5 per week had not been paid in full. The association was bankrupt. Again, the officials made no effort to investigate the local chapters' activities. Keene thought the fraud order should stand. Basing its decision on the report of inspector Keene, on January 18, 1906, the Post Office Department denied the application for revocation.[24]

While the Association appealed to federal officials, developments in Congress further strengthened the Post Office Department's hand. Assistant Attorney General Tyner expressed the

*James Tyner, assistant attorney general for the
Post Office Department, authorized Harrison
Barrett, his nephew and assistant, to harass the
association with a fraud order. The order closed
the mails to the group.*

same concern that association lawyers and others had raised
about the postmaster issuing fraud orders without due process
and suggested that individuals should have the right to a speedy
appeal of such orders. However, Tyner was precisely the wrong
person to lead the cause, as he had been identified as one of the
principal corrupt officials in the Post Office Department.
Everyone assumed that Tyner, upon his imminent retirement,
wanted to protect clients from enforcement of the orders.[25]

However, Congressman Edgar Crumpacker of Indiana, as
persuaded as Mrs. House was that there was a due process
problem, followed up by introducing a bill that would have

impounded the mail while a hearing and judicial resolution took place. He complained that the number of fraud orders, most of which constrained business enterprises, had increased to 630 in the preceding two years, 71 more than in any four previous years. In addition, during the preceding year, every request for an injunction had been denied. The courts had said complainants could obtain a review of the decision but not of the facts to determine whether fraud actually existed. Crumpacker's bill required judicial review of the law and the facts. Although the Judiciary Committee supported it, at first unanimously in January 1907, the Post Office Department ultimately managed to kill the legislation.[26]

Postmaster General George Cortelyou went public in April 1907 in an article in the *North American Review,* vigorously defending the existing procedures as in the public interest. Cortelyou, who presumably had the support of the Roosevelt administration in whatever he did, had extensive connections within the president's party. A New Yorker, he had been secretary to several powerful men, including Presidents McKinley and Theodore Roosevelt. As chairman of the Republican National Committee in 1904, he had conducted the campaign that elected Roosevelt. He brooked no interference with or curtailment of his powers as postmaster general. Cortelyou also had Tyner's support of the legislation as an easy target. The postmaster insisted that fraudulent enterprises would simply continue to gouge the public during the legal appeals and that judicial review in advance would compromise the post office's work of protecting consumers. In response, the Senate simply buried the bill in the committee. The Congress and officials within the department and the Roosevelt administration had squelched attempts to introduce reform and thwarted a measure that might have given due process to the association. As a result, the post office remained unfettered in making unilateral decisions on the subject.²⁷

Mrs. House and the Association decided to try again to have the fraud order lifted. This time, on April 20, 1907, Attorney Thomas Jones, representing R. E. Gilchrist, born a slave in Virginia in 1847 and the Association's new secretary, wrote Assistant Attorney General R. F. Goodwin, asking that the fraud order be revoked. The letter explained that whatever had happened before, "future business methods here in Washington as elsewhere shall be clean." Gilchrist had not known of the fraud order when he was elected, but he also knew of no "wrongdoing" by Dickerson, Callie House, and others.²⁸

The board of the Association expelled Dickerson, despite no evidence of "wrongdoing" on his part, hoping that would please the officials. Being "embarrassed and interfered with," Gilchrist wanted the fraud order withdrawn. He still believed the ex-pension measure was "a just one, and should be agitated by every intelligent colored man, until sufficient sentiment is created as will cause the enactment of some measure to relieve." He pointed out that the group had new officers: A. W. Rogers of Williamstown, N.C., had been president of the association since May 1904, and Parker Moten, a Washington, D.C., shoemaker served as treasurer. When Rogers arrived in Washington to lobby for the association, *The Washington Post* reported that he hoped to achieve passage of a law to pension the ex-slaves.²⁹

Despite her previous experiences, Mrs. House harbored a faint hope that this time the effort would succeed. No one involved with the Association realized that no matter what they said or did, the government was bent on suppressing the pension movement. But then the assistant attorney general's response on May 16, 1907, made clear that the problem was the very existence of the pension movement. He pointed out that in the meeting on April 18, Gilchrist had "state[d] plainly his intention of continuing to promote the same business." The letter stated that not only would the department decline to revoke fraud orders against businesses and other institutions, it would not permit Gilchrist to use the mails individually unless he withdrew altogether from the pension movement. Just as the Post Office Department had done with Mrs. House, Dickerson, and other officials, the Association's new leader could not personally send or receive mail. Gilchrist refused to withdraw from the association, and the order remained in force.[30]

The Association reorganized twice, to no avail. It clarified its mutual-aid function in their certificates and literature and elected new officers—excluding Callie House—hoping to reduce any antagonism caused by her defiance and the outspoken letters she had written to officials. The second reorganization and the expulsion of Dickerson had still garnered nothing. They did not understand at first how deeply committed the officials were to stopping the movement. Prosecution of obvious impostors and fraud orders against bona fide leaders in the movement provided a rationale for cutting off all financial support and mail, even from leaders' friends and family, until the Association leaders had no alternative except to stop the work. Pension Bureau and postal officials repeatedly made a judgment that the pension idea undermined the national interest, which was keeping African Americans passive; the Association, the officials asserted, misled "credulous" African Americans, who did not understand that legislation would never pass. Because the organization and its leaders must agree that they would fail, they engaged in fraud by continuing to operate as if they had a chance to succeed. By the same standard any organization devoted to a remote, or an improbable legislative goal,

In an effort to satisfy federal officials, this new certificate displays prominently the mutual assistance work of the association chapters.

was at risk. Gauged by such a measure, the NAACP's long and unsuccessful struggle to gain an antilynching law could have been considered fraudulent.

Over the next few years, federal officials continued to fill their files with "sightings" of persons erroneously identified as Dickerson or Callie House. These imposters used their names to collect money from freedpeople. For example, on January 24, 1905, the president signed Senate Bill 2009, giving a pension to white veteran Richard Dunn of Cambridge, Maryland. Richard Dunn "colored," of Chattanooga, wrote to the bureau that someone he identified as "L. Dickerson" had put a mark on the *Congressional Record* by the white Dunn, told him he represented the government, collected one dollar, and claimed that they, as ex-slaves, would receive a pension. He said Dickerson also collected from other "colored" men. He wanted to know if pensions had been enacted. He described Dickerson as about forty years old, five feet, four inches tall, and weighing about 160 pounds. Even H. V. Cuddy, chief of the Law Division of the Pension Bureau, admitted that Dickerson did not fit the description of the man described but in passing described Dickerson as "an extremely smooth talker" with "the delivery of a trained orator." He did not know Dickerson's whereabouts, but the Washington office had been closed for more than a year. Cuddy noted that Dickerson had worked with Callie House, but erroneously described her as "a thin-faced mulatto, who writes a fairly plain hand, and is an excellent talker." Callie House was in fact a dark, heavyset woman. Cuddy thought that bureau officials should take testimony from Dunn to see if they could establish that he had given Dickerson money because he represented himself as a government employee. If so, they could prosecute Dickerson, Cuddy hoped.[31]

The post office seemed to view every piece of information it received as another opportunity to cast suspicion on Callie House. On December 28, 1906, Nashville Postmaster Wills wrote to Washington that he had a letter addressed to Thomas House that had previously been sent to her from the same address and returned to sender. On December 26, 1906, the superintendent of letter carriers told Wills that he thought the writer wanted to reach her by using Thomas House as an addressee, which "I believe to be a fictitious name used by Callie House." On March 11, 1907, Wills responded that even though he had made no investigation he thought the letters addressed to "her brother" Thomas belonged to her and that the mailing "indicates to me she still continues the fraudulent business, and I think the case should be investigated at an early date." Callie House, indeed, asked correspondents to send letters to her children, including Thomas, hoping to communicate with the chapters. However, they could have easily ascertained Thomas's identity. The Nashville City Directory included the information that Callie House and Thomas House, her son, who worked as a railroad car cleaner, lived at the same address.[32]

The association continued to hold annual conventions without interruption despite the federal harassment. At the June 1907 convention in Washington, D.C., at Miles Memorial Church, A. W. Rogers of Newbern, North Carolina, presided as president. Reverend L. E. B. Rosser, pastor of the church, spoke, as did Armond Scott, a Washington attorney. The resolution endorsing the pension bill took a new tack; adding the rationale pushed originally by Vaughan: "to refill the depleted treasury of the South, made so by the ravages of war." The strategy did not gain more support in Congress.[33]

On November 26, 1907, when inspector W. E. Greenaway asked what "is the status of this case?" Wills, the Nashville chief postmaster, replied, "Petered out entirely. The parties have evidently quit business—because we made it too hot to continue." The post office believed it had successfully killed the organization by stopping its mail.[34]

A change in the White House after the 1908 election did not change the government's stance toward the association. However, Mrs. House and other advocates continued to collect signatures and to organize in the ex-slave pension cause, even though the new Taft administration appointees and career officials in the Pension Bureau and Post Office Department continued their harassment. After Dickerson's death in 1909, Mrs. House, described in the 1910 Census as a "traveling Lecturer" for the National Ex-Slave Mutual Relief, Bounty and Pension Association, stayed on the road even more than before. Her children were able to care for themselves; the youngest child, Annie, was sixteen, and Mrs. House's brother and his wife still lived next door. Mrs. House collected funds personally at local meetings and carefully stretched whatever she received to pay her fare to the next place. She met with agents and supervised their work. She stayed with local chapter members and had them send correspondence to her family. The group also had to hold more frequent local meetings to share information, instead of distributing flyers and other materials because of the government harassment. Association officers also tried to use intermediaries to send and receive mail pertaining to headquarters operations. None of these special efforts was easy and their movement suffered.[35]

Nevertheless, the association's work in the field continued, as did the petition drive. In December 1909, the U.S. Senate took note of another set of petitions from ex-slaves that arrived at the Capitol but took no action. The petitions asked, as earlier ones had, for the passage of the bill by Senator Mason of Illinois, first introduced on June 6, 1898, and reintroduced in each Congress thereafter. The petition stated that the petitioners had seen service as slaves and believed they deserved pensions, just as did unknown and deceased soldiers. Only a few of the petitions remain in the government's files. As with previous petitions, the pension seekers included their names, the names of their former owners, their ages, and their present addresses.[36]

From time to time the Post Office Department and the Pension Bureau would record rumors about Mrs. House and continuing meetings of people in the movement. On January 2,

1911, a constituent from Tuskegee, Alabama, M. A. Warren, sent Congressman Thomas Heflin a circular printed by a "negro preacher, for the purpose, I think, of fraudulently obtaining money from these negroes." Warren thought the preacher had promised that money had already been appropriated in order to collect $5. He told Heflin, "I think you represent these old negroes in Congress as well as us white people, and if these claims of his are fraudulent, I think you ought to have the government put a stop to him and his association." The local U.S. attorney told the assistant attorney general that under the "meager facts submitted" the state and not the federal government had jurisdiction so he should give it to the local prosecuting attorney. Still, neither the U.S. attorney nor local officials made any attempt to investigate whether the local chapter engaged in bona fide activities.[37]

A few complaints of alleged imposters continued to trickle in and the government used the complaints to reinforce the conclusion that the association was engaging in fraud. On April 24, 1911, the postmaster general, F. H. Hitchcock, responded to the secretary of the interior concerning a complaint by Henry Parrish of Jackson, Mississippi, that alleged the use of the mails to defraud by two women, one of whom claimed to be Callie House of Nashville, Tennessee. He referred it to the chief inspector for handling. But the description of the woman did not fit Mrs. House. Congressman Swagar Sherley of Kentucky reported to the attorney general, based on a constituent's letter, that "one of the negroes" employed by the Ohio River Saw Mill Company had given to an ex-slave association. He wanted to know if this violated the law because he believed that "ignorant negroes are being fleeced." Assistant Attorney General W. R. Hair replied that they were sending the complaint to the Post Office for investigation because they had responsibility for the federal law that covered schemes to defraud through the mails. These complaints were simply acknowledged as additional evidence that the association still operated and as a reason to keep the fraud order in place.[38]

Even more positive political change in Nashville failed to attract the support for the pension cause Mrs. House still hoped for from African-American leaders. Locally, after William Howard Taft's election to the presidency in 1908, division among the Democrats in the 1910 election permitted the first Republican governor since 1883, Ben W. Hooper, to take office. He named an African-American adviser, a new man in town, Benjamin Carr. Also, President Taft revived James Napier's political fortunes by naming him register of the Treasury, making him the first nationally recognized black leader from Nashville. Ben Carr was responsible for having Tennessee Agricultural and Industrial, the state college for "negroes," located in Nashville. He also engineered the city purchase of the John L. Hadley former slave plantation and its development as the first public park for African Americans, dedicated in 1912. But Carr showed no interest in the pension cause. Federal departments did not modify their behavior toward blacks, and matters worsened when the staunch segregationist Woodrow Wilson became president.[39]

The association held its Nineteenth Annual Convention on November 23–27, 1914. House managed to distribute a report to members despite the federal harassment. She reported that they met at Mount Gilead Baptist Church in Nashville, pastored by Reverend R. Page. Reverend William Atkins of Lynchburg, Virginia, served as president. "Two white friends" visited the convention before the opening of the meetings and assured them that the movement would succeed someday in having the ex-slaves paid. She asked that contributors continue their commitment to the work and asked that they send any funds to pay expenses. Attempting to bypass the scrutiny of Nashville postmaster Wills, Mrs. House asked that they reply to 1219 William Street in Chattanooga.[40]

Despite the barriers they faced, the movement had kept up a level of momentum since its inception—albeit inhibited. The chapters continued to provide mutual assistance, and Mrs. House and local chapters continued to gather petitions and work for the legislation. However, even though members kept sending petitions to Congress, passage of the ex-slave pension legislation seemed increasingly unlikely. The movement needed another strategy.[41]

CHAPTER 7

The Association Goes
to Federal Court

*"We deserve for the government to pay us as an indemnity
for the work we and our foreparents was rob[bed] of from
the Declaration of Independ[ence] down to the Emancipation."*

CALLIE HOUSE
(1899)

DESPITE THE FEDERAL government's attacks on the movement, Callie House continued to lecture to local chapters and
mobilize membership in the National Ex-Slave Mutual Relief,
Bounty and Pension Association. Her family responsibilities
were alleviated because her children, now grown, had their own
jobs and could better fend for themselves. Her brother and his
wife, who lived next door, could lend a hand, if needed, when
she was away on association business. However, by now Mrs.
House could see that the efforts in behalf of the always embattled poor rural and urban African Americans could only go so
far. The association could have pension legislation introduced,
but it did not have the resources to gain its passage. Further, at

the Pension Bureau's instigation, the whole reparations idea had been denounced by key members of Congress. In addition, the association leaders had to worry about fraud charges against local agents brought by state prosecutors, urged on by the Justice Department. Local chapters maintained their mutual assistance programs, but the communications barriers and attacks on their leaders made effective organizing toward the reparations goal increasingly difficult. The fraud order made fund-raising perilous. Through use of expensive commercial delivery services, solicitations at meetings, and occasional mailings to intermediaries, Association leaders kept a bare trickle of financial support flowing to the national office. Clearly, the movement needed another strategy. At this juncture, according to federal officials, Callie House "instigated and paid for" a reparations lawsuit.[1]

This new tactic taken after they had practically destroyed the movement infuriated federal officials; it provided yet another reason to harass House. They denounced the litigation as part of a continuing moneymaking scheme to defraud "credulous" ignorant ex-slaves. Mrs. House saw the courts as responsible for deciding claims of injustice when legislative lobbying failed. Even though the courts had proved inhospitable to suits seeking protection for blacks under the Fourteenth Amendment, judicial protection of minority rights was firmly embedded in the Constitution. And the Constitution was the rock on which all of Mrs. House's claims of political agency and citizenship rights for the ex-slaves stood. This lawsuit offered another route to establish their claims legally. Besides, even if the effort failed, it might engender more public understanding of the pensions cause. Turning to the judiciary was just another example of using whatever weapons came to hand.[2]

From Mrs. House's perspective, the national political climate after the election of Woodrow Wilson on the Democratic Party ticket in 1912 had made bad matters worse. The ex-slaves living in the poor communities where she lived and worked were without the right to vote, without land, and without means of support beyond meager wages for their labor; many were disabled and suffered in their feeble old age.

She understood that some leading African Americans had changed parties to vote for Wilson, hoping to attract more attention to the need to end lynching and disenfranchisement. However, the Wilson administration's New Freedom agenda did not extend to African Americans. In Washington, D.C., where black employees had worked freely with whites in the federal workforce, the Wilson administration instituted segregation. The downturn in the fortunes of African Americans coincided with the continued harassment of the ex-slave pension movement by federal officials during the Wilson years.[3]

Mrs. House understood that the people she represented needed inspiration. They must not give up in discouragement. She thought that recording ex-slaves' claims in the petitions continued to be important and the movement effectively served local ends. Members helped one another to survive and the movement also gave ex-slaves and their families a larger vision that the slave experience validly justified compensation for their suffering. The courts offered another venue to argue their case.

The Association had been in court supporting Isaiah Dickerson's successful appeal of his Georgia criminal conviction, but this marked its first foray into civil litigation. They knew that Homer Plessy had achieved a victory in a civil case in the lower court before ultimately losing at the appellate level. After deciding on a suit, Mrs. House faced the challenge of identifying a competent lawyer to handle the case. She identified Cornelius Jones, an experienced litigator. Jones and Wilford Smith were the African Americans usually discussed as the best-known and most successful African-American attorneys in the Mississippi bar. Both had gained bar admission at the same time, and both argued separate cases before the U.S. Supreme Court on December 13, 1895, challenging the exclusion of blacks from grand juries. Newspaper publisher Calvin Chase's *Washington Bee* reported that this marked the first time that more than one black lawyer had appeared before the Supreme Court in different cases on the same day. It was a time when, among the small number of African-American lawyers, few had argued before the nation's highest court. Chase considered this a major indication of racial "progress."[4]

Jones, both an active politician and a practicing lawyer, had served one term in the Mississippi legislature in the 1890s. He lost a disputed contest for a congressional seat in 1896 after claiming unsuccessfully that he had been elected with votes from 40,000 black voters and 10,000 whites. Hailing Jones as "a superb Constitutional Lawyer," publisher Edward Cooper's *Colored American* lamented the failure of Congress to act on his 1896 election challenge and noted Jones's role as one of the first African Americans to openly oppose black disenfranchisement. The paper identified him as "the first and only Negro lawyer appearing in the Supreme Court of the United States, unsupported by a white lawyer" in defense of the rights of the "Negro," under the Thirteenth, Fourteenth, and Fifteenth Amendments. Jones's work with Emanuel D. Molyneaux Hewlett, one of the leading African-American lawyers at the bar, in a 1896 Supreme Court case, *Gibson v. Mississippi,* led to a decision that excluding blacks from grand juries violated the Fourteenth Amendment.[5]

Hewlett, a graduate of Boston University School of Law

Cornelius Jones was one of the widely known and respected African-American civil and criminal trial lawyers. Callie House chose him to sue the government for reparations from the cotton tax.

Calvin Chase, editor of the Washington Bee, *an opponent of the ex-slave petition movement but a proponent of Jones. He published favorable stories about the cotton tax suit but not about Callie House and the Association.*

and admitted to the District of Columbia Bar in 1883, was one of only six black lawyers practicing in the city in 1885. He became a highly successful criminal defense attorney and stayed well connected in Republican political circles. He served as a justice of the peace from the Harrison administration through the presidency of Theodore Roosevelt. When he died in 1929, the Supreme Court of the District of Columbia adjourned out of respect for him, an honor reserved only for the most respected members of the bar. For Mrs. House, engaging Jones to seek compensation, she hoped, would not only ensure effective representation but might encourage the support of leading African Americans who had ignored or denounced the pension cause.[6]

Jones agreed with House that congressional action afforded the most reasonable approach to gaining reparations, but since that strategy had failed, he would develop the best possible case to bring before the courts. She and Jones decided to aim the court attack at the widely discussed cotton tax. The proceeds from the sale for federal tax payments of cotton confiscated by federal troops had been the subject of reports in black newspapers. The reports noted that ex-Confederates who had tracked the funds found that they lay untouched in the Treasury. When the Civil War began, the cotton had already been picked and stored. Congress enacted the tax first, in 1862, at two and one-half cents per pound on raw cotton, for the ostensible purpose of paying war debts. In 1866, Congress increased the tax to three cents a pound. This time Congress designated no specific purpose for the money. The newspapers also reported that southern senators unsuccessfully sought legislation to return the funds to the ex-slaveholders. Jones wanted this identifiable fund distributed among the old ex-slaves.[7]

"COTTON PILE NEAR THE WORTHINGTON PLANTATION—COLLECTING CONFISCATED COTTON."

Rolling Cotton on Board the "Tatum."

The cotton raised and gathered by the hands of slaves was the source of funds sought in the tax suit. "Rolling Cotton on Board the 'Tatum,'" Harper's Weekly, May 2, 1863.

First Jones wanted to make sure the cotton tax funds still existed. In May 1915, before filing the case, he wrote to Secretary of the Treasury William G. McAdoo, asking about cotton tax revenue. Assistant Secretary William S. Malburn responded that the courts had never decided whether the tax had been constitutional in the first place. Malburn concluded that "though bills for a refund of the cotton tax have been introduced in Congress from time to time, no legislation has been enacted; and the subject is one within the jurisdiction of Congress."[8]

Consequently, the suit Callie House inspired claimed that the Treasury Department owed African Americans $68,073,388.99, collected in cotton taxes between 1862 and 1868 and demanded repayment of the debt. In July 1915, Attorney Cornelius Jones filed the association's class action suit in federal court in the District of Columbia against Secretary of the Treasury McAdoo, claiming a specific debt owed from the production of certain cotton crops during slavery. Because this cotton had been identified when it was taxed, it could be traced in the Treasury, and thus the suit avoided the issue of whether Congress would appropriate funds to pay for pensions as compensation for the ex-slaves. Jones cited by analogy Indian monies held in the Treasury that were payable under specific Indian treaties. Jones wanted this identifiable fund distributed among the old ex-slaves.[9]

Jones avoided specific references to Reconstruction or developments during slavery to support the claim for debt repayment to African Americans. Callie House, Frederick Douglass, and other advocates did not discuss specific Reconstruction policies or failures either. They knew that the Freedmen's Bureau had never really controlled any significant land in the South. Besides, President Andrew Johnson's Amnesty

Proclamation of 1865 had forced the restoration to ex-slaveholders of what the agency did control. Frederick Douglass, in insisting on reparations, emphasized that "the Russian serf was provided with farming tools and three acres of land with which to begin life,—but the Negro has neither spoils, implements nor lands." House talked routinely of how the old ex-slaves had received nothing for their labor.[10]

In the suit, Jones avoided novel arguments and any focus on Jim Crow, the rights of blacks, or the horrors of slavery. Instead, he strategically formulated the suit in sterile, formal legal terms common in the period. His strategic arguments reflected the negative racial climate of the times. He and Mrs. House knew by the time they brought the case that African Americans had endured the reversal of positive uses of Reconstruction civil rights legislation. By this time, the courts had routinely affirmed the use of the Fourteenth Amendment to defend corporations, not African Americans.[11]

Jones knew that legal rules, such as governmental immunity—the legal principle that the government cannot be sued without its consent—limited his case. That is why he kept insisting that though the government held the tax revenue, the proceeds always belonged to the ex-slaves. Surely, he argued, the ex-slaves had a right to the funds generated by their labor even though they could not exercise that right during their enslavement.[12]

In response to the suit the Treasury Department went on a public relations offensive. In a press statement of October 15, 1915, the department insisted the government had a right to keep the tax money and that if the ex-slaves "had any claim it would be against their masters." The Treasury Department expected to win based on governmental immunity since "the usual fate of such suits is to be thrown out of court because of lack of jurisdiction." The statement warned anyone who gave to a fund for prosecuting the suit against "throwing their money away."[13]

Despite the earlier letter to Jones from Malburn, the Treasury Department not only slammed the lawsuit but denied the existence of the monies sought by the ex-slaves. Secretary of the Treasury McAdoo wrote to Jones denying the existence of the cotton tax revenue. He also asserted that "the United States Supreme Court decided the tax of 1862–68 was unconstitutional, and that the money collected as a Civil War revenue tax has been treated as part of the general receipts of the Government and applied to payment of government debts." McAdoo stated, "There is no fund of $68,000,000 or any other sum in the Treasury of the United States for ex-slaves, or those who worked in the cotton fields of the South." Jones denounced McAdoo's response, insisting that either sometime after writing to him in June, Treasury had spent the funds, or the government still had them in the account and McAdoo was denying their existence to defeat the lawsuit.[14]

The District of Columbia Court of Appeals rejected Jones's claim in the cotton tax case on the grounds of governmental immunity. The United States could not be sued without its consent. Jones filed an appeal to the U.S. Supreme Court but lost. The justices upheld the lower court decision.[15]

The freedpeople lost the case because the court would not let them overcome the government's procedural objection to having a trial to determine who owned the funds. Today waivers of governmental immunity might allow such a claim to avoid immediate rejection in the courts. However, Jones's plea failed because the court decided that governmental immunity superceded a determination as to whether African Americans might receive the funds.[16]

Out of regard for Jones's prestige, black newspapers that usually ignored or denounced Callie House and the Association commented favorably on the suit when it was filed. However, the *Washington Bee,* still deeply committed to denigrating Mrs. House and the Ex-Slave Association and knowing of the federal government's enmity toward the pension movement, insisted the case had no connection with the "agitation of freedmen" for pensions. Other African-American papers expressed the same view, or did not mention the association at all in the news coverage about the suit.[17]

After Jones filed the case, he circulated information about it to potential claimants and asked for support. Jones and the Ex-Slave Association asked for local chapters and general public contributions. Jones, in a letter, asked African Americans to contribute $1.75 each to support the suit and explained that ex-slaves would share in the proceeds if the case succeeded. Federal officials chose to characterize movement leaders' efforts to publicize the case to their grassroots constituency as further evidence of criminality. Federal officials reported that, "renewed activity on the part of Callie D. House and other persons who had been connected with the ex-slave pension movement at once became apparent."[18]

Although the case was lost, Jones, by representing the ex-slaves, made himself a target of the governmental officials already attacking Mrs. House and the Association—the hostile Post Office Department and Pension Bureau officials. Angered by the lawsuit, government officials tried a strategy against Jones that they planned to use against Mrs. House. Just as they could not harass her for exercising her citizenship rights to petition the government, they could not prosecute Jones for litigating the cotton tax suit at her instigation. Instead Post Office Department officials decided to prosecute him for violating the Postal Code by using the mails to defraud. They made this decision while Jones was appealing the cotton tax case to the U.S. Supreme Court.

Congress had enacted modifications in the postal fraud law to ease prosecution of fraudulent land and mining deals that were quite prevalent at the time, and the new Postal Code language made it possible to obtain a conviction even when no "scheme or artifice to defraud" had transpired. The new provision exacted a penalty of $1,000 or imprisonment for not more than five years or both for obtaining money or property by false or fraudulent pretenses or promises, by "placing or causing to be placed, any letter . . . in any post office." Under this language, in 1914, the U.S. Supreme Court decided the postmaster did not need to prove a scheme to defraud. The placing of a letter in the mails concerning what the postmaster considered a fraudulent project provided sufficient proof. Using the mails to carry out a scheme, by making promises the postmaster considered impossible to perform—or promises the defendant had no intention of performing—constituted using the mails to defraud. The government charged Jones with fraud for mailing letters seeking support from African Americans who might benefit from the lawsuit. The government sought to punish Jones for having the temerity to bring the lawsuit and for his connection to the Ex-Slave Association.[19]

Alexander R. Pitts, the U.S. attorney in the Southern District of Alabama, wrote Justice Department headquarters enclosing a circular that J. D. Watson, an agent collecting funds for Jones, to support the case, had allegedly distributed. Pitts concluded that Jones's agents had been "going through the country collecting hard-earned money from poor negroes" in violation of the Postal Code. Pitts volunteered that he could provide "plenty of witnesses" who had made contributions. He had called in Watson and directed him to produce receipts and communications from Jones soliciting contributions. Pitts later informed headquarters that he had enough evidence to prosecute Jones in either Memphis or Selma, and a decision was made to proceed in Memphis.[20]

After the U.S. attorney in Memphis, Hubert Fisher, filed charges, he vacillated on whether to actually seek punishment. His uneasiness about prosecuting the case probably resulted from his background and professional aspirations. A Democrat, born in 1877, Fisher graduated from the University of Mississippi at Oxford ("Ole Miss") and attended Princeton for a year. He read law and began a practice in Memphis. He became politically active, serving as a delegate to the Democratic National Convention in 1912 and later in the State Senate. President Wilson appointed him U.S. attorney in 1914. If he aspired to a federal appointment, he would need positive responses from respected members of the bar in addition to political connections. He first sought a postponement because "the cotton tax case, *Johnson v. McAdoo,* has not been decided by the U.S. Supreme Court." Then he told the court he had decided not to prosecute at all, but later he went forward with the complaint against Jones. In the proceedings, the jury returned a guilty verdict.[21]

Instead of accepting the jury verdict, Judge John Ethridge McCall, who presided over the case, ordered a new trial. McCall appeared as uneasy as Fisher about the government prosecution of a lawyer on such a minor charge while the lawyer was suing the government in the underlying matter of the tax case then before the U.S. Supreme Court. McCall cared about the reputation of the judicial branch. A sixty-year-old Republican and native Tennessean, he attended the University of Tennessee and read law. After admission to the bar he began editing a newspaper, *The Tennessee Republican.* He savored the reputation of having "distinguished himself as a fearless fighter for principles which he believed to be right." He also practiced law privately for about two years and served one two-year term in the state legislature before accepting a succession of political posts. He served as U.S. attorney, one term as a member of Congress, and ran unsuccessfully for governor in 1900. President McKinley had appointed McCall as a district collector of internal revenue before President Theodore Roosevelt nominated him to the district court. According to the *Memphis Commercial Appeal,* locals saw him as "a courageous foe of the liquor traffic back in the days when it required courage to take a stand against the system. He fought the liquor interests from the platform with great effectiveness and many Memphians will remember his forensic assaults here 15 years ago during the wide-open regime." He thought it important that his behavior at all times reinforce public confidence in the integrity of the court.[22]

Thus McCall was reluctant to accept a conviction, and in the next term U.S. Attorney Fisher decided not to prosecute the case further. Jones's reputation and connections served him well. Each time Fisher had moved forward with the prosecution, a number of respectable African-American witnesses had gathered in Memphis to testify for Jones, including Calvin Chase of the *Washington Bee* and the Washington, D.C., justice of the peace Emanuel Hewlett. Their support, naturally, contrasted sharply with the negative racial tone of reports in the local *Memphis Commercial Appeal.* One article began, "The members of the race have been prone from time immemorial to strive to get something for nothing." Now the government had charged Jones with "fleecing thousands of the members of his race out of hard earned dollars." If he had confined his efforts to personal appeals, the newspaper concluded, Jones might have escaped, but the letter writing had sent the postal authorities after him. The newspaper likened Jones and Mrs. House's suit to stories Harris Dickson of Vicksburg wrote regularly in *The Saturday Evening Post* that portrayed his belief in the stupidity, laziness, dishonesty, and childlike behavior of "big, black, credulous" African Americans. According to the *Commercial Appeal,* Dickson's work included a series of "negro get-rich-quick schemes revolving about one Rev. Criddle and Virgil Custard" that "rocked the sides of readers of a well known publication for many a month."[23]

The *Memphis Commercial Appeal* of January 18, 1917, reported the first delay in the prosecution with a headline saying that Jones had been "Released but Warned." The newspaper inadvertently gave evidence of the grassroots support for the movement, reporting that the ex-slave pension cause had become quite popular, with huge numbers of African Americans turning out for meetings. In Canton, Mississippi, in September 1916, masses gathered to hear Jones who composed a song for the occasion and sold copies for five cents each to support the cause. "Every emotion, which would stir the negro soul, was brought out in the several stanzas and chorus contained within the covers of the little pamphlet." Under the title "Voices from the Tomb of the Slaves," the first stanza expressed the mission of the ex-slave movement:

> Do you hear those voices calling
> From their lone and musty graves

Urging us to note the toilings
Of the poor neglected slaves?

Despite the hostile press, the government's final decision not to prosecute Jones ended the matter. The lawyers involved survived the experience and even prospered. Hubert Fisher's reputation remained intact; elected and reelected, he served in Congress from 1917 to 1931. Despite the Post Office Department's threats to pursue Jones, no record has surfaced of any further prosecution of Jones in the Southern District of Alabama or elsewhere. The *Washington Bee* reported in 1920 that Jones, described as chief counsel of the cotton case, wanted to revive the issue of a home for ex-slaves in the District of Columbia. He also participated in subsequent litigation against segregated schools in Oklahoma.[24]

The effort to gain pensions had failed again, but Callie House had been correct in her belief that the litigation would help to grow the movement. Ex-slaves were even more firmly convinced that they should continue to gather petitions seeking pensions and to continue to strengthen the Association's local chapters. In addition, the cause gained favorable publicity among African-American leaders based on Jones's respectable reputation. Because he was a successful male professional, blacks applauded his leadership role. With the failure of the litigation, the movement again concentrated on pursuing legislation.

However, there was still another case under way as the government was prosecuting Jones and as he pursued an appeal to the Supreme Court in the cotton tax case. At the same time that the government decided to prosecute Jones they also decided to bring charges against Callie House. Mrs. House lacked Jones's status of black male respectability, and she did not have his legal standing as attorney representing a client in a case before the federal courts. Mrs. House was just a black woman with the audacity—and no money—to stand firmly on claims of citizenship rights for herself and freedmen and -women. She had much to fear.

CHAPTER 8

Jailed for Justice

[I]f the government were to punish all those who use the mails to defraud, it would round up those energetic business men who flood the mails with promises to give eternal youth and beauty to aging fat matrons, to make Carusos and Galli Curcis of members of church choirs, and to make masterminds of morons.

E. FRANKLIN FRAZIER
(1926)

WHILE CALLIE HOUSE REJOICED over the positive effect the cotton tax court fight had on the grassroots ex-slave pension movement, federal government officials saw the matter differently. In their view, the cotton tax suit was further evidence of Mrs. House's arrogance and refusal to submit. At this point, the broad public was concentrating on "the War to End all Wars," in which Jim Crowed African Americans served. Blacks at home remained economically deprived and subject to lynching and disfranchisement, and in the midst of all this Mrs. House struggled to keep the ex-slave pension movement alive. But government officials by now had decided to stop the movement once and for all. They would break her spirit and end her defiance and the pension cause. They would jail Callie House.[1]

Even in the face of this climactic attack, African-American newspapers and civil rights leaders still did not speak out to aid or defend Mrs. House or the pension movement. African-American leaders' praise was limited to Cornelius Jones; it did not extend to his clients, the ex-slaves. And the endorsement of the reparations effort by a credible star did not translate into increased acceptability for the movement.[2]

Perhaps the unusual nature of Mrs. House's role as a leader of the association undermined the group's acceptance. There had been militant organizations of black women before. As early as 1866, laundresses in Jackson, Mississippi, announced a collective agreement to maintain prices of $1.50 a week and $15 a month for a family's washing. Eleven years later, women in Galveston, Texas, organized when threatened by Chinese laundries and steam laundries. In 1881, in Atlanta, washerwomen struck, joined by cooks, nurses, and servants. Like these women Callie House was also a laundress and seamstress, and she, too, was poorly educated and working class. Unlike them, however, Mrs. House became the leader of a membership organization of black men and women, one not defined by occupation but an explicit political cause.[3]

In addition, she was a single head of household, a widow with children. Mrs. House went when and where she pleased to advocate the pension cause, and seemed oblivious to criticism. Perhaps her lack of what Melinda Chateauvert and Evelyn Brooks-Higginbotham describe as "respectability" in the education and gendered manners displayed by middle-class contemporaries did not help. However, so-called respectability did not always suffice, as Ida Wells-Barnett, a leader of antilynching campaigns, learned when the founders of the NAACP in 1908 studiously failed to include her. Mary White Ovington, the only woman among the five charter members (which included only one African American, W. E. B. Du Bois), wrote later that Wells-Barnett was a "powerful" personality, "Perhaps not suited to the restraints of organization." Perhaps, the acknowledged power and influence of Booker T. Washington over everything concerning African Americans played a role in Mrs. House's isolation. Washington opposed the pension movement as undermining his accommodationist, up-by-the-bootstraps philosophy. Perhaps, independently, African-American leaders and newspapers simply believed the federal government's claims that the entire pension movement was misguided and probably crooked besides.[4]

For whatever reasons, African-American leaders uttered no objections when in February 1916, federal prosecutors used the strategy they had practiced against Jones. Instead of relying on fraud orders to strangle the movement, they decided to prosecute Callie House. Essentially the government punished her for exercising her constitutional right to petition the government and teach the other ex-slaves to do so. Mrs. House, like Cornelius Jones, was charged with obtaining money or property by false or fraudulent pretenses or promises, by "placing or causing to be placed, any letter . . . in any post office." She had, in the government prosecutors' view, used the mails to promise that which the postmaster considered impossible to perform and which she had no intention of performing. Using the mails to defraud exacted a penalty of $1,000 or imprisonment for not more than five years or both. Callie House and the association saw the freedpeople as victims of slavery whose exploitation needed reparation. Federal officials also characterized ex-slaves as victimized—but by the ex-slave pension movement.[5]

However, federal officials still had no evidence that House

actually intended to obtain funds by claiming Congress had passed a pension bill or that she had assured payment to the ex-slaves. Then, in February 1916, Alexander Pitts, the U.S. attorney in Mobile, Alabama, suggested to the Justice Department that the newer modified fraud law language could possibly be used to prosecute Mrs. House. This, federal officials reasoned, would kill the association once and for all.[6]

Postmaster General Albert Sidney Burleson, a former Texas congressman appointed by President Wilson, agreed. Burleson wrote Attorney General Thomas Gregory that the association had been "investigated for years and now was the time to get an indictment in order to close the case." He ordered the U.S. attorney in Nashville, Lee Douglas, to investigate and to prepare indictments in the case. He also ordered Mrs. House and other association officers arrested. Burleson calculated that the arrests would lead to some confessions and this would place the government in the advantageous position of not having to prove a violation. Douglas had no qualms about violating House's citizenship rights. He believed she was automatically guilty because the movement's cause was impossible. In the charges he included the unfounded, unsupported assertion of his belief that "most, if not all, of the profits of this scheme have been collected and converted by Callie House."[7]

Douglas presented the case against House to a federal grand jury in Nashville in March 1916. As before, he claimed she had collected dues and fees knowing that pensions would never be awarded. He introduced no evidence of her wealth or income and nothing on the association's expenditures for lobbying efforts, its lawsuit, officers' salaries, or locally funded burials and medical care. Essentially, he simply speculated that Mrs. House had used organizational funds for herself. Three months later, the all-white, male grand jury returned an indictment charging House with violating the postal laws of the United States. The indictment charged her with obtaining money from a number of ex-slaves "by means of false and fraudulent pretenses" sent through the mails of the United States. Callie House, individually and in conspiracy with others in the organization, according to the indictment, had acted to obtain money from "ignorant, illiterate, aged, and credulous" freedmen, by means of false and fraudulent pretenses. House had sent through the mails the Association's printed matter that used a "descriptive insignia" that could appear to "ignorant, illiterate" African Americans to represent a connection to the U.S. government, according to the charges.

The indictment alleged that Mrs. House had guaranteed the payment of pensions and promised that holders of certificates issued by the Association would be paid before non–certificate holders. The indictment identified no one who had actually been victimized by the association's alleged fraudulent scheme. Instead, the government charged that Mrs. House had mailed a misleading circular to Mrs. Alice Williams, a black woman, at the Hotel Imperial in Knoxville, Tennessee. The supposedly misleading circular contained an eagle in the upper-left-hand corner but included nothing regarding a forthcoming federal pension payment. Apparently, by federal standards the condemning words from Mrs. House were that "the national convention was represented from every section of the government by delegates and many proxies."[8]

In preparation for the trial, U.S. attorney Douglas used photographic copies of House's handwriting to compare it with other Association materials. The Association's membership badge also became evidence. This badge consisted "of a scroll from which is suspended a crescent upon which is the legend National Ex-Slave Mutual Relief, Bounty and Pension Assn." A

The official badge of the association. It was cited by the prosecution against House as misleading members into thinking the group was an official government body because of its design containing the words "of the U.S.A."

star within the crescent read "of the U.S.A." Projecting the worst possible interpretation of Mrs. House's actions, Douglas described the use of patriotic symbols to represent the organization as a means of fooling a largely illiterate membership.

The complaint seemed to suggest that the government was unaware that national political parties and other organizations routinely used the American eagle on promotional literature.[9]

On Thursday afternoon, August 3, 1916, Deputy U.S. Marshal James M. Southall arrested Callie House at her home in South Nashville. The *Tennessee American,* in reporting the arrest, described her as "a dusky woman of ample avoirdupois." In addition to noting Mrs. House's weight, the paper invoked from the grave the judgment of the Wizard of Tuskegee against her, surmising, "It is said the organization was denounced by Booker T. Washington a short time before his death."[10]

If House had enriched herself by collecting thousands of hard-earned dollars from the old ex-slaves, her lifestyle showed no signs of it. Her family still lived in the same house in the same poor working-class neighborhood she had lived in since coming to Nashville. The Association had to scrape together resources to pay her travel expenses, and her grown children worked as laborers, pressers, servants, or taking in laundry. After Mrs. House had spent two weeks in jail, her son, Thomas House, persuaded a local pawnbroker and bondsman to post her $3,000 bond. U.S. District Judge Edward T. Sanford set a trial date in September 1916.[11]

In the days leading up to the trial, House hired H. P. Stephens, a local white attorney, to defend her. Prosecutor Douglas exulted to his superiors that this was good news. He thought Stephens had persuaded her to enter a guilty plea in exchange for a light sentence. Stephens, who had represented Callie House for some years with federal investigators, knew that long ago they had determined to punish her and that no amount of information concerning the legality of association activities would dissuade the government from its attack. Apparently this was enough for those who had dealt with

Stephens to assume he would advise her to plea bargain. Prosecutor Douglas, certain of her acceptance, told various postal and pension officials that they would not have to appear in court.[12]

However, the government's plans went awry. If Stephens did urge Mrs. House to plead guilty in exchange for a light sentence, it was to no avail. When House stood before Judge Sanford, she denied the charges against her. Douglas angrily reported to his superiors in Washington that she "denied any moral turpitude." Judge Sanford seemed to believe that she was puzzled about the actual stages of congressional action. Callie House asserted that "she was merely rendering a service to the negroes in making it possible with little effort to secure the money the Congress had appropriated for them." Since she denied any guilt, Judge Sanford rejected the attorneys' statements that she wished to plead guilty and ordered her placed on trial.[13]

In his eagerness to put Mrs. House away, Douglas did not reckon on her independence or Judge Sanford's predilections. Edward T. Sanford, later an associate justice of the U.S. Supreme Court from 1923 to 1930, is remembered, if at all, for his majority opinion in the 1925 case *Gitlow v. United States*. This First Amendment case was the first to apply one of the guarantees of the Bill of Rights to the states. Sanford saw himself as a benevolent judge who overtly tried to act with scrupulous fairness no matter the status of the client. He gloried in being called the most impartial judge in the South.[14]

Like other federal judges, Sanford came from an upper-middle-class background. Born in Knoxville, Tennessee, on July 23, 1865, he had the best education available. He went to private schools, the University of Tennessee, Harvard College, and Harvard Law School, where he served as editor of the *Har-*

vard Law Review. After some years of corporate practice, in 1905 he agreed to serve as an assistant attorney general in the U.S. Justice Department, litigating major cases.[15]

Sanford was certainly not a civil rights activist, but he opposed lynching and demonstrated as a prosecutor a conscious interest in avoiding racial bias. During Theodore Roosevelt's administration Sanford tried a Chattanooga sheriff, his deputies, and members of a lynch mob for the lynching of a black defendant, despite a stay issued by the U.S. Supreme Court. Douglas reported to his superiors that when Mrs. House appeared before Judge Sanford, she would plead guilty for the light sentence of "one year and one day in a penitentiary—where I do not know but probably Atlanta." Instead Mrs. House denied any wrongdoing; her lawyer stated that she knew bills had been in Congress and committees and told everyone the "business has not been completed." Sanford decided Mrs. House's letters might mean nothing more than the Association needed to keep working until passage of the legislation. Considering the factual dispute, he decided he had no alternative but to set the matter for trial.[16] Sanford had prior experience with fraud cases and had shown a concern for keeping the defendant's circumstances in mind. In one case, after a jury found a defendant guilty of mail fraud, Sanford imposed a sentence of eighteen months. Upon being informed that the defendant's wife, who had repeatedly fainted in court, had heart trouble, Sanford reduced the sentence to a fine.[17]

Federal prosecutors saw no need to devote more resources to jailing Mrs. House. They viewed her refusal to plead guilty as more evidence of her arrogance. Severely disappointed at Sanford's refusal to agree with their strategy, the U.S. attorney's office tried to persuade Stephens to make her return to court again and, without comment, simply to plead guilty. House continued to refuse, and Sanford set a new trial date for March 22 or 29, 1917.[18]

In order to pressure a guilty plea from Mrs. House, the government indicted Reverend Augustus Clark, an agent for the association, hoping he would implicate her. Clark had gathered petitions and organized chapters in Texas and Louisiana. For this organizing work, he was charged with impersonating an officer of the U.S. government. A letter introduced in his case was later used as a major piece of evidence against House. Special Pension Examiner U. A. Biller, operating from New Orleans, reported that he had attempted to question Clark at his Texas home but found he had left to organize chapters in Louisiana. Bon Wier, Texas, chapter members of the association said that Clark had recruited them and collected their dues but said nothing about being a government official. Biller described Clark as "shrewd and unscrupulous" and believed that if he had been "imposed upon" by Callie House "he was willing to be imposed on provided he got his money." The official reported that he had obtained "one letter from Clark's niece that Callie D. House had written him" that could be used to prosecute Clark and House.[19]

Even without the evidence of the Bon Wier chapter members, the federal government charged Clark with obtaining money by impersonating an officer of the government. Prosecuting Clark's case was Clarence Merritt, the well-connected son of a Texas county sheriff and state legislator. Merritt, a delegate to the Democratic National Convention in 1916, had supported the nomination of Woodrow Wilson through forty-six ballots. The president had rewarded him with his job as U.S. attorney for the Eastern District of Texas. Merritt eagerly joined in the Post Office Department, Justice Department, and Pension Bureau effort to stop the ex-slave movement once and for all.[20]

Merritt convened a grand jury and gathered witnesses from Bon Wier, along with government officials, to testify against Clark. Merritt charged that Clark had told nine ex-slaves that he had the authority to enroll their names so that they might receive a government pension. Like other agents, Clark always carried the association's circulars bearing the insignia of an eagle. The members signed their names and each paid him a membership fee of one dollar.

In the trial before Judge Gordon James Russell, Merritt tried to prove that Clark had collected some $200 to $400 from ex-slaves in the area, implying that they would receive pensions from already appropriated funds. Even though the postal inspector found no one to testify that Clark had said he was a government agent, Merritt alleged that what he termed "bent and enfeebled 'uncles' and old black 'mammies'" began to complain when they received no pension payments. He offered as evidence the letter the inspector had taken from Clark's niece: "mailed on the Nashville & Memphis R.P.O. on June 6, 1916, addressed to the accused at Bon Wier, Texas, which is in the handwriting of Callie D. House, of Nashville, Tenn., and bears her genuine signature." According to Merritt, Mrs. House had advised Clark on how he should handle the cases of persons "who did not reside in places where there was a sufficient number of victims to constitute a club." Although the association itself was victimized by government harassment, Merritt, like government officials before him, characterized the ex-slaves as victims of those who attempted to organize them to demand that the government remedy its continued mass victimization. Using the term "ex-slaves" made sense to

House, for it focused on their enslavement. However, the critical public and government officials used the term to reinforce the idea that the recruited members were ignorant, childlike consumers who needed protection from the association.

Callie House's handwritten letter to Clark introduced by Merritt actually stated something quite different from what he charged. She said, "I tell the people that there has been something done in Congress for the ex-slaves, regardless of what anyone says, white or colored, but the business has not been completed. If it had, we would not have appointed you [Reverend A. Clark] as agent to give the ex-slaves a chance to get in the movement before the work is finished, which we are expecting at any time." She expressed her hopes and her optimism that legislation would eventually pass.

Merritt focused on House's statement that "there has been something done in Congress" rather than "the business has not been completed." He argued that the letter promised the impossible; that the bill had passed and if ex-slaves became members, they would receive payment. He rejected the alternative interpretation, acknowledged by Judge Sanford during Callie House's failed plea-bargain proceedings. Sanford's interpretation had been otherwise. In his view her language meant that Mrs. House knew bills had been introduced repeatedly, hoped eventually one would pass, and organized ex-slaves to support the effort in their own interest. Callie House's letter to Clark "authorized him to canvass all of Texas and four parishes of Louisiana for the purpose of organizing ex-slaves."[21]

To encourage a belief that Clark's guilt could be presumed, Merritt falsely claimed that Mrs. House had pled guilty before Judge Sanford. However, Merritt's flimsy case against Clark collapsed before House's trial was held. Merritt had presented no evidence that Clark had ever claimed to be a government agent and the letter, which had been seen by the allegedly defrauded members, made no such statements. Clark, described in the press as the "aged negro" defendant did not try to rebut Merritt's case. He assumed Merritt was telling the truth when he said Mrs. House had, for some strategic reason, pleaded guilty. Consequently, using no lawyer and pleading his own case, Clark portrayed himself as a "victim" of House. He claimed to be the "innocent hireling" of Mrs. House, a black Amazon. "Uncle Tomming," Clark invoked the racial paternalism of the white jury; he said he was "nothing but an unsophisticated old darky, unversed in the ways of the world and was the innocent dupe of Callie House, the notorious Negro from Nashville." Paternalistic powers should protect a "silly negro" from this already convicted felon, pleaded Clark, not punish him.[22]

Five months after Clark's April trial, Mrs. House appeared in court as her three-day trial began on the fourth Monday of September 1917. The *Tennessean*, unsurprisingly, sensationalized the trial, calling her, as the prosecutors did throughout, "Aunt Callie," in keeping with the time when black adults were "Aunt" or "Uncle" to whites. Under the headline "Aunt Callie, Head of Ex-Slave Relief Body Ready for Trial," the subheading read "Two hundred and Twenty Pound Negro Woman Gloriously Garbed, Center of Attraction in Federal Court—Members of Association Charge Fraud." She might have been "gloriously garbed" but it was the federal government, not members of the association, that was charging fraud. The paper went on to describe Mrs. House as discomfited briefly by the narrow doorway because of her weight. In her new black silk dress, "her velvet Merry Widow with the little touch of lavender, had become tilted to a decidedly undignified angle, Aunt Callie had begun to sweat." The audience, "distracted by other cases being disposed of gave her time to compose herself sit at the counsel's table and to take out a fan whereupon she assumed an air of bored tolerance."[23]

In the hope that they would call themselves victims of Mrs. House, as Augustus Clark had in the Texas case, the prosecutors presented Reverend William Atkins of Lynchburg, Virginia, the president of the association, and Reverend Doc Parchment of Okolona, Mississippi, as witnesses. These men, unlike Clark, knew that Mrs. House had not pleaded guilty. Reverend Parchment attested to the authenticity of the certificate of membership beautifully embossed with the words "Love One Another" and stamped with a golden seal. The certificate indicated that the membership fees would be used to "aid the movement in securing the passage of the Ex-Slave Bounty and Pension bill" and to "aid the sick and bury the dead."

The *Tennessean* reported that "The Rev. Doc was not quite certain just when it was Aunt Callie had led him to believe he was to receive the pension funds from the government." But letters exchanged indicated he should not be "discouraged." He testified that he could think of no evidence of fraud.[24]

Reverend Atkins's testimony was also a "sore disappointment" to the prosecution. He had attended the movement's conventions, heard the financial accounting, and observed the allocation of funds and swore in court to "Everything having been open and above board." Affirming the association's commitment to an open process and defending the organization's operating procedures, Reverend Atkins testified that he saw nothing wrong with Callie House's presence on the committees that made recommendations to the association's convention so long as the convention approved the work. Government officials countered, telling the court that the fraud order was issued after "many certificates had been sent to the Pension Bureau by ex-slaves who insisted on having their bounties and benefits paid." However, the government prosecutors presented no evidence of any ex-slaves who had been told by House that they could collect a pension.[25]

Reverend J. W. Clift of Alabama testified about the Petersburg, Virginia, convention that pretended it had "expelled" House and "I. S. Dixon [Dickerson] Callie's right-hand man in an effort to satisfy the government after the issuance of the fraud order." He and the other Association officers told of how they had reorganized as recommended by attorney Robert Abraham Lincoln Dick in the hope of having the fraud order lifted.

Callie House, on the witness stand, "maintained an air of self assurance throughout several hours of examination and grilling cross examination," according to the *Tennessean*.[26] She answered the prosecution's questions about the association, trying to interject explanations about their local chapters' work. Mrs. House testified how, despite the federal harassment, the chapters had continued to bury the dead and aid the sick, while agents and members also had continued to collect petitions. The prosecutor, Lee Douglas, pressed her to tell how money had been collected and sent to the national treasurer. She explained that since the imposition of the fraud order had been imposed, they had used most of the national office funds for travel expenses. The association paid House $50 per month—when they could afford to. She insisted that "she had not received yearly more than about $150.00 over and above the expenses connected with the national office expenses."[27]

The prosecution focused on damning the Association's political activities as fraudulent with no attention to the local charitable work of the chapters. Prosecutor Douglas denounced the movement's "so-called" national conventions and "so-called" reports from local clubs, saying they deceived the "ignorant and illiterate negroes." However, even with the two typed letters, the only letters not in Mrs. House's handwriting in the government's files, the evidence was inconclusive. In the absence of any evidence of income or expenditures, any funds collected by the national organization could easily have been used to pay for the agents; expenses for House and other national officers; for the conventions held in every state where they were active; and for mailings and circulars.[28]

In his charge to the jury after the three-day trial, Judge Sanford explained the government's theory that she had used the mails to defraud and collected large sums. Defense attorney Stephens argued that she engaged in bona fide work to gain a worthwhile legal, legislative objective, whether she succeeded or not. The prosecution insisted Mrs. House was guilty and that she had conceived of the organization for the purpose of defrauding persons, "by making it appear ostensibly that persons would receive a benefit, when she alone would profit thereby." The all-white, male jury found her guilty. The offense was punishable by a fine of $1,000 or imprisonment for up to five years or both. Mrs. House lacked the resources to pay a fine. When she stood before Judge Sanford, he sentenced her to only one year in prison, apparently no more persuaded of her criminality than at the failed plea-bargain proceeding.[29]

Callie House's conviction, like the story of the hundreds of thousands of African Americans who sought pensions, was mostly ignored. The Nashville papers reported her sentencing, but the papers around the nation focused on the war and preparedness and overlooked the story. Those stories about African Americans included the *Chicago Tribune*'s: "Negro Women Car Washers Take Men's Places in Chicago Plant." The only discussion of "civil rights" was actually about efforts to pass a bill guaranteeing insurance for soldiers who paid no premiums during the war or up to one year thereafter. African-American newspapers totally ignored the pension cause and the case.[30]

Outside the courtroom on the day of Mrs. House's sentencing Reverend Atkins commented that without her, "the guiding spirit," he had no idea what would become of the association. His expressed sentiment affirmed what everyone involved knew, Callie House was "the secret" on which the organization depended. Poor African Americans gathered outside the courtroom murmuring aloud as Reverend Atkins cried, "She kept it alive." The collection of petitions, the finances, the local chapters, the lobbying and litigation—Callie House had kept it alive.[31]

In November 1917, upon the instructions of Attorney General Thomas Gregory, "the colored woman" Callie D. House, age fifty-two, entered the Missouri State Prison at Jefferson City, Missouri, to serve a one-year sentence. Prison records described her as "Negro," "Baptist, Lecturer," "educated," and with black hair, brown eyes, and a "nut brown complexion."

She was sent to the Jefferson City prison because the federal government had no facility available for female prisoners. Mrs. House was lucky that she was not incarcerated in a southern state prison. Female state prisoners were whipped, sexually abused, made the personal servants of contractors, and put to hard work in mines and farms.[32]

About six months after House's incarceration, the federal government sentenced another female political prisoner to the Jefferson City facility. This woman, born to Jewish parents in Rochester, New York, also a seamstress by trade, was sentenced for protesting the military draft. One of the most famous radi-

*Callie House was placed in the Jefferson City, Missouri,
Penitentiary Women's Wing because there was no federal prison for women.*

cals of her age, Emma Goldman had become an anarchist, war resister, sympathizer with the Soviet Union, and feminist. In the women's wing, where these two activists lived, two thirds of their fellow prisoners were African Americans.[33]

Mrs. House left no written record of her time in prison, but Goldman's autobiography, *Living My Life,* prison records, and other materials describe the conditions in detail. Located in Jefferson City, the state capital, about one hundred miles from St. Louis on bluffs overlooking the Missouri River, the state prison was the largest in the United States. The facility housed 2,300 inmates, mostly male. In a period when prison reform was a major political and social welfare concern, Goldman saw the prison as "a model in many respects." Compared to the "pest holes of 1893" on Blackwells Island in New York City, where she served a previous sentence, the Missouri prison cells had double the space.[34]

However, the Jefferson City cells lacked light and ventilation. The prisoners were made more miserable by the warden's refusal to open the corridor windows except in very hot weather. But Goldman liked it that the prisoners had single cells and did not have to share. Still, the facility was overcrowded, with low sanitary standards, bad working conditions in the shops, poor medical services, and harsh disciplinary methods. The facility had no educational programs beyond two months of training to sew clothes for state profit.[35]

The women's department housing Goldman, House, and ninety other female prisoners consisted of a long building with a cage of cells, four high and two deep facing in opposite directions in the center. Each cell measured seven feet wide, eight feet deep, and seven feet high, with solid steel ceilings, cement floors, and steel-barred fronts. Each had a toilet, a sink with running cold water, and a steel bunk fastened to the wall, with

Emma Goldman was imprisoned for her antiwar efforts and served at the same time as House. Goldman wrote a memoir in which she described the prison.

two bags of straw, one to use for a mattress, the other for a pillow. The remainder of the furnishings consisted of a crude table, chair, broom, and dustpan. Each woman received raspy brown muslin prison garb to replace her own clothes, which the matrons confiscated. The dresses, long and wide in 1890s style, fit like a tent. Cheap, uncomfortable shoes completed the outer garments.[36]

Discipline and routine, the hallmarks of prevailing penal theory, governed the women's movements day and night. Awakened every morning at 5:00 A.M. except Sunday, the prisoners ate breakfast at 6:15.

Prison food, never wholesome or sufficient to sustain the laboring prisoners, was often rancid, cold, and infested with insects. The inmates especially hated Tuesdays and Fridays, when they had "fish that was neither fresh nor plentiful." The prisoners ate in a large, gloomy, cockroach-infested dining room with rows of long wooden tables and benches each seating eight women. They used rusty tin dishes and cast-iron knives and forks. Breakfast consisted of corn syrup, bread, "hash," and weak coffee. For lunch they had "meat, vegetable, bread and water, and supper a light meal of bread, and perhaps stewed fruit." Almost all the food contained vermin.[37]

Work started in the sewing shop by 6:30 A.M., continuing until lunch. The inmates then had a rest period from 11:30 to 12:30 and then went back to work again until 4:30, the end of their nine-hour workday. After work, supper lasted until 6:00 P.M. and then the guards allowed the prisoners to walk outside in the yard. Friday after work, they cleaned their cells and bathed. On Sunday they ate breakfast later, then had church services and an outdoor exercise period. The inmates had to remain silent and could talk only during limited recreation periods. The men's wing had a library, but women could not use it for the matron feared they could not be trusted to go there alone.[38]

The nine-hour shift six days a week in the sewing shop was consistent with the period when workingmen were required to put in a nine-hour day. House and Goldman were both seamstresses. However, the inmates trained two months to sew wearing apparel the state contracted for revenue. The prisoners received assigned tasks, or quotas, of work to complete each day. They sewed jackets, overalls, jumpers, and suspenders for delivery by the state to retailers. Operating in a double row of old "out of date" sewing machines in a narrow, badly lighted room, each inmate would be assigned to sew 45 to 100 jackets or 9 to 18 dozen suspenders in a day. In the clothing, the jailed women sewed the labels of private firms across the country. Goldman found the work onerous and tedious.[39]

G. R. Gilvin, the acting warden, pressed the women hard to produce their daily quotas. To compound the harsh labor conditions, the state prisoners received time off their sentences for good behavior if they made or exceeded their tasks. But this promise did not automatically extend to federal prisoners such as Callie House and Emma Goldman. The shop foreman, an unnamed twenty-one-year-old who had been in the job since age sixteen, would insult and intimidate the women verbally to keep them hard at work. The shop matron displayed a considerate attitude toward the inmates, but the head matron, Lilah Smith, in her forties and an employee of penal institutions since her teens, exuded hostility, except toward those who became her favorites.[40]

The earlier practice of flogging the prisoners had been dropped for the more "enlightened" practice of isolation in a cell for forty-eight hours from Saturday to Monday on a bread-and-water diet. The worst punishment consisted of the blind cell, an entirely dark hole four by eight feet in size. With one blanket, two slices of bread, and two cups of water a day, a prisoner might be kept there from three to twenty-two days.[41]

Emma Goldman appears not to have noticed Callie House among the sixty other inmates of color. Goldman described her fellow prisoners as "poor wretches of the world of poverty and drabness." She wrote, "Colored or white, most of them had been driven to crime by conditions that had greeted them at birth." She saw them as victims of economics and/or society and not as possible political actors like her. An unnamed "Chinese girl," imprisoned for having killed her husband, warned Goldman against being so friendly with the "colored" inmates, whom she thought "inferior and dishonest." Challenging the woman's racial stereotyping, Goldman reminded her that Chinese men and women had been attacked in California by mobs, just as "colored" people were in the South. The "Chinese girl" said she knew this but whites had been mistaken because Chinese people "no smell. No ignorant, different people."[42]

Goldman relied on the African-American prisoners, who helped her in "making the full task" quota. "The kindness of several coloured girls in the shop," plus her five cents per jacket paid to these "girls" who usually finished their quotas an hour earlier than others, permitted Goldman to finish her shift. She thought perhaps they had greater physical strength or had done the work longer, but she did note that African-American women did the work much better than the white women. Most white prisoners could not afford a nickel to pay for help, but Goldman lent them money since they would not accept payment because she shared food and books with them.[43]

Goldman declared that she "never had any prejudice against coloured people," but the race question had not been part of her politics. And she apparently missed the opportunity for sharing with her fellow federal political prisoner Callie House and learning about her fight for reparations.[44]

The foreman graded the prisoners' work. The highest score, "A," resulted in as much as half time off one's sentence. Although sentence reduction applied only to state prisoners, Mrs. House somehow gained early release for her good work and was discharged from prison on August 1, 1918.[45]

The indictment of Callie House claimed that she had "fraudulently converted money to her own use" but noted that the government could not determine the "amount of money collected or converted." The prosecution introduced no evidence of wealth. Nashville property deeds record that Mrs. House and her son Thomas House jointly purchased a lot in 1909 for $200. They paid $35 down and agreed to pay $4 a month for forty months, and then $5 for the last month plus 6 percent interest for the property on Currey Street in South Nashville. Seven months after her release from prison, Thomas sold his mother the lot for one dollar and "in consideration of the love and affection" he held for her. Whatever Mrs. House did in the ex-slave pension movement, she and her family did not profit financially from it.[46]

The federal government expected to destroy the reparations idea embodied in the ex-slave movement by jailing Callie House. But hundreds of thousands of African Americans had the same idea. Too many people had seen and heard Callie House and believed in the principle. "She kept it alive for years," but other African Americans were willing to defend it in her stead.

CHAPTER 9

Passing the Torch

*My Whole soul and body are for this ex-slave movement
and are willing to sacrifice for it.*

CALLIE HOUSE
(1899)

IN AUGUST 1918, after her release from prison, Callie House
returned to her family home in South Nashville. It was the
same shotgun frame house she had lived in since a few months
after moving from Murfreesboro in 1898 at the start of the
national ex-slave pension movement. For the next ten years,
until her death, Mrs. House worked once more as a washerwoman and seamstress in her neighborhood of porters, laborers, washerwomen, and domestic servants.[1]

Mrs. House's conviction had killed the national legislative
activities of the Ex-Slave Association. But the work of the local
chapters and the reparations movement continued. Mrs.
House's work did not occur in a vacuum. The final decades of
her life came at a time when conservative Republicans and
Democrats dominated politics; liberal social trends vied with
religious fundamentalism for political attention. In the
African-American community, art and literature exploded in

the creativity of the Harlem Renaissance while brutal repression, in the form of lynching and racial riots, seemed to increase. The NAACP began a concerted effort to end racism and bigotry, which included an initiative focused at obtaining a federal antilynching law.[2]

In Nashville, the city and the Carnegie Foundation opened a "Negro" library. The "colored" Young Men's Christian Association occupied a large building in the heart of the African-American business district, and national African-American organizations such as the Baptist Convention and National Medical Association held their conventions in the southern city. African-American civic organizations abounded, their activities dutifully reported by the black-owned *Globe* newspaper. The state operated a segregated tuberculosis hospital to address the disease many whites saw as a "Negro disease." Black churches flourished. So did taxpayer-supported all-black institutions, including Pearl High School, Tennessee A&I College for Negroes, which my eldest brother and numerous cousins attended in the 1950s and 1960s, and Hadley Park. These stood as accomplishments that local African Americans had requested successfully from politicians. In 1917, in response to another African-American demand, the state of Tennessee permitted a Nashville colored National Guard to mobilize for service in World War I.[3]

In the years following Mrs. House's release from prison, the great migration of blacks to the North and West during and after World War I grew from a trickle to a stream. African Americans were drawn to economic opportunities made available because the war reduced European immigration and increased demands for workers in industry for military preparedness. About a half million African Americans left the South between 1916 and 1919, and nearly a million followed in the 1920s. In addition, within the South, many moved from rural areas to cities.

Mrs. House lived to witness the growth of South Nashville as thousands of African-American sharecroppers and other rural blacks moved into the city, either permanently or as a way station on the trip north. The local African-American population grew by 25 percent to 42,836 in 1930. Many of these migrants moved into South Nashville, where Mrs. House lived, in neighborhoods blacks had developed since the Civil War. Former tenant farmers and sharecroppers without other occupational skills, the migrants worked in low-wage, unskilled jobs like their neighbors. African-American women maintained their overwhelming presence in the low-wage workforce. Well over half of the Nashville female black population worked mainly in domestic or personal service occupations or as washerwomen like Mrs. House. Only a small number of black women were professionally employed; 57 African-American women held jobs as teachers or doctors, or in insurance and real estate, with 526 working in some area of the clothing and textile sector. Those African Americans in the professional and business class lived nowhere near Callie House's neighborhood.[4]

Black business in Nashville and elsewhere reached its peak in the favorable national economy of the 1920s. Black downtown, Cedar Street (now Charlotte), from Fourth to Tenth Avenue, boasted the two black banks, physician and law offices, churches, printing and publishing houses, retail stores, the colored YMCA, and the Negro Opera House.[5]

The business and professional institutions were led by a coterie of younger black lawyers, doctors, public school teachers, college professors, and businessmen, who emerged to pick up the mantle left by James Napier, Richard Boyd, and Preston

Taylor. These emerging leaders belonged to the NAACP, made ending segregation a major goal, and also showed great interest in the culture and literature of the Harlem Renaissance. They supported the student strike against the white president of Fisk in 1925, which took energy and time. After the city sent in policemen to beat the student protestors, working-class black Nashvillians joined the protests. Some 2,500 local blacks attended a rally at St. John's A.M.E. Church to support the students and roundly denounced police brutality. The college's white trustees refused to give in to the students; it was not until 1946 that Charles S. Johnson became the first African-American president of Fisk. In this period as in the past, except for the protest against police abuse, the activities of bourgeois African Americans mostly bypassed Callie House and other working-class residents of Nashville.[6]

On June 6, 1928, Callie House died at age sixty-seven. Living at home and "keeping house," she had been hemorrhaging from uterine cancer for almost six months. According to her physician, George M. Kendrick, who saw her daily, she had bled for a week. Although Dr. Kendrick and his partners treated patients whether they could pay or not, an operation for Mrs. House was thought either not useful or too expensive. Her funeral was handled by P. M. Ransom and A. Morris, undertakers, an African-American firm.[7]

Callie House lies buried in Mt. Ararat Cemetery, organized in 1869 by the Sons of Relief (No. 1) and the Colored Benevolent Society as the city's first black cemetery. Mt. Ararat is a thousand feet north of the junction of Murfreesboro Pike and Elm Hill Pike, next to the still existing dairy. Although the property was later sold to Greenwood Cemetery owner Preston Taylor, a historic plaque marks the Mt. Ararat location, but there is no map of the burial sites and no record of where individuals' graves are located. Among the graves many markers are worn away. My nephew and I have tramped the entire grounds repeatedly, vainly seeking a marker for Callie House.[8]

Mrs. House's funeral most likely took place at the same church where services were later held for her brother, Charles Guy, who died in 1933. Charles, an itinerant Primitive Baptist preacher, like most among the denomination's clergy, supported his family as a laborer.[9]

The funeral arrangements for Mrs. House's brother were handled by the most flamboyant Primitive Baptist minister in Nashville, Reverend Zema W. Hill, the charismatic pastor of Hill's Tabernacle Primitive Baptist Church. Born in rural Franklin County, Hill joined a local church and became a preacher as a teenager. After he moved to Nashville in 1916, his "elegance, good looks and magnetic preaching style" quickly developed a large following. By 1919, he had started Hill's Tabernacle and his funeral home. Unlike other black Primitive Baptist churches—"primitive" wood structures with potbellied stoves—Hill built his tabernacle of brick with two furnaces; congregants could look down through the registers and see the coals burning. His congregation of washerwomen, domestics, and laborers contributed their mites. Hill's "civic minded zeal" led him to arrange funerals for the destitute where he would pass a plate in a "silver service" to collect contributions from the congregation. His new funeral home, with six-foot concrete polar bears at the entrance, and his fleet of automobiles, with his name in gold letters, attracted attention and more customers.[10]

White and black civic and political leaders attended the church services, sitting among the working-class congregation. When she arrived in Nashville "from the country" in the early

1930s, my mother, Frances Southall Berry, joined Hill's Tabernacle. My brother and I attended services there while we lived in the neighborhood with my mother's eldest sister, Aunt Everleaner, and her family. The famous and the infamous showed up at Hill's Sunday services, including my uncles—my mother's brothers—inveterate sinners who drank and partied when not at work but would not have missed Reverend Hill's church services on Sunday. My uncles used to tease my mother, saying that before Zema Hill even said anything, excited women threw their pocketbooks at him. During services those who could not squeeze inside the building stood or sat outside in good weather. In a period before air-conditioning, the congregation fanned itself with paper fans advertising local businesses as they sweltered in summer, and those outside poked their heads through the wide-open windows to see the spectacle.[11]

After her death, Mrs. House's family can be traced through the city directories for the next few years. In 1929, the House family still lived at 1307 10th Avenue South, while her brother, Charles Guy, and his family remained nearby. Guy worked as a laborer until his death, and Mrs. House's younger son, William, worked as a clothes cleaner at a shop on Fourth Avenue North downtown. In 1929, Thomas, Mrs. House's eldest son, pressed clothes at the Just Rite Tailor Shop; William's wife worked as a domestic, and Charles's wife took in laundry.

In 1933, Callie House's daughter Annie rented a place on Vernon Street, where Callie and Charles and their families had first rented rooms in Nashville when Mrs. House began taking in washing. In the same year, William's wife was working as a maid at the James Robertson Hotel. Annie worked as a maid and Ross as a houseman. Thomas lived on Vernon Street also, with Annie and Ross, probably her son. The 1957 directory recorded their names as Howse. However, when Mrs. House's daughter Mattie died in 1971, her last name was recorded as House in the official city death records.[12]

Howse was the most popular spelling of the House name in Nashville. A white Howse family, including Mayor Hilary Howse and his relatives, had owned slaves. Like many African Americans, descendants of the Howses kept the name. Hilary Ewing House, born into a slaveholding Rutherford County family in 1866, served as mayor of Nashville from 1909 to 1915 and again from 1924 to 1938. The African-American Howses and the few Houses who live in Nashville today claim to know nothing about Callie House.[13]

Even though Mrs. House appears to have stopped working in the reparations movement after her imprisonment, some of the local chapters of the Ex-Slave Association continued their self-help activities in the ensuing years. The Atlanta council, led by Professor Brunsey R. Holmes, president of the Holmes Institute, held fund-raising drives to provide mutual assistance for the old ex-slaves in the form of "Warm clothing and something good to eat." The affiliate repeatedly asked the public to send groceries, old clothes, or money and held "tag days" (yard sales) to raise funds. Two of Holmes's female relatives, Savannah and Kizza, taught at the school where Professor Holmes served as the principal. *The Atlanta Constitution* published a photograph of "Holmes of The Ex-Slave Association," which apparently gave weekly allowances for fuel, groceries, and clothing to old ex-slaves right before Christmas. The chapter, organized in the early 1900s, engaged in such self-help activities as late as 1931.[14]

Although the federal government defeated the legislative goals of the Association, the hope for and belief in pensions on the part of old ex-slaves remained alive. Their children and

Even after Callie House's jailing and death, old ex-slaves like these kept writing the government to demand pensions for their bondage and forced labor. Sarah Graves, Edgar and Minerva Bendy, Tiney Shaw, and Molly Ammond.

*Some of the local chapters continued to work after Callie
House's jailing. This Atlanta chapter lasted at least
until 1932. Brunsey R. Holmes, their president,
is shown giving funds to the needy.*

grandchildren also remembered the demand. In April 1928,
some relatives of a freedman in Wetumka, Oklahoma, asked
the U.S. attorney general, "Is there any money set aside for old
ex-slaves by the U.S. Government?" An Arkansas freedman
asked in December 1930, "Had there Ben a law in Congress
that we people should draw a pension by being own by southern people?"[15]

A freedwoman in Holmes County, Mississippi, wrote to President Herbert Hoover, wanting to know if the pension bill had ever been passed. She "were a girl the age of 16 when freeman [freedom] were taken place and now am an old lady blind can't see and if there ever were a person kneads assistance I know its me. My owners in slavery were Mr. Jeff Poole who lived in Moreland, Miss."[16]

In 1934, a number of old ex-slaves wrote President Franklin D. Roosevelt, "Is there any way to consider the old slaves?" One asked specifically, whatever happened to the idea of "giving us pensions in payment for our long days of servitude?" The government officials replied that no legislation existed. Their letters attest to the interest in pensions. They also affirm Callie House's insistence during federal investigations and prosecution that she had told ex-slaves only that the association wanted to gain the enactment of a federal pension law. Members had not been told that Congress had passed a law.[17]

As late as 1937, the attorney Richard Broxton of New York City asked the Treasury Department and the attorney general whether the law prohibited "forming an Organization designed for the purpose of having the Government appropriate funds for the payment of the services of those held in involuntary servitude—such funds, if available, to be paid to the descendants of such ex-slaves, if located." His inquiry and others concerning the legal issues received a standard response: "The Attorney General is authorized by law to give opinions only to the President and heads of the Executive Departments."[18]

The interest of the ex-slaves and their descendants in pensions persisted. Callie House gave voice to their pleas and her "whole soul and body to the movement." African Americans, who carried the message of the movement with them as they migrated out of the South, carried the struggle with them to live for another day.[19]

In the years since the demise of the Ex-Slave Mutual Relief, Bounty and Pension Association, scholarly analysis of social movements has shed additional light on the fate of the organization and Mrs. House. The "changes in the political environment" that a social movement confronts, rather than "the internal characteristics of the movement ['s] organization and the social base upon which it drew," determine its success or failure, according to sociologist Charles Perrow and others. Perhaps reparations for African Americans will never become a reality, but the 1890s proved a decidedly negative time for the ex-slave pension movement. Mrs. House believed that the aging condition and social deprivation of the ex-slave population called for a remedy. Also, pensions had been given quite freely to white Union veterans, and even Confederate states paid pensions. However, most public attention to the unfinished business of the Civil War focused on achieving national reconciliation and reunion consensus, bringing closure to the divisions of whites North and South.[20]

By the time Mrs. House and her associates were working for ex-slave pensions, the Reconstruction-era interest in blacks and freedmen and -women had become a distant memory. So had the national refusal, in the immediate aftermath of emancipation, to give land or other property to the freedpeople to start them on their way. Except for praising loyal retainers, the "Mammies and Uncles," of plantation lore, talking about slavery symbolized a refusal to forget and an offensive insistence on still waving the "Bloody Shirt" of civil war. The bloodiest war in American history, in which more than 400,000 soldiers laid down their lives, no longer was viewed as a war to save the Union that had become a war to free the slaves.[21]

Reconciliation and reunion between North and South focused on the broken bonds of brotherhood, not the travail of combat, much less the fate of the ex-slaves. Though poorly armed, clothed, and fed, and often denied their pay, black Union soldiers fought and died to save the Union and to earn freedom for themselves and other African Americans, yet the claims of more than 186,000 African Americans who served in the Union ranks went unacknowledged, banned from the national debate.[22]

President Abraham Lincoln's words in the Gettysburg Address, delivered on November 19, 1863, gave hope of reparations when he described the task before the nation as finishing the work so that those who died had not died in vain. He saw the goal as ensuring "that this nation, under God, shall have a new birth of freedom." By war's end, his meaning, described by Confederate officials as slavery and the South's determination to preserve it, had been accepted by millions of northern whites and almost all African Americans. The Lincolnian idea that Emancipation would result in a new birth of freedom, in a reunited nation, and a new charter of equal rights in the Fourteenth and Fifteenth Amendments to the Constitution, receded in the face of a new national disposition. Those who wanted to cite Lincoln's sentiments and reject any measures beyond emancipation for African Americans could cite the president's second inaugural address, in which he seemed to equate the sacrifice of battle with reparations for enslavement. Lincoln said he hoped the war would end quickly but God might will that "it continue until all the wealth piled up by the bondsman's two hundred years of unrequited toil shall be sunk, and until every drop of blood drawn by the lash shall be paid by another drawn with the sword, as was said three thousand years ago."[23]

As historians Nina Silber and David Blight explain, the custodians of Confederate memory won a postwar battle to celebrate the South's lost cause as a valiant crusade for constitutional liberties and states' rights that lost only to brute force. In this version of history, slavery had little to do with causing the war, and reconciliation of the two sections that had fought a "brother's war" deserved concentrated attention instead of discussing the consequences of abolition.[24]

In 1888, only four years after he had pleaded for a memory of abolition among causes and consequences of the Civil War, Albion Tourgee, the white Massachusetts lawyer who had gone south to serve as a judge after the war, conceded defeat. In the "field of American fiction today," he wrote, "the Confederate soldier is the popular hero. Our literature has become not only Southern in type, but distinctly Confederate in sympathy."[25]

With sad inevitability, forces that emphasized reconciliation and those with white supremacist visions merged to overwhelm any "New Birth of Freedom" in the future of African Americans. By 1913, "a combination of white supremacist and reconciliationist memories had conquered all others," according to Blight. In that year, the fiftieth anniversary commemoration of Gettysburg attracted five thousand aging veterans and many more spectators, and took place, Blight notes, "as a national ritual in which the ghost of slavery, the very questions of cause and consequence, might be exorcized once and for all, and an epic conflict among whites elevated into national mythology." In such a climate, redress for the defeated white southerners, not reparations for African Americans, became a more acceptable objective. Whites in the North and South sought to heal the harm they had done to each other.[26]

Essentially, the view of the Civil War and Reconstruction portrayed in D. W. Griffith's 1915 movie *Birth of a Nation*, which demonized African Americans and depicted white southerners as victims, prevailed throughout the country. Based on Thomas Dixon's *The Clansman,* a novel about Reconstruction that appeared in 1905, *Birth of a Nation* told a story of how heroic whites had redeemed the South from efforts to Africanize it by black brutes unleashed by the abolition of slavery. The movie faithfully followed the book. The movie was the first motion picture to be shown at the White House. The southern segregationist president Woodrow Wilson called the film "like writing history with lightning." Meanwhile, as the newly founded National Association for the Advancement of Colored People protested unsuccessfully against the film's showing, millions of people saw it and forever viewed themselves and the country in the context of the film's contrived political appeals.[27]

Reflecting the growth of a general southern nostalgic movement, there was some sentiment for establishing monuments and memorials to the "old black mammies, "and some Confederate veterans endorsed the idea of pensions to reward those slaves who "peaceably cultivated the plantations of their masters" during their absence and showed absolute "fidelity." But even their efforts were of no avail.[28]

In such a climate, the adoption of legal and practical racial segregation was not surprising. After the Civil War and Emancipation, and through the years of reconciliation and reunion, African Americans attempted to gain political and economic opportunity through various strategies, and a few people became relatively prosperous. However, African Americans' freedom did not bring economic, political, or social equality. In an effort to gain fair treatment and opportunity, some joined political protest groups such as the African American League, the Niagara Movement, and later the NAACP. Others boycotted segregated streetcars and struck against unequal wages. Some African-American factions placed more emphasis on self-help through mutual assistance, racial solidarity, emigration, and separatism. Still, the situation was so bad that the usually optimistic Frederick Douglass, who lived through this period of transformation in thought with its reshaping of memory and the forgotten aims of the Civil War, doubted aloud in the 1890s whether American justice and equality of rights would ever apply fully to African Americans.[29]

Despite the prevailing national mood and the powerful forces that fought her efforts, Callie House insisted that the nation acknowledge its debt to every old ex-slave. In the end, she paid dearly for her stubborn devotion to the cause.

Epilogue: The Reparations Movement Still Lives

Do you hear those voices calling
From their lone and musty graves
Urging us to note the toilings
Of the poor neglected slaves?

CORNELIUS JONES
(1916)

SINCE THE FOUNDING of the National Ex-Slave Mutual Relief, Bounty and Pension Association in 1896, the poorest African Americans have been the most consistent supporters of reparations for slavery. The black middle class has been mostly critical of the effort. However, there have been times, such as during the late 1960s and more recently, when some among the middle class have supported reparations and taken leadership in the cause. The political scientists Cathy Cohen and Michael Dawson argue that the black poor are detached from the American political system because it seems irrelevant to solving their problems. They point out that black nationalism is popular among poor African Americans, although they note that in particularly stressful times, others join in the nationalist cause. So long as African Americans endure discrimination and ill-treatment because of race, and so long as economic resources are distributed unequally and correlated with race, many African Americans will believe the government should pay compensation for 300 years of slavery.[1]

The right to vote, ensuring access to a quality education, fair employment, and contracting opportunities are issues supported by most African Americans now and in the past. Yet the visceral wrong that African Americans built the nation without compensation—assets to pass on—while others reaped the benefits both during and since slavery is maddening to some. That the nation has never apologized or fully acknowledged that debt is a thought too painful for many African Americans to bear.[2]

While former slaves still lived, Callie House and the Ex-Slave Association embodied the cause. But during the year Mrs. House spent in prison, another black leader arrived in the United States to stir up the masses of African Americans. His movement advanced the reparations cause. This new leader was Marcus Moziah Garvey, and his organization was the Universal Negro Improvement Association (UNIA). When Garvey arrived in 1916 from Jamaica, many African Americans, versed in the Ex-Slave Association, found that the UNIA was another organization through which they might press their aims. Garvey's movement drew from these ideas. Garvey saw the redemption of Africa as recompense for the exploitation of African peoples. The UNIA emphasized self-help, self-improvement, and the importance of racial pride and organization to success.[3]

Like the Ex-Slave Association, which had a chapter in New York City, his movement attracted the working poor. As future

Marcus Garvey. Some of the agents of the association became chapter heads in Garvey's Universal Negro Improvement Association, which supported reparations.

labor leader Asa Philip Randolph wrote sneeringly to Attorney General Harry M. Daugherty in 1923, Garvey's members came chiefly from "the most primitive and ignorant element of West Indian and American Negroes." In fact, these men and women were mostly not "primitive" or "ignorant." Many of the American members were ex-slaves or the children of ex-slaves who had also joined the ex-slave pension movement.[4]

Garvey, born in Jamaica in 1887, the grandson of an African slave, emigrated as a young man to London, where he lived for several years working as a printer. In London's colonial émigré community, Garvey became acquainted with native Africans, from whom he learned about the calculated exploitation of the continent and its immense potential. After returning to Jamaica and unsuccessfully attempting to organize a printers' strike, Garvey abandoned the trade union movement to promote industrial education modeled after Booker T. Washington's *Up from Slavery.*[5] The famed Tuskegeean, replying to his inquiries, encouraged Garvey to visit the United States, but Garvey did not arrive until after Washington's death. Garvey's initial basis for the UNIA came from West Indian immigrants in Harlem. A commanding, charismatic figure, Garvey insisted on "Africa for the Africans" and promoted racial solidarity. His programs encouraged blacks to support black businesses, and the UNIA itself organized a chain of groceries, restaurants, laundries, a hotel, a factory to make black dolls, and a printing plant. Thousands of blacks bought stock in the UNIA's Black Star Steamship Line, organized to establish a commercial link among the United States, the West Indies, and Africa. UNIA membership swelled to the tens of thousands as blacks paraded in the mass units of the African Legion and the Black Cross Nurses through Harlem, proudly waving the black, green, and red flag.[6]

Naming himself the provisional president of Africa in 1922, Garvey petitioned the League of Nations to turn over the former German colonies in Africa to the UNIA. A strong element of his appeal came from the militant black nationalist stance he inspired. For example, one of his chief lieutenants, Hubert Harrison, for a time associate editor of the *Negro World*, urged blacks to demand an eye for an eye in their struggles against discrimination and mob violence: "If white men are to kill unoffending Negroes, Negroes must kill white men in defense of their lives and property." This was a stance echoed by A. Philip Randolph, a critic of Garvey in his condemnation of the 1919 race riots.[7]

Garvey's influence was global. European and colonial administrations in Africa sought to suppress the UNIA. Even though he was a native of the British colony of Jamaica, in 1923 the British refused to give Garvey a visa to travel in British-controlled areas in Africa. The British Colonial Office explained that it believed he wanted "to stir up trouble and to incite sedition in Africa."[8]

Garvey attracted enemies not only among the European colonial powers, but also among African-American leaders, including Randolph and W. E. B. Du Bois. Garvey criticized light-skinned integrationists and middle- and upper-class blacks active in the NAACP for their shame about their ancestry. The criticism and the rapid growth of the UNIA raised fear and jealousy. Cyril Briggs, a Communist who had failed to draw UNIA members to his party, urged government officials to prosecute Garvey. Other African-American leaders called on the U.S. government to investigate irregularities in the management of the Black Star Steamship Line and demanded Garvey's arrest.[9]

The Black Star Line, founded to take African Americans to Africa, was a viable business idea executed by people with no expertise in the business. Unscrupulous ship owners had sold him worn-out vessels, unseaworthy crafts that could not make the promised voyages. The federal government indicted Garvey for using the mail to defraud, the same charge they used to jail Callie House. His subsequent imprisonment and deportation led to the collapse of his movement.[10]

Former members of the UNIA, inspired by the themes of racial pride, redemption, and organization, joined other nationalist organizations, including the Black Muslims. Many became vocal advocates of reparations. Sociologist E. Franklin Frazier, writing in 1926, said there was justice in the "halo that shines about" Garvey, a victim of selective federal prosecution. "[I]f the government were to punish all those who use the mails to defraud, it would round up those energetic business men who flood the mails with promises to give eternal youth and beauty to aging fat matrons . . . and to make masterminds of morons."[11]

The UNIA had great presence in urban centers. However, it established chapters including pension supporters in the same hamlets and towns where Mrs. House had organized her movement. The UNIA organized in the same way as the Ex-Slave Association. A dynamic speaker from UNIA headquarters or a popular minister would motivate a community to form a division. In some cases an inspired local layman or -woman would start a branch. High commissioners and designated organizers were assigned by the UNIA to organize and supervise the work of the divisions. In the wake of the Ex-Slave Association, the UNIA organized not just in New Orleans, Kansas City, and Atlanta but in Wetumka, Oklahoma; Suffolk, Virginia; Bullock County, Alabama; and Cairo, Illinois. Ex-Slave Association agents, including John Scott in Ohio and P. Powell in Ohio, were prominent in their state UNIA divisions.[12]

The messages of the UNIA and the Ex-Slave Association coincided in emphasizing the needs for African Americans to act for themselves. Pension supporters believed in a black-led movement, but they were not separatists. Mrs. House often talked of the white and black people she talked to and whites who supported the movement. Pension advocates, however, could embrace Garvey's nationalist self-help message. The UNIA attracted business and professional people who depended on an African-American clientele but looked with disdain at the pension movement. They liked the message of economic uplift and racial solidarity.

Marcus Garvey spoke in Nashville early in 1917, and the UNIA organized chapters in Tennessee, including one in Nashville. Reverend James Carruthers, probably a Primitive Baptist minister whose South Nashville church and home were both listed at the same address in the city directory, was the president. He was at various times a tailor, pressman, and clothes cleaner. The local African-American press ignored the UNIA just as they overlooked the Ex-Slave Association. However, the *Negro World,* Garvey's paper, reported that it attracted professional blacks. No connections with the UNIA were apparent, but a black-owned-and-operated ice cream factory remained solvent. Also, just as the UNIA ran a doll factory, the Nashville Negro Doll company was so successful that it had difficulty keeping up with the Christmas trade.[13]

In the period after the deportation of Garvey in 1927 and Mrs. House's death in 1928, black nationalists promoted reparations, although they often split over which groups best represented the cause. After the UNIA collapse, several movements picked up the banner, among them the Nation of Islam, which has always supported reparations. The Peace Movement of Ethiopia petitioned President Franklin D. Roosevelt and the Virginia legislature in the 1930s. Leaders went so far as to support the 1939 congressional bill introduced by Mississippi's racist senator Theodore Bilbo that would have provided federal funds to transport African Americans to Africa.[14]

In the spirit of Callie House, another woman, Audrey Moore, spent time in the Garvey movement, and then became the queen mother of the reparations cause. Born just after Mrs. House organized the association, in New Iberia, Louisiana, July 27, 1898, Moore was the descendant of former slaves. Her grandmother was the daughter of her master. Her grandfather had been lynched. Forced to quit school in the fourth grade, she went to work and then trained as a hairdresser to care for herself and her sisters. She came into contact with the Garvey movement in New Orleans. During the 1920s, she traveled around the country, finally settling in Harlem, where she became a member of UNIA and a community organizer.[15]

Like other African-American activists of the period, she vacillated between black nationalism and communism in groups organized by others and founded some of her own. Impressed by their defense of the defendants in the Scottsboro case, she joined the Communists but left when they could not translate words about black self-determination in the Black Belt into action. In 1955, she joined a small band of activists demanding reparations for slavery. She was honored as an Ashanti queen in Ghana when she attended the funeral of Kwame Nkrumah in 1972.[16]

When Queen Mother Moore called for reparations in 1955, few listened. But as the Black Muslims grew and established new mosques outside Detroit, so did calls for reparations.

*Queen Mother Moore spent time in the Garvey movement and
became a principal voice for reparations until her death in 1996.*

Malcolm X, the leader of Harlem's Mosque Number Seven,
expanded Moore's popular base. He made a dramatic demand
for reparations at Boston University in 1960, telling his audience that African Americans had "worked 300 years without a
pay day." Therefore, the United States must "compensate us for
the labor stolen from us." He asked for land. After his assassi-
nation in February 1965, other black nationalists and radicals
embraced the cause as their own. The Republic of New Africa,
a black nationalist group favoring a separate state within the

United States for African Americans, organized by Imari Obadele and his Malcolm X Society, called for $400 billion in slavery damages in 1968. In the same period, the African-American Repatriation League appealed for support for blacks to emigrate to Africa as compensation for slavery.[17]

Black leaders identified as pacifists and integrationists also called for reparations. In 1964, Martin Luther King justified the civil rights movement's continued activism on these grounds: "The moral justification for special measures for Negroes is rooted in slavery." The government should do something special for African-Americans since "our society has been doing something special against the Negro for hundreds of years." Affirmative action, based on many different rationales, constituted one of the "special measures." The pro–black business Urban League's Whitney Young suggested a Marshall Plan for African Americans.[18]

The 1960s saw the most vocal clear demands for reparations since Callie House's day. Unlike the ex-slave pension movement, James Forman, former executive director of the Student Nonviolent Coordinating Committee (SNCC), targeted religious institutions, not the federal government. Speaking in Detroit, in his Black Manifesto, Forman called for a "revolutionary black vanguard" to take control of the United States Government. To finance the revolution, Forman demanded $5 billion in reparations from the "white Christian churches and Jewish synagogues, which are part and parcel of the system of capitalism." Lambasted by most whites, Forman's manifesto received a respectful reading in such journals as *Commonweal, Christian Century,* and *World Outlook. Christian Century* typified such views: "We do not believe the idea of reparations is ridiculous. This generation of blacks continues to pay the price of earlier generations' slavery and subjugation; this generation of whites continues to enjoy the profits of racial exploitation." Some white Protestant churches responded to the manifesto by increasing their annual contributions to black organizations by $1 million.[19]

Black capitalists have had their own form of reparations. Some proposed black economic development through tax credits, and the establishment of preferred markets for black corporations and businesses. In 1969, President Richard Nixon launched a campaign for "Black Capitalism" to give blacks a greater stake in the economy, as a form of reparations. This "piece of the pie" approach had negligible results for the black elite and almost nothing for the poor. For example, in 1973, the government extended $26 billion in credits to white corporations but granted less than $1 billion to black-owned businesses. According to the Nixon administration, a special effort went toward increasing the assets of black-owned banks. Yet the thirty-five black banks received an average of only $3 million each. The "Black Capitalism" campaign, intentionally or not, was a colossal hoax. Republicans used it as propaganda to attract black voters to their party. *The New York Times* concluded in 1973, "The Nixon administration's program to provide funds and other aid to minority businessmen was turned in 1972 into the vehicle by which the president's re-election effort sought nonwhite support. Not only did minority businessmen sustain intense pressure from the White House and the president's campaign staff to support him, few minorities received awarded contracts last year without at least an attempted political quid pro quo . . ." "Besides political misuse of the program, there were instances of money set aside for minorities ending up with whites." In the aftermath, some of those African Americans who had once supported set-asides became reparationists.[20]

*Labor activist and community activist Christopher Alston, shown
here (standing left) with fellow organizers of a sit-down strike,
heard about the movement and Callie House from an elderly
man who had moved from the South to Detroit. Alston became
a leading activist in the reparations cause.*

In Detroit in the 1960s and 1970s, Christopher Alston, a
child of the 1940s radical labor movement, tried to keep up
awareness of the Ex-Slave Association, as a major grassroots
movement, in public consciousness. As a young Packard
foundryman and a member of the Young Communist League,
Alston had led black workers to shut down the foundry to
demand that union leaders take more forceful action against
recalcitrant whites who opposed black workers' advancement
during World War II. Their militancy paid off; by the end of

1943, they had desegregated job classifications, moving five hundred blacks out of the Packard foundry and into heretofore all-white production jobs. Alston remained a union and community organizer for the rest of his life. When I met him in the late 1960s, he told me he had met "an old man who could have been ninety" and who, he recalled, had come to Detroit from the South and remembered that "there was once a great movement to get pensions for the ex-slaves run by a woman." Alston remained committed to "the principle of the thing"—reparations—as a necessary goal for African Americans.[21]

The early-twenty-first-century interest in reparations stemmed from continued discontent. Many African Americans saw the slow rate of progress toward equality of opportunity and attacks on remedial measures such as affirmative action and contract set-asides as showing the need for more drastic solutions. The resurgent interest in reparations gained its greatest impetus, however, from the Japanese-American Redress ordered by the Congress. The federal government made several efforts to address the internment of Japanese Americans during World War II. In 1948, a law provided for compensation for property damage as a result of the evacuation. The Justice Department received about 26,500 claims, and the federal government paid out approximately $37 million. In 1976, President Gerald Ford formally revoked Executive Order 9066, which had authorized the evacuation and internment program.[22]

In 1980, Congress established the Commission on Wartime Relocation and Internment of Civilians, which recommended that although "no amount of money can fully compensate the excluded people for their losses and sufferings," a national apology should be made, those convicted should be pardoned, and other attempts at redress should be undertaken. In 1983, in

Hohri v. United States, nineteen Japanese Americans, former World War II internees or their living representatives, brought a class action suit against the United States, seeking money damages and a declaratory judgment on twenty-two claims based on constitutional violations, tort, and breach of contract and fiduciary duties. The district court dismissed the claims, holding that all but one, based on the Fifth Amendment ban against the government's taking private property without compensation, were excluded by "sovereign immunity," the rule that the government cannot be sued without its permission. The court then held that even the Fifth Amendment Takings Clause claim could not proceed. It was too old—barred by the statute of limitations. The court also found that the government had not waived its immunity to being sued without its consent.[23]

The Court of Appeals for the District of Columbia Circuit reversed, and then the Supreme Court held that the Japanese Americans had sought appeal in the wrong court: they should have gone to the Court of Appeals for the Federal Circuit rather than the District of Columbia Circuit Court of Appeals. The court, however, refused to address the factual issues, and they affirmed the district court's decision throwing out the claims. Judge J. Skelly Wright suggested in his lower-court ruling that by exhausting their judicial options they had made a case for congressional action. Congress then passed the Civil Liberties Act of 1988, providing for a formal apology and benefits, including redress payments of $20,000, to citizens and permanent residents of the United States interned during World War II. It established an Office of Redress Administration in the Civil Rights Division of the Justice Department to administer it.[24]

As a result of the Japanese-American Redress Law, in 1989

Congressman John Conyers of Detroit introduced his own bill to establish a commission to consider reparations for African Americans. Conyers had long been urged by Christopher Alston and "Reparations" Ray Jenkins, a self-employed businessman and community activist who led the cause after Alston's death, to introduce legislation. Jenkins promoted the idea in churches, in community meetings, at the NAACP, and wherever people gathered. At first people "laughed" at his persistent devotion.[25]

In 1988, Imari Obadele and Adjoa Aiyetoro, with other black nationalists, founded National Coalition of Blacks for Reparations in America (N'COBRA). N'COBRA initiates legislation, publishes a newsletter, sponsors national and regional conferences, and has its own Web site. Harvard Law professor Charles Ogletree became counsel for the organization.[26]

With new interest in the cause and congressional action remote, African-American plaintiffs filed a suit for reparations in the Federal District Court in California. They did so with no legal assistance. The Lawyers Committee for Civil Rights Under Law stepped in to handle the appeal after the court dismissed their claim. However, they confronted the same problem that had defeated Callie House and counsel Cornelius Jones in the cotton tax case and the Japanese Americans in the internment case: the court decided that the government cannot be sued without its consent. Therefore, just as in the ex-slave cotton tax case the court did not reach the substantive issue of whether slavery reparations are a debt owed to African Americans.[27]

In a second case, Imari Obadele, as the head of the Republic of New Africa, successfully won an indirect consideration of the legality of reparations in the federal court of claims. He and two other members of RNA demanded payment under the

Japanese-American Redress Law, arguing that the enslavement of their ancestors and the continuing failure of the U.S. government to recognize African Americans' rights of self-determination supported their claim. To decide their claim, the court had to decide whether the Japanese-American Redress Law was illegal because it applied only to Japanese Americans, excluding others on the basis of race.[28]

In analyzing the issues the court ended up discussing the status of African Americans and slavery. The court asked whether congressional failure to enact a claims process for African Americans constituted unlawful preferential treatment for Japanese Americans. Also, the court decided that the claims law did not permit dismissal without considering the facts in the case. This did not mean that African Americans could win. However, the government's effort to have the suit immediately dismissed failed. In deciding against the claim, however, Chief Judge Bashir concluded that the plaintiffs had made a powerful case for redress as representatives of a racial group other than Americans of Japanese ancestry. "The treatment of African Americans enslaved, oppressed, and disenfranchised is a long and deplorable chapter in this nation's history. Their plight may well be the subject of future legislation providing for reparations for slavery." However, he noted, "Plaintiffs must make a legal case, which is far different from the political case they would make in Congress."[29]

In recent years, turning against suing the federal government, lawyers who support reparations have targeted insurers or employers of slaves. Deadria Farmer-Paellmann sued Aetna Insurance Company, Fleet Boston Financial, and the CSX Railroad. The claim alleged that these companies conspired with slave traders and illegally profited from slavery. Fleet Boston is the successor of Providence Bank, founded by Rhode

Island businessman and slave trader John Brown. Providence Bank lent substantial sums to Brown, financing and profiting from his slave trade, and also collected custom fees from ships transporting slaves. A predecessor company of Aetna insured slave owners against the loss of their slave chattel. CSX is the successor of several railroads constructed or run in part by slave labor. Even if they do not win these cases, the advocates hoped the public relations impact might influence the implementation of at least the study commission proposed by Congressman Conyers.[30]

Reparationists also succeeded in having resolutions passed in city councils in Los Angeles, Chicago, Detroit, and other cities requiring companies that do business with the city to disclose their profits made from slavery. Chicago city councilwoman Dorothy Tillman led the campaign for local legislation, and during Black History Month 2002, the New York City Council took up the Queen Mother Moore Reparations Resolution for Descendants of Enslaved Africans. Lawyers hoped the data collected as a result of these resolutions would provide information to strengthen the reparations claims in court or in the Congress.[31]

Focusing on other historical wrongs against African Americans, in 2003 a legal "dream" team of African-American attorneys, including Johnnie Cochran of O. J. Simpson case fame; Willie Gary, one of the most successful plaintiffs' negligence lawyers; and Harvard law professor and N'COBRA counsel Charles Ogletree filed a reparations suit on behalf of 126 living survivors of the 1921 Tulsa, Oklahoma, riot. The oldest of their clients was 102 and the youngest 81. The argument presented was that state and city officials abetted the actions of a rampaging white mob that burned and looted much of Tulsa's black community. The mob killed as many as three hundred people. The 1921 riot started with a confrontation between whites who had gone to Tulsa's courthouse to lynch an African-American man accused of sexually assaulting a white woman and black men who showed up to stop them. Many members of the white mob received weapons from local law enforcement officials and were deputized, according to the 2001 report of a state commission that investigated the riot. The plaintiff's lawyers argued that this "state" action violated the due process clause of the Fourteenth Amendment.[32]

A historical study of the Tulsa riot led the state to establish a commission to make recommendations for a response. The commission reported two years ago in favor of reparations for the victims. However, the legislature has refused to enact legislation for the payment of compensation. The "Dream Team" lawyers used the fact finding of the commission as a basis of a damage claim. They hoped that a victory would establish a legal basis for other reparations claims based on government culpability for the abuse or exploitation of African Americans.[33]

However elusive the possibility of obtaining any form of reparations for the descendants of African-American slaves, lawyers may eventually develop a viable litigation claim against the federal government. Some experts argue that the government's immunity to being sued without its consent, which confounded Callie House, is no barrier because the federal government gave consent to be sued when it passed legislation to protect freedpeople during Reconstruction. They cite the Freedmen's Bureau courts and the Civil Rights Act of 1866, which gave blacks the same rights as whites to sue and be sued, own property, make contracts, and conduct other routine activities. Because blacks are still discriminated against, they argue the government's consent to civil actions against itself in these instances is still relevant.[34]

Other experts argue that the Administrative Procedure Act of 1946 may be used to overcome the government's immunity to suits. The APA provides that a person who is wronged by a government agency action may have the government action reviewed in the courts. The act clearly states that the court cannot dismiss the action solely on the grounds that the government is being sued. The United States may be named as a defendant, and the court can issue a judgment against the United States. People suing have the opportunity, unlike the ex-slaves in the cotton tax case, to prove they have been harmed under a law permitting money damages in order to win payment. In such a case today, one of the Civil Rights Acts passed during Reconstruction, which include money damages, might be used to make a claim under the Administrative Procedure Act.[35]

Some advocates have proposed arguing that international law has been violated by the U.S. government because a universal consensus exists against genocide, enslavement, and systematic racial discrimination. Furthermore, the Nuremberg trials established that under international law, a state could be held criminally liable for the treatment of its own citizens. At Nuremberg, the four victorious powers of World War II tried German officials for "crimes against humanity." However, Germany's crimes against its own citizens took place during a war. In 1951, the Civil Rights Congress presented a petition to the United Nations charging genocide by the federal government against African Americans, but to no avail. Under international law, arguably to continue segregation under the charter meant a waiver of sovereign immunity. However, the United States signed the Covenant on Civil and Political Rights, with reservations, only in 1992.[36]

The interest in reparations has led some people to attempt collection prematurely, without benefit of law or court decision. In March 2002, the Internal Revenue Service admitted that it had mistakenly paid out some $30 million on more than 100,000 tax returns for a reparations tax credit. The agency paid for erroneous refunds in 2000 and 2001. The funds amounted to a "black tax credit" of about $43,209 for each individual return, an amount that *Essence* magazine suggested in 1993 would be the updated value of the promised forty acres and a mule that African Americans never received after Emancipation. The agency is taking steps to recoup the funds. Apparently some Internal Revenue Service employees received some of the refunds. The government successfully prosecuted professional tax preparer Gregory Bridges for aiding and assisting the preparation of tax returns for individuals who claimed the "black tax credit" in violation of the tax code.[37]

The continuity in the reparations cause, from Callie House to Queen Mother Moore to Christopher Alston and "Reparations" Ray, offers graphic historical testimony of the indelible memory of the unrequited labor of the slaves among African Americans. In August 2002, thousands arrived on the Mall in Washington for the "Millions for Reparations Rally." Chicago activist Conrad Worrill, chairman of the National Black United Front and one of the chief organizers, pointed out, "This is the first time there has been a mass rally demanding reparations" in the nation's capital. As John Conyers and "Reparations Ray" exulted, the crowd, "raising red, green, and black flags and clenched fists," demanded recompense for centuries of slavery and racism. They symbolically carried on the tradition started by the UNIA followers who first proudly

The time has come to say to the U.S., *"You Owe Us"*. The world has acknowledged the "Trans-Atlantic Slave Trade as a Crime Against Humanity", and the sons and daughters of former slaves are bringing that debt to your doorstep. We no longer see ourselves as beggars, pleading for your assistance. We come for our rightful earnings from your ill gotten gains.

We need Reparations to build our schools, homes, hospitals and industry for our peoples' sustainable development.

We are going to the Capitol of this nation, built with slave labor ,and the rightful place to declare our human and legal right to *Reparations...*

Join the Mobilization, We need... Millions For

REPARATIONS

National Rally Washington, DC August 17th 2002

Join the New York Organizing Committee Call _(718) 398-1766_ "You Owe Us"

Detroit follower of Christopher Alston, "Reparations" Ray, and others spoke at this first reparations march in the nation's capital organized by N'COBRA, the National Black United Front, and other organizations.

waved the black, green, and red association flag: black for skin, green for hope, and red for blood.[38]

Callie House wanted ex-slaves to have economic capital based on their work during slavery. Financial resources made available would strengthen mutual assistance organizations and provide a basis for economic development. She fought to address the poverty and subordination faced by ex-slaves. African Americans in later generations have made progress, but the underlying issue of appropriate payment is still unresolved. Mrs. House tried and failed to gain reparations for those African Americans still alive, who were the first generation to survive slavery.

Whatever the outcome of the modern case for reparations, there was a time when freedpeople believed in the possibility. Those who act in the cause today pay homage to their struggle and to the spirit of Callie House.

NOTES

Prologue

1. The defiant quote is from the postmaster of Nashville to the assistant attorney general for the Post Office Department on March 30, 1901. "Wild" and "anarchists" come from an assessment of the movement made by the Pension Bureau in connection with the investigation of an alleged imposter, W. L. Reid. Inspector to George Rice, Agent-in-Charge, Little Rock, May 21, 1899, case no. 273, 115c, Record Group 15, Pension Bureau, Department of the Interior, Ex-Slave Pensions, National Archives (hereafter referred to as R.G. 15).

1   We Need a Movement

1. This was the Third Annual Convention. "Notice to All Associations Chartered under the National Ex-Slave Mutual Relief, Bounty and Pension Association, 1898"; Constitution By-Laws and Membership Certificate, Bureau of Pensions, Department of the Interior, Record Group 15, Ex-Slave Pensions, National Archives. Flyer from 1898 Nashville Convention, "Greetings and History," Callie House's introduction to *Constitution and By-Laws of the National Ex-Slave Mutual Relief, Bounty and Pension Association of the United States of America* (Nashville: National Baptist Publishing House, 1899), Record Group 15, Pension Bureau, Department of the Interior, Ex-Slave Pensions, National Archives (hereafter referred to as R.G. 15).
2. Rayford Logan, *The Negro in American Life and Thought: The Nadir, 1877–1901* (New York: Dial Press, 1954); Senate Committee on Pen-

sions, January 16, 1900. 58th Congress, 1st session, report 75, estimated about 69,000 members by 1900. Federal prosecutors in their indictment of House in 1916 estimated almost 300,000 members. (See chapter eight.) The Association estimated a high of 600,000 members in the early 1900s.

3. Callie House to Harrison J. Barrett, acting assistant attorney general for the Post Office Department, September 29, 1899, Record Group 28, Records of the Postmaster General, Office of the Solicitor, Fraud Order Case Files 1894–1951.

4. In 1880, the U.S. Census recorded Callie Guy as a "school girl" and her birth date as 1861; National Archives film no. T9-1276, p. 223B. The 1910 United States Manuscript Census, Ed. 60, Sheet 12, L.30 reported her age as forty-eight, which would accord with the 1880 Census, but her death certificate recorded her age as sixty-three, which would place her birth date as 1865; State of Tennessee Board of Vital Statistics registration no. 21901, file no. 1391, death certificate no. 13311, Tennessee State Library and Archives, Nashville. Jim Leonhirth, *The Black Presence in Rutherford County: Fragments of a Past,* Rutherford County History of Families, Rutherford County Historical Society (Paducah, Ky.: Turner Publishing Company, 1976). See also Reverend Melvin E. Hughes, Sr., compiler and writer, *A History of Rutherford County's African American Community* (Murfreesboro, Tenn.: Allen Chapel A.M.E. Church, 1996).

5. James McPherson, *Battle Cry of Freedom: The Civil War Era* (New York: Oxford University Press, 1988), pp. 394–403, 579–581; "Tennessee Slave Narratives," Born in Slavery: Slave Narratives from the Federal Writers' Project, 1936–38, American Memory, Library of Congress, http://memory.loc.gov/cgi-bin/ampage.

6. McPherson, *Battle Cry of Freedom,* pp. 394–403, 579–581; *The Roster of Union Soldiers, 1861–1865, United States Colored Troops,* edited by Janet B. Hewett, 98 reels, National Archives, 2 vols. (Wilmington, N.C.: Broadfoot Publishing, 1997).

7. Ira Berlin and Leslie Rowland, eds., *Families and Freedom: A Documentary History of African-American Kinship in the Civil War Era* (New York: New Press, 1997), pp. 140–147.

8. *Liberator,* February 24, 1865; quoted in McPherson, *Battle Cry of Freedom,* p. 841. See also Steven Hahn, *A Nation Under Our Feet: Black*

Political Struggles from Slavery to the Great Migration (Cambridge, Mass.: Harvard University Press, 2003), p. 145.

9. McPherson, *Battle Cry of Freedom,* p. 842; United States, *Statues at Large* (Washington, D.C.: U.S. Government Printing Office, 1867), XIII, 507–509.

10. Freedmen's response quoted in the *National Anti-Slavery Standard,* October 7, 1865; James McPherson, *The Struggle for Equality: Abolitionists and the Negro in the Civil War and Reconstruction* (Princeton, N.J.: Princeton University Press, 1964), pp. 408–409; "Tennessee Slave Narratives."

11. Article by Reverend John Savary in the *National Anti-Slavery Standard,* November 3, 1866, quoted in McPherson, *The Struggle for Equality,* p. 410. Abolitionists finally achieved a provision in a new Homestead Act that opened up government lands for the freedmen, but the return of land to the slaveholders meant the government had few acres under its control and what was avilable consisted of the worst, most unrproductive soil. Further, the freedmen had no capital to buy tools or to support themselves as they tried to grow a crop.

12. Mary Frances Berry and John W. Blassingame, *Long Memory: The Black Experience in America* (New York: Oxford University Press, 1982), pp. 94–96; Leon Litwack, *Been in the Storm So Long: The Aftermath of Slavery* (New York: Alfred A. Knopf, 1979), p. 454.

13. Leonhirth, *The Black Presence in Rutherford County.* See also Hughes, *Rutherford County's African American Community;* Bertram Wyatt Brown, "Black Schooling During Reconstruction," in Walter J. Fraser, Jr., R. Frank Saunders, Jr., and Jon Wakelyn, eds., *The Web of Southern Social Relations: Women, Family and Education* (Athens: University of Georgia Press, 1985), pp. 146–166: Heather Andrea Williams, "Clothing Themselves in Intelligence: The Freedpeople, Schooling, and Northern Teachers, 1861–1871," *The Journal of African American History* 87 (Fall 2002): 372–389; Berry and Blassingame, *Long Memory,* pp. 262–264.

14. "Tennessee Slave Narratives"; Paul David Phillips, "Education of Blacks in Tennessee During Reconstruction, 1865–1870," *Tennessee Historical Quarterly* 46 (1987): 98–109; Hahn, *A Nation Under Our Feet,* pp. 277–280.

15. Phillips, "Education of Blacks in Tennessee During Reconstruction, 1865–1870."

16. Laura Jarmon, *Arbors to Bricks: A Hundred Years of African American Education in Rutherford County, Tennessee, 1865–1965* (Murfreesboro: Middle Tennessee State University Division of Continuing Studies and Public Service, 1994), pp. 27, 54–55. Uniform textbooks were mandated by the state in 1888; however, in Rutherford County well into the twentieth century, African-American students had to buy their own books. The schools provided education through the eighth grade. In 1891, the state directed exactly what eight-grade schools had to teach. Every secondary eight-grade school was to teach orthography, reading, writing, arithmetic, grammar, geography, history of Tennessee and history of the United States, including the U.S. Constitution, vocal music, elocution (the art of public speaking), and nothing else.

17. Jarmon, *Arbors to Bricks;* Bertram Wyatt Brown, "Black Schooling During Reconstruction," pp. 146–166.

18. W. E. B. Du Bois, *The Autobiography of W. E. B. DuBois: A Soliloquy on Viewing My Life from the Last Decade of Its First Century* (New York: International Publishers, 1968), pp. 116–118; quote is on p. 118.

19. Hahn, *A Nation Under Our Feet,* pp. 106–108; Berry and Blassingame, *Long Memory,* p. 150.

20. Eric Foner, *Reconstruction: America's Unfinished Revolution* (New York: Harper & Row, 1988), p. 48 and note 25.

21. Ibid., pp. 64, 331–332.

22. Hahn, *A Nation Under Our Feet,* p. 107.

23. Berry and Blassingame, *Long Memory,* p. 150. See also Hahn, *A Nation Under Our Feet,* p. 120, which quotes Reverend James D. Lynch as saying, "We have met here to impress upon the white men of Tennessee, of the United States and the world that we are part and parcel of the American Republic."

24. Hahn, *A Nation Under Our Feet,* pp. 178, 233.

25. E. Franklin Frazier, *The Negro Family in the United States* (Chicago: University of Chicago Press, 1939), pp. 125–145.

26. Hahn, *A Nation Under Our Feet,* p. 213, also cites Thomas Bayne in Virginia, but see Foner, *Reconstruction,* pp. 87–88.

27. Jarmon, *Arbors to Bricks;* Bobby Lovett, *The African American History of Nashville: Elites and Dilemmas* (Fayetteville: University of Arkansas

Press, 1999), pp. 85–89, 214–224; C. C. Henderson, *The Story of Murfreesboro* (Murfreesboro, Tenn.: News-Banner Publishing Company, 1929).

28. Jarmon, *Arbors to Bricks;* Carlton C. Sims, ed., *A History of Rutherford County* (Murfreesboro, Tenn., 1947), p. 43.

29. Hahn, *A Nation Under Our Feet,* pp. 418–451.

30. Ibid., pp. 441–450; Berry and Blassingame, *Long Memory,* pp. 160–161.

31. 1880 United States Census T9-1276, p. 223B, Rutherford County Roll 223B, National Archives Film Number T9-1276, p. 223B.

32. 1880 United States Census T9-1276, p. 223B, Rutherford County Roll 223B, 1883 marriage record Rutherford County Marriages and Births, 1883, roll 44, box no. 218, p. 9, and 1910 Census extrapolating ages and dates of birth. In addition to Thomas, the children also included William, born in 1888, and three daughters, Delphia, born in 1886; Mattie, born in 1892; and Annie, born in 1894. Acts of Tennessee 1881 (chap. 155), p. 212, was preceded by an 1875 Tennessee statute that permitted public officials to discriminate if they wished. Acts of Tennessee, 1875 (chap. 130), p. 216.

33. Berry and Blassingame, *Long Memory,* p. 399.

34. Ibid., p. 400.

35. Ibid., p. 405.

36. V. P. Franklin, *Black Self-Determination: A Cultural History of the Faith of the Fathers* (Westport, Conn.: Lawrence Hill, 1984), pp. 133–144; Hahn, *A Nation Under Our Feet,* pp. 320–322, 332.

37. Berry and Blassingame, *Long Memory,* p. 403.

38. Ibid., pp. 403–404. See in general Nell Painter, *Exodusters: Black Migration to Kansas After Reconstruction* (New York: Alfred A. Knopf, 1976). On Singleton and Henry Adams, see Berry and Blassingame, *Long Memory,* p. 403.

39. Berry and Blassingame, *Long Memory,* pp. 404–405.

40. Hahn, *A Nation Under Our Feet,* pp. 318–363.

41. Ibid., p. 355.

42. Ibid., p. 452.

43. Berry and Blassingame, *Long Memory,* p. 405.

44. Walter R. Vaughan, *Freedmen's Pension Bill: A Plea for American Freedmen* (Chicago, 1891), p. 32, copy in Moorland Springarn Collection, Howard University Library.

45. See H.R. 11119, *Congressional Record*, 51st Congress, 1st Session (1889–90); S. 1389, *Congressional Record*, 53rd Congress, 2nd Session (1894–5); S. 1978, *Congressional Record*, 54th Congress, 1st Session (1895–6); S. 1176, *Congressional Record*, 56th Congress, 1st Session (1899–1900); H.R. 11404, 57th Congress, 1st Session (1901–2). All the bills contained the same provisions.

46. Vaughn, *Freedmen's Pension Bill*. See in general Nina Silber, *The Romance of Reconstruction: Northerners and the South, 1865–1900* (Chapel Hill: University of North Carolina Press, 1992), and David Blight, *Race and Reunion: The Civil War in American Memory* (Cambridge, Mass.: Harvard University Press, 2001), pp. 1–5.

47. Letter from Douglass to Vaughan in Vaughan, *Freedmen's Pension Bill*, p. 150.

48. R.G. 15, Veterans Administration, Correspondence and Reports Pertaining to Ex-Slave Pension Movement, 1892–1916, National Archives.

49. Rayford W. Logan and Michael R. Winston, *Dictionary of American Negro Biography* (New York: W. W. Norton, 1982), pp. 102–103.

50. Ibid., pp. 439–440.

51. Ibid., pp. 382–384; R.G. 15.

52. Mary Frances Berry, *Black Resistance/White Law: A History of Constitutional Racism in America* (New York: Penguin Books, 1994), pp. 89–91.

53. Ibid.

54. Albion Tourgee, "Is Liberty Worth Preserving?," published by the Inter Ocean, Chicago, Ill., 1892, in African American Perspectives: Pamphlets from the Daniel A. P. Murray Collection, 1818–1907. The pamphlet was written to benefit the National Citizens Rights Association Mayville, Chautauqua, N.Y.

55. Walter Fleming, "Ex-Slave Pension Frauds," *South Atlantic Quarterly*, April 11, 1910, p. 126; Reverend Isaiah Dickerson claimed Murfreesboro as his birthplace.

56. Ibid.; R.G. 15.

57. R.G. 15; "Ex-Slaves Pension Bill," *The Washington Post*, April 24, 1897, W. R.

58. "To Pension Ex-Slaves," *Nashville American*, August 31, 1897, Deposition of Isaiah Dickerson, May 12, 1902, Record Group 15, Veterans Administration, box no. 2, Correspondence and Reports Pertaining to the Ex-slave Pension Movement.

59. Theda Skocpol, *Protecting Soldiers and Mothers: The Political Origins of Social Policy in the United States* (Cambridge, Mass.: Harvard University Press, 1992), pp. 110–111, 128.

60. Stephen Ochs, *A Black Patriot and a White Priest: André Cailloux and Claude Paschal Maistre in Civil War New Orleans* (Baton Rouge: Louisiana State University Press, 2000); Donald R. Shaffer, "I Do Not Suppose Uncle Sam Looks at the Skin: African Americans and the Civil War Pension System, 1865–1934," *Civil War History* 46, no. 2 (June 1, 2000): 132–147; Elizabeth Ann Regosin, "Slave Custom and White Law: Ex-Slave Families and the Civil War Pension System, 1865–1900," Ph.D. dissertation, University of California at Irvine, 1995, pp. 26, 50, 56–70, describes the operations of the pension agents and racial considerations. On Harriet Tubman, see Logan and Winston, *Dictionary of American Negro Biography*, pp. 606–607; "Harriet Tubman's Family Seeks Civil War Pension," *The New York Times*, November 1, 2003, p. B17.

2 *Organizing the National Ex-Slave Mutual Relief, Bounty and Pension Association*

1. Aldon Morris, *Origins of the Civil Rights Movement: Black Communities Organizing for Change* (New York: Free Press, 1984), pp. 4–7.

2. Bobby L. Lovett, *The African American History of Nashville: Elites and Dilemmas* (Fayetteville: University of Arkansas Press, 1999), pp. 85–89.

3. In 1899, the Post Office Department placed Callie House at 1003 Vernon, but she is not in the Census in 1900. In 1902, she was listed in the Nashville City Directory as a widow, at 1003 Vernon, with Charles Guy as a boarder. By the 1910 Census, they were both residing on Tenth Avenue South, where they remained in subsequent censuses and directories. The 1920 Census lists House as a seamstress; 1920 Census roll no. 1735. There are two African Americans named William House in the 1880 Census in Murfreesboro, Rutherford County; both were laborers; Tennessee Census, National Archives, film no. 1255276, pp. 224C, 120C.

4. Nashville City Directory, 1902; 1920 Tennessee Census, National Archives, Roll no. 1735.

5. Sarah Hill, ed., "Bea: the Washerwoman," Federal Writer's Project

Papers 1936–40 (1998 Southern Historical Society Collections); University of North Carolina, Chapel Hill, "Sixty-five Years a Washer and Ironer," Clifton H. Johnston, ed., *God Struck Me Dead: Religious Conversion Experiences and Autobiographies of Ex-Slaves* (Philadelphia and Boston: Pilgrim Press, 1969), pp. 116–120; Tera A. W. Hunter, *To 'Joy My Freedom': Southern Black Women's Lives and Labors after the Civil War* (Cambridge, Mass.: Harvard University Press, 1997), pp. 56–57; *Crisis*, I (Nov. 1910), 8 (April 1911), p. 6. The description of how the laundry was done is taken from my own observations and my mother's recollections. See also Carter G. Woodson, "The Negro Washerwoman, A Vanishing Figure" *Journal of Negro History* 15 (1930): 269–277

6. Ibid. The quote is reported in Leon Litwack, *Trouble in Mind: Black Southerners in the Age of Jim Crow* (New York: Alfred A. Knopf, 1998), p. 234.

7. Thirteenth United States Census, 1910, Part of Sixteenth Ward Enumeration District 60, and Fourteenth United States Census, 1920, Nashville, Tennessee, Part of Sixteenth Ward Enumeration District 64.

8. Bobby L. Lovett, ed., *From Winter to Winter: The Afro-American History of Nashville, Tennessee, 1870–1930* (Nashville: Department of History and Geography, Tennessee State University, 1981), p. 107.

9. Lovett, *African American History of Nashville*, pp. 72–74. Edgefield Camp sat across the Cumberland River in East Nashville near the present site of the Tennessee Titans football stadium. "Black Bottom" referred not to African Americans but to the foul water from frequent flooding and the ever-present black mud. These stagnant pools lay just south of Broad Street between Front and Cherry, south of the capitol. Black Bottom predated the Civil War and had moved from being white to black and then from working-class and middle-class black to poor and black. An area of rental houses, brothels, gambling joints, saloons, and small retail businesses, it became the sort of slum that existed in every large southern town. Nearby lay Trimble Bottom, to the east off Lafayette Street, and northwest, the largest camp, in which a thousand contraband lived in plank buildings between Church and Cedar (today Charlotte) Streets from Tenth to Eighteenth Avenues North. James Somerville, "The City and the Slum: 'Black Bottom' in the Develop-

ment of South Nashville," *Tennessee Historical Quarterly* 40, no. 182 (1981).

10. Ibid.

11. Don H. Doyle, *Nashville in the New South, 1880–1930* (Knoxville: University of Tennessee Press, 1985).

12. Ibid.

13. Lovett, *From Winter to Winter,* pp. 108–109.

14. Lovett, *African American History of Nashville,* chapter 10.

15. The incorporation papers were filed in Nashville for the Ex-Slave Bounty and Pension Association of Tennessee, registered on February 8, 1898, vol. 197, page 400, charters of incorporation, Tennessee State Library and Archives, Nashville, Tennessee.

16. Luke Mason had also been a county magistrate. His wife kept house, and he had five grown children. Squire Mason, a sixty-two-year-old shoemaker, had operated a downtown shop for almost twenty years. His wife kept house, and they also had five grown children. Reverend McNairy appeared in the Nashville City Directory, but not with a congregation of his own; Twelfth Manuscript Census of the United States, 1900, Tennessee, Sumner County, 11th District, lines 128–129, Nashville National Archives Film, T9-1250, pp. 267D, 190A; Nashville City Directory, 1890, 1899, 1900. Gosling, the last incorporator, has not been found in the Census or the city directories.

17. Mary Frances Berry and John W. Blassingame, *Long Memory: The Black Experience in America* (New York: Oxford University Press, 1982), p. 64; "Greetings and History," flyer from 1898 Nashville Convention; Callie House, introduction to *Constitution and By-Laws of the National Ex-Slave Mutual Relief, Bounty and Pension Association of the United States of America* (Nashville: National Baptist Publishing House, 1899), Record Group 15, Pension Bureau, Department of the Interior, Ex-Slave Pensions, National Archives (hereafter referred to as R.G. 15).

18. Light McGhee to Commissioner on Pensions, April 1, 1898, R.G. 15, Ex-Slave Pensions; William Glasson, *Federal Military Pensions in the United States* (New York: Oxford University Press, 1918), p. 234.

19. Drew Smith, *New Day Begun: The Public Influences of African American Churches* (Durham, N.C.: Duke University Press, 2003), p. 3, explains that the concept of secondary reliance on mediating institutions prob-

ably does not apply easily to African Americans, for whom churches and mutual-aid associations have always been a first resort. Government help instead of suppression is only a mid-twentieth-century development.

20. Leslie J. Pollard, "Black Beneficial Societies and the Home for Aged and Infirm Colored Persons: A Research Note," *Phylon* 4 (1980): 230–334.

21. Although the Ex-Slave Association was one among many African-American mutual-assistance organizations in the late nineteenth and early twentieth centuries, studies have focused primarily on women's associations. For example, Avery Chapel African Methodist Episcopal Church, in Memphis, which my youngest brother pastored in the 1990s, hired a physician for $200 a year to treat ill members. Nannie Helen Burroughs developed an association of black female wage earners in Washington, D.C., and led the women's convention of the National Baptist Convention. The members of these associations included the wives of skilled workers and professional men as well as laundresses, domestics, and similar low-paid working women. Males dominated some organizations, while others worked independently of male leadership. Elsa Barkley Brown describes the Independent Order of St. Luke, led by the banker Maggie Lena Walker, that began as a women's association but admitted men. As women's work, Callie House's leadership in the mutual-aid mission of the Ex-Slave Association was unremarkable. In the African-American community, her leadership in the political campaign for pensions—"men's work"—was a different matter. See Kathleen Berkeley, "Colored Ladies Also Contributed: Black Women's Activities from Benevolence to Social Welfare, 1866–1896," in Walter J. Fraser, Jr., R. Frank Saunders, Jr., and Jon Wakelyn, eds., *The Web of Southern Social Relations: Women, Family and Education* (Athens: University of Georgia, 1985), pp. 184–185; Armistead Robinson, "Plans Dat Comed from God: Institution Building and the Emergence of Black Leadership in Reconstruction Memphis, in Orville Vernon Burton and Robert McMath, Jr., eds., *Toward a New South*, pp. 71–102. See also Anne Firor Scott, "Most Invisible of All: Black Women's Voluntary Associations," *Journal of Southern History* 56, no. 1 (1990) 3–22; Evelyn Brooks Higginbotham, *Righteous Discontent: The Women's Movement in the Black Baptist Church, 1880–1920*

(Cambridge, Mass.: Harvard University Press, 1992); Elsa Barkley Brown, "Womanist Consciousness: Maggie Lena Walker and the Independent Order of St. Luke," *Signs* 14, no. 3 (Spring 1989): 610–615, 630–633. The Pullman Porters Benevolent Association, established to provide for old retired porters, was the first independent porters' organization. The concept of burial assistance was so traditional that the men in the Tuskegee Syphilis Study participated in part because they were offered burial assistance. The heads of major civil rights organizations today are men. Elaine Jones, who headed the NAACP-LDF, a small nonmembership public interest law firm, was exceptional; see the discussion in Linda Faye Williams, "Power and Gender: A Glass Ceiling Limits the Role of Black Women in the Civil Rights Community," *Emerge*, December–January 1995, pp. 63–65; Carter G. Woodson, "Insurance Business Among Negroes," *Journal of Negro History* 14 (April 1919): 202–206; Pollard, "Black Beneficial Societies," pp. 230–234.

22. Lovett, *From Winter to Winter,* p. 109.
23. Lovett, *The African American History of Nashville,* pp. 93–96.
24. *Ibid.,* pp. 127–34; see, e.g., "A Brief Survey of the Negro Building," *Nashville American,* April 5, 1897; "In and Around the Negro Building," *Nashville American,* April 6, 1897; "One Massachusetts Negro Trying to Get in Front of the Engine," *Nashville American,* February 27, 1897
25. John Hope Franklin and Alfred Moss, Jr., *From Slavery to Freedom* (New York: Alfred A. Knopf, 1988), p. 246.
26. Rayford W. Logan and Michael R. Winston, *Dictionary of American Negro Biography* (New York: W. W. Norton, 1982), pp. 470–471.
27. Lovett, ed. *From Winter to Winter,* p. 129.
28. Ibid., pp. 127–134; see, e.g., "A Brief Survey of the Negro Building, *Nashville American,* April 6, 1897, and "In and Around the Negro Building, *Nashville American,* April 5, 1897.
29. "Notice to All Associations Chartered Under the Ex-Slave Mutual Relief Bounty and Pension Association," 1898; Constitution By-Laws and Membership Certificate, R.G. 15; Charter of Ex-Slave Bounty and Pension Association of Tennessee, Registered February 8, 1898, *Charters of Incorporation,* vol. 197, page 400, Nashville Metro Archives.
30. "Leaders of Afro-American Nashville, Preston Taylor, 1849–1931," *The*

Nashville Colored Directory Biographical, Statistical, p. 22; *Black Yellow Pages,* Nashville Metro Archives; author's interviews with Pastor William Crowder, New Covenant Church, Nashville, Tenn., September–October 2002, and March 19, 2003.

31. This was the Third Annual Convention. "Notice to All Associations Chartered under the Ex-Slave Mutual Relief Bounty and Pension Association, 1898"; Constitution By-Laws and Membership Certificate, R.G. 15; Lovett, *From Winter to Winter.*

32. *Constitution and By-Laws,* p. 23. P. F. Hill was either a member of the African Methodist Episcopal Church or associated with the denomination. He was a member of the committee on address to the country and on resolutions when a Race Council meeting affirmed support for Washington's policies, while denouncing lynching and disenfranchisement at St. John A.M.E. church, where Bishop Henry Turner spoke; "The American Negro Union," *Nashville American,* September 3, 1897.

33. 55th Congress, 2nd Session, p. 2516, March 1, 1898; flyer, 1898 Association Convention, R.G. 15.

34. "National Home for Aged and Infirm Colored People," S. 2140, *Congressional Record,* 56th Congress, 2nd Session, pp. 3503–3504, 7775–7776.

35. Ibid.

36. "McNairy's Master Stroke for the Ex-Slaves, Reverend D. D. McNairy President of the National Ex-Slave Mutual Relief, Bounty and Pension Association, February 20, 1899, flyer concerning the Home for Ex-Slaves bill, R.G. 15.

37. *Congressional Record,* 56th Congress, 2nd Session, pp. 7775–7777.

38. Ibid.

39. Minutes, Third Annual Convention, *Constitution and By-Laws,* 1899, R.G. 15. See also H.R. 11119, *Congressional Record,* 51st Congress, 1st Session (1889–90); S. 1389, *Congressional Record,* 53rd Congress, 2nd Session (1894–5); S. 1978, *Congressional Record,* 54th Congress, 1st Session (1895–6); S. 4718, 55th Congress, 2nd Session (1897–8); S. 1176, *Congressional Record,* 56th Congress, 1st Session (1899–1900). All the bills contained the same provisions. There were a number of organizations in various states that operated only locally. In May 1899, Pension Bureau inspectors reported on their investigation of an organization that they described as an obvious scam, using it to defame any pension

lobbying effort as fraudulent. In 1897, Isaac Walton, an African American in Madison, Arkansas, organized The "Ex-Slave Assembly" and obtained a certificate of incorporation from the Arkansas secretary of state. He had 12,381 members signed up at twenty-five cents each. He had a newspaper called *The Ex-Slave* that he sold for $1 a copy. The Post Office Department planned to prosecute Walton at the October term of court in Helena, Arkansas, although Jacob Trieber, the U.S. attorney in Little Rock, thought Walton's publication and distribution of a newspaper to promote the pension cause to be a valid use of the funds he collected. However, the Post Office Department could, of course, use its unreviewable authority to issue a fraud order.

40. Membership certificates, *Constitution and By-Laws*, R.G. 15, Ex-Slave Pensions.

41. Minutes, 1899 Convention, R.G. 15, Ex-Slave Pensions; House to Acting Assistant Attorney General Harrison Barrett, September 29, 1899.

42. Callie House to Acting Assistant Attorney General Harrison Barrett, September 29, 1899, Record Group 28, Records of the Postmaster General, Office of the Solicitor, Fraud Order Case Files 1894–1951.

3 *The Association Under Attack*

1. Harrison J. Barrett, Acting Assistant Attorney General for the Post Office Department, Washington, D.C., Record Group 28, Records of the Postmaster General, Office of the Solicitor, Fraud Order Case Files 1894–1951, hereafter referred to as R.G. 28. Barrett was actually assistant to the assistant attorney general, James Tyner, who was his uncle by marriage, Harrison J. Barrett, Post Office Department File, National Personnel Records Center, Civilian Records, St. Louis, Missouri.

2. Dorothy Garfield Fowler, *Unmailable: Congress and the Post Office* (Athens: University of Georgia Press, 1977), pp. 55–56; Record Group 15, Pension Bureau, Department of the Interior, Ex-Slave Pensions, National Archives (hereafter referred to as R.G. 15).

3. J. L. Davenport to Mr. Alfred Lathan, Hammond, Louisiana, November 20, 1897, R.G. 15.

4. Reid, Inspector, to George Rice, Agent in Charge, Little Rock, May 21, 1899, case no. 273, 115C, R.G. 15.

5. Harrison J. Barrett, circular no. 260, Office of the Assistant Attorney

General for the Post Office Department, Washington, D.C., October 16, 1899, R.G. 15.

6. Wills served as postmaster from 1890 to 1914; see http://politicalgrave-yard.com/parties/R/1900/index.html; *Who's Who in Tennessee, 1911* (Memphis: Paul & Douglass Co., 1911); United States Census, 1880, National Archives film T9-1249, p. 129D; 1885 Nashville City Directory, Wills, Andrew W., Atty & Claims Agent; 1888 Nashville City Directory, Wills, Andrew W., President, National Manufacturing Co. (cotton yarn manufacturers) Attorney and Claims Agent. Marshall Cushing, in *The Story of Our Post Office: The Greatest Government in All Its Phases* (Boston: A. M. Thayer, 1893), pp. 725–726, praises Wills and everything else about the Post Office Department.

7. Fowler, *Unmailable,* pp. 55–56.

8. Helen Lefkowitz Horowitz, *Rereading Sex: Battles over Sexual Knowledge and Suppression in Nineteenth-Century America* (New York: Alfred A. Knopf, 2002), pp. 358–385 has a useful description and interpretation of Comstock's work.

9. Section 149, 1872 Post Office Department Law; Fowler, *Unmailable,* pp. 55–56.

10. Fowler, *Unmailable,* pp. 55–56. The law also forbade the transfer of lottery tickets in interstate commerce. See *Champion v. Ames,* 188 US 321 (1903).

11. Ibid.; *Public Clearing House v. Coyne,* 194 U.S. 497 (1904).

12. Inquiries received by the Post Office Department concerning ex-slave pensions, Record Group 32.

13. Callie House to Harrison J. Barrett, acting assistant attorney general for the Post Office Department, September 29, 1899, Record Group 28, Records of the Postmaster General, Office of the Solicitor, Fraud Order Case Files 1894–1951.

14. Leon Litwack, *Trouble in Mind: Black Southerners in the Age of Jim Crow* (New York: Alfred A. Knopf, 1998), pp. 321–322; Mary Frances Berry, *The Pig Farmer's Daughter and Other Tales of Law and Justice* (New York: Alfred A. Knopf, 1999), pp. 208, 213.

15. Barrett, circular no. 260.

16. Ibid.

17. In her history of Washington's race relations, Constance Green describes Chase as "not from one of the old mulatto "first families" but occupying a place in the upper stratum of the rank just below"; Con-

stance McLaughlin Green, *The Secret City: A History of Race Relations in the Nation's Capital* (Princeton, N.J.: Princeton University Press, 1967), p. 139. See also Rayford W. Logan and Michael Winston, eds., *Dictionary of American Negro Biography* (New York: W. W. Norton, 1982), pp. 98–101.

18. Ward Churchill, *Agents of Repression: The FBI's Secret War Against the Black Panthers and the American Indian Movement* (Boston: South End Press, 1988). John Johnson's *Jet* magazine similarly cooperated with the FBI over a long period of years. "Deluding the Freedmen," *The Evening Star,* September 21, 1899; "Gigantic Fraud Being Pushed by Base White Men," *The Nashville Banner,* January 28, 1899; Nell Painter, *Exodusters: Black Migration to Kansas After Reconstruction* (New York: Alfred A. Knopf, 1976).

19. Deposition G, Criminal Conduct of Charles H. Dixon, November 13, 1899, taken by P. W. Rawles special examiner. This was presented by the bureau to the Senate Committee on Pensions for its report Congressional Serial Set Volume 3886, Senate Adverse Report "Pensions for Freedmen, Etc.," 56th Congress, 1st Session, report no. 75, January 1900, R.G. 15.

20. Barrett, circular no. 260. After years of tolerating Vaughan's activities, the staff noted that they were issuing no order against Vaughan's association because he was no longer operating. Historian Walter Fleming, who saw the reparations idea as irrational and crackpot, opined in a 1916 article that Vaughan was "probably ill-balanced mentally" for promoting the idea; Fleming, "Ex-Slave Pension Frauds," *South Atlantic Quarterly,* April 11, 1910, p. 126.

21. Barrett, circular no. 260. The city directories and the Census confirm that House's immediate family members were always employed in low-wage jobs while she worked in the movement. Also, local property records show no evidence of wealth possessed by her or her children.

4   Voices of the Ex-Slaves

1. Ledger Book, Boone County Lodge no. 1, Veterans Administration Correspondence and Reports Pertaining to Ex-Slave Pension Movements 1892–1916, Record Group 15, National Archives (hereafter referred to as R.G. 15).

2. Robert Dick, deposition, R.G. 15; Theda Skocpol, *Protecting Soldiers and Mothers: The Political Origins of Social Policy in the United States* (Cambridge, Mass.: Harvard University Press, 1992), p. 115–117. Senate Committee on Pensions, 58th Congress, 1st Session, Report 75, January 15, 1900, on membership numbers.

3. Robert Dick, Deposition, R.G. 15.

4. Suzanna Maria Grenz, "The Black Community in Boone County, Missouri, 1850–1900," Ph.D. dissertation, University of Missouri, 1979, pp. 1, 222.

5. Born in Slavery: Slave Narratives from the Federal Writers' Project, 1936–38, American Memory, Library of Congress, http://memory.loc .gov/cgi-bin/ampage. The stories cited below are from this collection.

6. Harriett Casey and Matilda Pehy Montgomery, "Missouri Slave Narratives," Born in Slavery.

7. One ex-slave woman's strongest memory was the words her mother said to her when she was four. Her mother had been sold and was permitted to say good-bye before the trader took her away. "Ellaine, honey momma's goin way off and ain't never goin to see her baby agin." "An I can see myself holding on to my momma and both of us cryin—and then she was gone and I never seed her since." The old ex-slave, at ninety-seven, said, "I hopes I goin to see my good mama some day, I do yes." Ellaine Wright, Born in Slavery.

   "Even a Bellerin Cow Will Forget Her Calf," "Missouri Slave Narratives," Born in Slavery.

   Grenz, "The Black Community in Boone County," pp. 177–179.

8. Ibid., p. 1.

9. Ibid., pp. 26, 27, 173, 185.

10. James McPherson, *Battle Cry of Freedom: The Civil War Era* (New York: Oxford University Press, 1988), pp. 291–292, 783–786.

11. One ex-slave remembered that his master dealt with the guerrilla warfare this way: "When de Rebel Sojers came by our place old master had the table set for them and treat em fine—cause he's a rebel—den when the Yankee's come along he give dem the bes he had, and treat em fine 'cuse he's a Yankee. Therefore, none of the Sojers ever bothered the place." "Missouri Slave Narratives," Born in Slavery, p. 227. See also Perry McGee's story.

12. Perry McGee and Harriett Casey, "Missouri Slave Narratives," Born in Slavery.

13. Grenz, "The Black Community in Boone County," pp. 27–30.

14. Ibid.

15. Matilda Pethy Montgomery said, "The morning we was set free we didn't have nothing." Louis Hill believed the government should have made some provision for the aid of the Negroes during the early days after Emancipation. He "was too young to know what to expect from freedom." His mother "picked up and left the white folks in the night and took the kids with her." The masters would not let them leave in the day time "very handy." They did not pay her anything. William Black said his master "didn't give us nothing but some clothes and five dollars." He told them they could stay but they was so glad to be free that they left.

Delicia Patterson said her master told her she was free and he wanted her to stay but she could leave if she pleased but her mistress said no she is still yours you paid $1500 for her. That "made her mad" so she left right away. The rest of her life some of the master's children would come to visit her but they never gave her anything. She had married before the war and had a three-year-old baby. They took her husband into the army and he died. She "hired" herself out to a family for $3 a week and "living on the place." She left when the mistress misplaced her silver thimble and accused her of stealing it. She didn't remember "what the ex-slaves expected," but she knew "they didn't get anything." After the war, ex-slaves "just wandered from place to place, working for food and a place to stay. Now and then we got a little money but very little."

Perry McGee said one day the master came out and said not to call him master any more they were free. "Only one colored family left"; the rest stayed. There were about seventy slaves. The master said there was plenty of land and they could all stay and work as they had been. He paid them ten cents a day or three dollars a month and board. McGee did every kind of job. He carried water on his head the water was in a "piggins," a well bucket with one handle so you could catch it with one hand and set it up on your head." They were made of wood and could hold eight gallons of water.

These interviews are in Missouri Slave Narratives "Born in Slavery."

16. The material in the following sections until the next note is based on Grenz, "The Black Community in Boone County," pp. 37–40, 240–245, 265, except for the information on Sanford Estes, a laborer and preacher who joined the Ex-Slave Association lodge, Ledger Book, Boone County Lodge no. 4, 1880, R. G. 15.
17. Grenz, "The Black Community in Boone County," p. 168.
18. Ibid., pp. 39–41. The material in the following section before the next note is based on pp. 30–31, 50–51.
19. Ibid., pp. 240, 245, 248–250, 265.
20. George Bryant was fifty-five in 1880; if he was alive in 1896, he was then seventy-one; he had a son, George; a wife who was forty-one in 1880, which meant she was fifty-seven in 1896; and two male boarders. Sanford Estes was a laborer in 1880, age twenty-eight. His wife, Elizabeth, was twenty-six, and he had two children. By 1896, he would have been forty-four, his wife forty-two, and the children grown. 1880 United States Census, National Archives Film, No. T9-0676, pp. 92A, 109D, 110A, 118B, 141A, 151B. Twelfth Census of the United States, 1900, vol. 8, Enumeration District 24, sheet six, line 100; Ledger Book, Lodge No. 1, R.G. 15. On April 20, 1900, the state chapter filed for incorporation as a benevolent institution for fifty years; charter no. B002308, Ex-Slave Mutual Relief, Bounty and Pension Association of Missouri, Office of Missouri Secretary of State.
21. Minutes and ledger book, Lodge no. 1, R.G. 15.
22. Ibid.
23. Eric Arnesen, *Waterfront Workers of New Orleans: Race, Class and Politics, 1863–1923* (Urbana: University of Illinois Press, 1991, 1994), pp. 118, 147–148; J. Morgan Kousser, *The Shaping of Southern Politics: Suffrage Restriction and the Establishment of the One Party South, 1880–1910* (New Haven, Conn.: Yale University Press, 1974), pp. 152–165; John Hope Franklin, *From Slavery to Freedom* (New York: Alfred A. Knopf, 1987), pp. 236–238.
24. Marvin Fletcher, "The Black Volunteers in the Spanish American War," *Military Affairs* 38 (April 1974): 48–53.
25. "Act of Incorporation of the Ex-Slave Mutual Relief, Bounty and Pension Association of Louisiana," vol. 3, Louis Martinet's notarial volumes: 1899, Act. no. 20, June 22, 1899, Notarial Archives, New Orleans; Senate Bill no. 4718 known as the "Mason Bill." The charter

noted that the bill was first introduced in the House of Representatives by Congressman W. J. Connell of Nebraska on June 24, 1890, as House Bill no. 1119 and in the Senate on February 6, 1896, as Senate Bill no. 1978 by Senator J. M. Thurston of Nebraska and then reintroduced in 1898 as Senate Bill no. 4718 by Senator Mason of Illinois; Harry Joseph Walker, "Negro Benevolent Societies in New Orleans: A Study of Their Structure, Function, and Membership," master's thesis, Fisk University, 1937. Between 1900 and 1930, two to three hundred such mutual-assistance societies operated for short or longer periods of time. Further, the incorporators of the association, based on the names in the military records, did not appear related to any of the participants in the group of Louisiana African Americans who served in Cuba. Thanks to Rebecca Scott for sharing information about the charter.

26. J. Clay Smith, *Emancipation: The Making of the Black Lawyer, 1844–1944* (Philadelphia: University of Pennsylvania Press, 1993), pp. 283–285. Beyond the fact that Martinet notarized and prepared the legal papers for the incorporation of the Ex-Slave Association chapter, no apparent political connection has surfaced between those who organized the pension and self-help movement and the committee organized to end segregation in public transportation.

27. Diamond, age forty-two, was listed in the New Orleans City Directory as a recorder. He lived with his wife, Matilda, his stepson, Louis, his mother, and an aunt, Susan Campbell, at 705 Delachaise in New Orleans. They were all born in Louisiana. Phillip Burton lived alone at age sixty-five. Marcellin Zephilin, age sixty-three, was recorded in the Census as born in 1836 in Louisiana, but his wife, Martha, was from Virginia. They reported that they had each been married previously to spouses since deceased. They lived on Landon Avenue in New Orleans. Henry Boyd, age sixty-three, was born in Kentucky, and his wife, Lottie, age fifty, was from Virginia. Two twenty-year-old nieces, one born in Louisiana and one in Mississippi, Lillie Belle, lived with them on Prieur Street. The charter members were Diamond, Burton, Jones, Jackson, Green, Zephilin, Lottie Boyd, and Bell. U.S. Census 1900 Soundex; Diamond, roll no. T1048, vol. 39, sheet 11, line 37; Burton, T1048, Zephilin, vol. 27, sheet 12, line 51, Marriage certificates, New Orleans Public Library, Louisiana Divi-

sion, March 21, 1878, VEC678, p. 85; Death Certificate, Diamond FF420, August 10, 1927, age seventy-five; New Orleans Public Library Louisiana Division. Green's service on Executive Committee noted in letter from Dick to Reverend A. B. Webb, president of the association, February 27, 1902, Record Group 28, Records of the Postmaster General, Office of the Solicitor, Fraud Order Case Files 1894–1951.

28. Joseph G. Dawson III, ed., *The Louisiana Governors from Iberville to Edwards* (Baton Rouge: Louisiana State University Press, 1990), pp. 118–124.

29. Soldier's Certificate no. 883907, Veteran Marcellin Zephilin, Can no. 18128, bundle 38, Veterans Pensions Records, National Archives.

30. Elizabeth Ann Regosin, "Slave Custom and White Law: Ex-Slave Families and the Civil War Pension System, 1865–1900," Ph.D. dissertation, University of California at Irvine, 1995, pp. 26, 50, 56–70, describes the operations of the pension agents and their racial perspectives.

5   *The Movement Fights Back*

1. "Convicted Dickerson, Ex-Slave Pension Fraud Gets a Year or $100 Fine," *Nashville Banner*, March 6, 1901.

2. Callie House to Acting Assistant Attorney General Harrison Barrett, September 29, 1899, Record Group 28, Records of the Postmaster General, Office of the Solicitor, Fraud Order Case Files 1894–1951 (hereafter referred to as R.G. 28). The letters to and from federal officials are all in these files unless noted otherwise.

3. Ibid.

4. Wills served as postmaster from 1890 to 1914; see http://politicalgraveyard.com/parties/R/1900/index.html; *Who's Who in Tennessee, 1911* (Memphis: Paul & Douglass Co., 1911); United States Census, 1880, National Archives Film, T9-1249, p. 129D; 1885 Nashville City Directory, Wills Andrew W. Atty & Claims Agent; 1888 Nashville City Directory, Wills, Andrew W., President, National Manufacturing Co. (cotton yarn manufacturers) Attorney and Claims Agent.

5. Wills to Barrett, October 2, 1899.

6. House to Barrett, September 29, 1899.

7. Dickerson to Willis, November 9, 1899.

8. House to Harrison J. Barrett, November 23, 1899.

9. Dickerson to Wills, November 9, 1899; House to Barrett, November 1899.

10. See chapter four on the Boone County and New Orleans chapters.

11. Barrett to Lawson, December 9, 1899.

12. House to Barrett, December 18, 1899.

13. Ibid.

14. "Fraud upon Negroes," *The Washington Post,* December 12, 1899.

15. January 16, 1900, 58th Congress, 1st Session, report 75; "Ex-Slaves Are Defrauded: Pension Swindle Is Now Reaching Great Proportions," *The New York Times,* January 23, 1900. William C. Basil, Post Office Inspector, to Paul E. Williams, Inspector in Charge, September 7, 1899; he found no evidence that Vaughan or P. H. Hill were engaged in organizing or any other pension work.

16. In 1900, Reverend Richard Henry Boyd warned the black ministers of Tennessee that unless they aggressively guarded the interests of African Americans, white politicians would "turn the hand backward on the political dial of a century." Boyd referred to the hardening of racial lines and the beginning of the long reign of segregation. Bobby L. Lovett, ed., *From Winter to Winter: The Afro-American History of Nashville, Tennessee, 1870–1930* (Nashville: Department of History and Geography, Tennessee State University, 1981), p. 136.

17. "No Pensions for Ex-Slaves," *The Colored American* (Washington, D.C.), April 21, 1900.

18. House to Barrett, April 5, 1900; David Rutherford, *Bench and Bar* (Nashville: Davidson County, 1981), p. 66.

19. H. P. Stephens to Barrett, April 30, 1900.

20. Tyner to H. P. Stephens, May 3, 1900; Stephens to John W. Griggs, attorney general, March 15, 1901; Administrative Procedure Act, 60 Stat. 237 5 U.S.C.A.

21. From the assistant attorney general to Congressman Livingstone and others; Wilson, postmaster, to superintendent Nashville, February 26, 1901.

22. J. B. Mullins to Charles Emory Smith, March 5, 1901; letter sent to McNairy returned stamped "Found in bed dead," May 1, 1900.

23. J. B. Mullins to Charles Emory Smith, March 5, 1901.

24. J. B. Mullins to William McKinley, March 15, 1901.

25. A. W. Wills to George C. Christiancy, March 30, 1901.

26. Ibid.

27. The lower court opinion was by Judge Calhoun; "Limit of Law Is Insufficient in This Case—Judge Calhoun," *Atlanta Constitution,* March 6, 1901, clippings forwarded on March 7, 1901. "Convicted, Dickinson, Ex-Slave Pension Fraud Gets a Year or $1,000 Fine," *Nashville Banner,* March 6, 1901; Commissioner Evans to secretary of interior, March 13, 1901,

28. Wills to acting assistant attorney general, August 6, 1901, enclosing news clipping; *Dickerson v. State,* 39 SE 426 (1901).

29. *Dickerson v. State,* 39 SE 426 (1901); Judge Andrew Cobb routinely construed statutes narrowly in criminal cases. On his background, see "In Memoriam," Supreme Court of Georgia, May 17, 1926. See in general Mary Frances Berry, *The Pig Farmer's Daughter and Other Tales of American Justice: Episodes of Racism and Sexism in the Courts, 1865 to the Present* (New York: Alfred A. Knopf, 1999) on the behavior of State Supreme Court justices in cases involving African Americans. Wills to acting assistant attorney general, August 6, 1901, enclosing news clippings.

30. Hitchcock to the postmaster general, March 18, 1901, enclosing letter from Commissioner Evans to Hitchcock. J. I. Bristow to Tyner, March 21, 1901.

31. Wills to Christiancy, March 30, 1901.

32. A. W. Washington to Delphia House, September 25, 1910; Postmaster Arcola J. Gankstone to the Nashville postmaster, September 25, 1901.

33. Gerald Cullinan, *The Post Office Department* (New York: F. A. Praeger, 1968), pp. 116–117; *Tyner v. United States Barrett v. United States* 23 App. D.C. 324, 1904 WL 15862 App. D. C. April 5, 1904. Barrett's initial fee was a $1,000 retainer and $100 a month. See also *Report of the Postmaster-General in the Matter of the Investigation of the Post-Office Department* (Washington, D.C.: U.S. Government Printing Office, 1903). Barrett and Tyner were indicted three times, but the state did not include the punishment of federal officials.

34. Ibid.

6 *Avoiding Destruction*

1. Mary Frances Berry, *Black Resistance/White Law: A History of Constitutional Racism in America* (New York: Penguin, 1994), pp. 97–98.
2. The conclusion about the press coverage is based on reading the newspapers in the black newspaper file at the Library of Congress and local white newspapers in Nashville, Chicago, Washington, and Atlanta for this period and the Tuskegee Institute news clippings file [microfilm], Division of Behavioral Science Research, Carver Research Foundation, Tuskegee Institute (Sanford, N.C.: Microfilming Corporation of America, 1976); "Says Negro Held Her Prisoner for Five Years," *Chicago Tribune,* October 8, 1917, p. 1; "What the Negro Is Doing: Matters of Interest Among the Colored People," *Atlanta Constitution,* January 6, 1901.
3. Bobby L. Lovett, ed., *From Winter to Winter: The Afro-American History of Nashville, Tennessee, 1870–1930* (Nashville: Department of History and Geography, Tennessee State University, 1981), chapter 4.
4. Berry, *Black Resistance/White Law,* p. 97.
5. Dick and Dickerson, depositions, Record Group 15, Veterans Administration Correspondence and Reports Pertaining to Ex-Slave Pension Movements 1892–1916, National Archives (hereafter referred to as R.G. 15).
6. Interrogatories responded to by Robert Dick sometime between November 1901 and February 1902, R.G. 15.
7. Campbell Gibson and Kay Jung, "Historical Census Statistics on Population Totals by Race, 1790 to 1990, and by Hispanic Origin, 1970 to 1990, for the United States, Regions, Divisions, and States," Population Division Working Paper no. 56, U.S. Census Bureau, Washington, D.C. (September 2002), Tables 1, 57, A-12, A-13-18.
8. H.R. 11404, 57th Congress, 1st Session, February 17, 1902.
9. Dick to Reverend A. B. Webb, vice president, National Ex-Slave Mutual Relief, Bounty and Pension Association of the United States, February 27, 1902, R.G. 15; "Ex-Slaves Organize," *The Washington Post,* February 7, 1902.
10. Commissioner of pensions to Eliakam (Ell.) Torrance, Commander in Chief, Grand Army of the Republic, February 7, 1902, R.G. 15; History

of the Ninth Pennsylvania Reserve Corps, www.contrib.andrew.cmu
.edu.

11. Dick to Hadley Boyd, March 21, 1902, R.G. 15; "Vaughan's Justice
Party," *Washington Post,* April 20, 1902.

12. Dick to Reverend A. B. Webb, vice president, National Ex-Slave
Mutual Relief, Bounty and Pension Association of the United States,
February 27, 1902, R.G. 15.

13. Dickerson, deposition, R.G. 15. In response to a line of questions,
Dickerson described himself as forty-four years old, and told them
that as a small boy he had been called Isaiah Murphy rather than
Dickerson in his birthplace, Rutherford County, Tennessee. He had
married but had last seen his wife in Union City, Tennessee, where
they had separated. He attested to his role in organizing the Ex-Slave
Association, formerly housed at 708 Gay Street in Nashville, in 1897.
They had white attorneys or advisers, but the members were all "colored people." W. H. Wills of 312 Indiana Avenue published their
trade paper in Washington, D.C., called the *National Capital.* They
asked him about his conviction in Georgia for "swindling," whereupon he reminded them that it had been reversed by the State
Supreme Court.

14. Dickerson deposition. Asked if he knew of other organizations that
were working on the passage of the "so-called" ex-slave pension bills, he
identified Stanley P. Mitchell, president of the National Industrial
Council, a small pension lobby group. Mitchell had been formerly in
Indianapolis and Lexington, Kentucky, where he had been chairman of
the executive committee of Vaughan's Justice Party. Dickerson thought
that Isaac Walton of Madison, Arkansas—already identified by the
bureau as another "swindler"—might be associated with him. He knew
little if anything about their operations and "had no connection with
them." In fact, Mitchell and Walton tried unsuccessfully to persuade
the association to consolidate with their organizations; "New Colored
Party," *The Washington Post,* January 7, 1903; "Hitch Among Ex-
Slaves," *The Washington Post,* January 9, 1903.

15. Wills to Greenaway, February 9, 1903, Record Group 28, Records of
the Postmaster General, Office of the Solicitor, Fraud Order Case Files
1894–1951, National Archives (hereafter referred to as R.G. 28).

16. *Freedmen's Headlight,* R.G. 28.

17. "Ex-Slaves Defrauded," *The Nashville Tenn Daily News,* February 6, 1903, R.G. 28.

18. "Ex-Slave Pension Matters," *The New York Times,* February 10, 1903; "Ex-Slaves Approve," *The Washington Post,* February 13, 1903. They also passed a resolution introduced by Stanley Mitchell of the National Council. A minor eruption occurred when he made a speech describing his organization and asked the body to endorse a resolution he had prepared instead of the one before the meeting. Dickerson and R. E. Gilchrist handled the situation by seeking approval for both motions, which the attendees passed enthusiastically. Vaughan, still interested in having legislation passed, continued to work on southern support for the cause as a way to help the white South.

19. Wilson, Inspector, to Captain W. B. Smith, inspector in charge, Washington, D.C., R.G. 15.

20. H. G. Payne, Postmaster, order no. 1064, Post Office Department, October 28, 1903, R.G. 15.

21. Dorothy Garfield Fowler, *Unmailable: Congress and the Post Office* (Athens: University of Georgia Press, 1977), pp. 88–89; *American School of Magnetic Healing v. J. M. McAnnulty,* 187 U.S. 94 (1902).

22. Fowler, *Unmailable,* pp. 55–56; *Public Clearing House v. Coyne,* 194 US 497 (1904).

23. Lovett, *From Winter to Winter,* pp. 158–160.

24. Report of Inspector Keene on the application for revocation denied; a letter from C. B. Keene, Inspector, to Captain William B. Smith, January 13, 1906, stated that the assistant attorney general had requested the investigation. R.G. 15.

25. See discussion of Tyner's corrupt behavior in chapter five.

26. Fowler, *Unmailable,* pp. 94–96.

27. Ibid.

28. Thomas Jones to R. P. Goodwin, assistant attorney general, April 26, 1907, R.G. 15.

29. "Would Pension Ex-Slaves," *The Washington Post,* December 9, 1905; 1880 United States Census, Washington, D.C.

30. Assistant Attorney General Goodwin to Thomas Jones, R.G. 15.

31. H. V. Cuddy to Chief of the Southeastern Division, December 5, 1904, Chief of Law Division, Bureau of Pensions, Department of the Interior, R.G. 15.

32. A. W. Wills to first assistant postmaster general, December 28, 1906; J. M. Thompson, superintendent of carriers, to Major A. W. Wills, Postmaster, December 26, 1906, R.G. 15.

33. "Ex-Slaves Want Pensions," *The Washington Post,* June 5, 1906.

34. Wills to Greenaway, November 26, 1907, R.G. 15.

35. 1910 Manuscript Census of the United States, ED 60, sheet 12, L 30, National Archives.

36. Senate Journal, 61st Congress, 2nd Session, December 7, 1909, p. 14; Senator Mason of Illinois's bill no. 4718, first introduced on June 6, 1898, in the 55th Congress, Record Group 46, box 150, Records of the U.S. Senate Committee on Pensions.

37. M. A. Warren, Tuskegee, Alabama, to Congressman Thomas J. Heflin, January 2, 1911; Assistant Attorney General to Warren S. Reese, United States Attorney, February 16, 1911, R.G. 15.

38. Hitchcock to secretary of interior, April 24, 1911; Sherley to Wickersham, attorney general, April 20, 1912; Assistant Attorney General Harris to Sherley, April 23, 1912; W. R. Harris to postmaster general, April 23, 1912, R.G. 15.

39. Lovett, ed., *From Winter to Winter,* pp. 165–170.

40. Report of the Nineteenth Annual Convention, Record Group 21, U.S. District Court, Middle District of Tennessee, Criminal Action no. 521, box 17, R.G. 15.

41. See H.R. 11119, *Congressional Record,* 1st Congress, 1st Session (1889–90); S. 1389, *Congressional Record,* 3rd Congress, 2nd Session (1894–5); S. 1978, *Congressional Record,* 54th Congress, 1st Session (1895–6); S. 4718, 55th Congress; S. 1176, *Congressional Record,* 56th Congress, 1st Session (1899–1900), H.R. 11404, 57th Congress, 1st Session, February 17, 1902.

7   The Association Goes to Federal Court

1. *United States v. Augustus Clark,* U.S. District Court, Eastern District of Texas, docket no. 239, p. 177, filed November 1916, April 10, 1917, History of the Case, pp. 3–4.

2. Ibid.

3. Mary Frances Berry, *Black Resistance/White Law: A History of Constitutional Racism in America* (New York: Penguin, 1994), pp. 108–109.

4. Constance McLaughlin Green, *The Secret City: A History of Race Rela-*

tions in the Nation's Capital (Princeton, N.J.: Princeton University Press, 1967), p. 139; Rayford W. Logan and Michael Winston, eds., *Dictionary of American Negro Biography* (New York: W. W. Norton, 1982), pp. 98–101; "Cornelius J. Jones, "America Must Redeem Her National Pledge of 'Sacred Honor'—Called to the Bar of Her Own Courts for an Accounting," *Washington Bee,* October 23, 1915.

5. J. Clay Smith, *Emancipation: The Making of the Black Lawyer, 1844–1944* (Philadelphia: University of Pennsylvania Press, 1993), pp. 131–132, 305, n. 26; *Gibson v. Mississippi,* 162 U.S. 565 (1896); "He Should Be Seated, the Congressional Campaign of Hon. C. J. Jones—A Superb Constitutional Lawyer," *The Colored American,* July 16, 1898.

6. Smith, *Emancipation,* pp. 131–132, 305, n.26.

7. "Look Up Old Cotton Claim," *The People's Recorder,* published by S. H. Nix and L. E. Holmes in Columbia, South Carolina, January 27, 1900; *Johnson v. McAdoo,* 45 App. D.C. 440 (1916); 244 U.S. 643 (1917); "Cornelius J. Jones America Must Redeem Her National Pledge of 'Sacred Honor'—Called to the Bar of Her Own Courts for an Accounting," *Washington Bee,* October 23, 1915.

8. Jones, "America Must Redeem."

9. *Johnson v. McAdoo,* 45 App. D.C. 440 (1916); Mary F. Berry, "Reparations for Freedmen, 1890–1916: Fraudulent Practices or Justice Deferred," *Journal of Negro History* 57 (July 1972): 219–230; Smith, *Emancipation,* pp. 296–297; Jones, "America Must Redeem,"

10. Jones, "America Must Redeem"; letter from Douglass to Vaughan in Vaughan, *Freedmen's Pension Bill,* p. 150; also published in newspapers and in Frederick Douglass papers online, Library of Congress, American Memory Web site discussed in chapter one.

11. As Boris Bittker did in *The Case for Black Reparations* (New York: Random House, 1973), he ignored approaches such as the Brandeis brief strategy, used by Louis Brandeis in seeking a limitation on hours of work for females in *Mueller v. Oregon,* which would have supported the inclusion of "social facts" concerning the plight of the old ex-slaves. Neither did Jones focus on the detrimental effects of segregation since slavery.

12. Jones characterized his claim as an equitable lien and avoided making a generalized claim for government money that would confront governmental immunity frontally, citing the government as the custodian of

funds belonging to the plaintiffs. He cited standard debt cases, including those where the creditor could not pursue a claim until much later, to support the ex-slaves' request for payment. For example, in *Wright v. Ellison,* 17 L. Ed. 555, 1 Wall 16 (1863), a maritime case, the court held that to constitute an equitable lien on a fund there must be some distinct appropriation of the fund by the debtor. Once that is identified, the holder of the fund is obligated to pay it. In *Christmas v. Russell,* 20 L. Ed. 76, 14 Wall 69 (1873), a mortgage debt case, the court held that to make an equitable assignment there must be an actual or constructive appropriation of the subject matter so as to confer a complete and present right on the party meant to be provided for, even if the circumstances do not permit immediate exercise of the right. McAdoo said the constitutionality of the tax had come before the courts in *Farrington v. Saunders, Collector,* tried in the U.S. Circuit Court, Western District of Tennessee, and appealed to the Supreme Court but not reported.

13. "No Fund for Ex-Slaves," *New York Evening Post,* October 15, 1915.

14. *Wright v. Ellison,* 17 L. Ed. 555, 1 Wall 16 (1863); *Christmas v. Russell,* 20 L. Ed. 76, 14 Wall 69 (1873); "The Cotton Tax," *Washington Bee,* November 13, 1915; "Look Up Old Cotton Claim," *The People's Recorder,* January 27, 1900.

15. *Johnson v. McAdoo,* 45 App. D.C. 440 (1916); 244 U.S. 643 (1917). In the *Blue Fox* case in 1999, the Supreme Court rejected a suit based on Jones's equitable lien theory, finding that what appeared to be a damage action was essentially a claim for money owed by the United States; *Department of the Army v. Blue Fox,* 525 U.S. 255; 119 S. Ct. 687 (1999). But it would be difficult to argue that the old ex-slaves' claim was contractual considering that slaves could not make contracts.

16. Jones agreed that a suit saying an officer should do a certain thing was a suit against the government and dismissible on the grounds of governmental immunity. Therefore he instead argued the equitable lien theory to show that the government had no direct interest in the suit. The fund in possession of the treasury secretary was there only for custodial purposes. He drew an analogy to Indian trust funds that were held in the Treasury until distributed to their rightful owners—location does not vest ownership. The arguments are taken from the brief filed in the Supreme Court, no. 897, October term (1916), *Johnson v. McAdoo,* per curiam judgment, affirmed 244 U.S. 643 (1917); *Postal*

Supply Co. v. Bruce, 194 U.S. 601, was a contract case in which the facts showed that the government was the defendant and would have been substantially interfered with, unlike the situation in the cotton tax case. In *Belknap v. Schild et al.,* 161 U.S. 10, the property in question was shown to belong to the United States, based on evidence at trial and not just a statement in the record. Getting to trial was precisely what Jones was asking to do. *State of Louisiana v. W. G. McAdoo, Secretary of Treasury,* 234 U.S. 627, was a case in which the state wanted to control the discretion exercised by the secretary under a statute. Jones cited cases to show that if the tax was illegal and the funds had been illegally collected by the government, they belonged to the ex-slaves. According to the decision by the Supreme Court in *Pollock v. Farmer's Loan and Trust Co.,* 157 601 (1895), in which an income tax was delcared unconstitutional, the cotton tax should have been apportioned. The Sixteenth Amendment, permitting a tax on income from whatever source derived, was not added to the Constitution in 1913. However, according to the *Pollock* decision, at the time the unapportioned cotton tax was collected it was illegal. This illegally collected tax, Jones argued, should be given back to the slaves who had produced it because slavery was illegal and the slave owners were rebels. However, the slaves were legally disabled from establishing a claim at the time.

17. For example, *Washington Bee,* July 24, 1915. In "Cotton Tax Suit Has No Merit," *The Chicago Defender,* November 6, 1915, reported Attorney General McAdoo's denunciation of the suit but let Jones reply on the front page in the next issue, "Cotton Tax Suit Has Merit." *The Defender* also ignored the Association; Record Group 15, Pension Bureau, Department of the Interior, Ex-Slave Pensions, National Archives (hereafter referred to as R.G. 15).

18. Quote is from complaint in the unsuccessful prosecution of Ex-Slave Association agent Augustus Clark, discussed in the next chapter; *United States v. Clark,* U.S. District Court, Eastern District of Texas, docket no. 239, p. 177, filed November 1916, April 10, 1917, p. 4.

19. Congress added the italicized language to Section 215, U.S. Criminal Code, the postal fraud statute: "*Whoever,* having devised or intending to devise any scheme or artifice to defraud or *for obtaining money or property by means of false or fraudulent pretenses, representations or promises . . . shall, for the purpose of executing such scheme or artifice, or*

attempting to do so place or cause to be placed, any letter . . . in any post office shall be fined not more than one thousand dollars or imprisoned not more than five years or both."

20. Letters from U.S. attorney, Southern District of Alabama, Alexander R. Pitts, February 28, 1916, March 2, 1916, to attorney general; letter from William Wallace, assistant attorney general, to Pitts, R.G. 15.

21. U.S. District Court, *United States v. Cornelius Jones* accounting ledger; Fisher died in 1941. See http://Bioguide.Congress.gov/scripts/biodisplay.pl?index=F000149.

22. *Memphis Commercial Appeal*, p. 1, August 9, 1920; www.fjc.gov/servlet/tGetInfo?jid=1520.

23. Harris Dickson, "Please Y'Onner," *The Saturday Evening Post*, July 1906–June 1907, vol. 179, nos. 1–52, microfilm reel no. 7: "The negro is emotional." "He does not mind being hanged, if only the execution is in public and people come from miles around to make a picnic day of it."; "The Mississippi Monarch," January–June 1913, vol. 185, nos. 27–52, reel no. 16: "Carpet-bag adventurers led these big black credulous children to believe that every ex-slave would be provided with forty acres and a mule." "Only the hungry ones could be induced to work, having got the fixed idea that as wards of Uncle Sam the nation must take care of them."

24. Smith, *Emancipation*, pp. 294–295, 318; *Washington Bee*, July 10, 1920. The *Philadelphia Public Ledger* criticized him for allegedly trying to organize petitioners to ask the government to legislate the cotton tax monies that he had not been able to obtain in court. Someone apparently was given or found a circular Jones had used to collect support for the case in 1915 that asked for a contribution of $1.75, "Asks Only $1.75 to Share Millions," *Philadelphia Public Ledger*, April 15, 1922, in Tuskegee Institute news clippings file [microfilm], Division of Behavioral Science Research, Carver Research Foundation, Tuskegee Institute (Sanford, N.C.: Microfilming Corporation of America, 1976).

8   *Jailed for Justice*

1. Mary Frances Berry, *Black Resistance/White Law: A History of Constitutional Racism in America* (New York: Penguin, 1994), pp. 108–110.

2. I. H. Dickerson was deceased; Pension Bureau memorandum on the

case March 21, 1917. An early handbill of the association denounced as "fakes and frauds" any black person or leader who opposed "a pension for past wrongs"; Record Group 15, Pension Bureau, Department of the Interior, Ex-Slave Pensions, National Archives (hereafter referred to as R.G. 15).

3. Paula Giddings, *When and Where I Enter: The Impact of Black Women on Race and Sex in America* (New York: Morrow, 1984); Anne Firor Scott, "Most Invisible of All"; "Black Women's Voluntary Associations," *Journal of Southern History* 56 (February, 1990): 3–22; Tera Hunter, *To 'Joy My Freedom; Southern Black Women's Lives and Labors After the Civil War* (Cambridge, Mass.: Harvard University Press, 1997).

4. Melinda Chateauvert, "Marching Together: Women of the Brotherhood of Sleeping Car Porters, 1925–1957," Ph.D. dissertation, University of Pennsylvania, 1992, pp. 36–40, 377–379; Evelyn Higginbotham, *Righteous Discontent: The Women's Movement in the Black Baptist Church* (Cambridge, Mass.: Harvard University Press, 1993), chapter 7. Rosalyn Terborg-Penn, *African American Women in the Struggle for the Vote, 1850–1920* (Bloomington: Indiana University Press, 1998), explains that black women in the movement wanted suffrage but also wanted to make sure they behaved only in a respectable manner while pursuing activism. On the background of women leaders, see, e.g., Beverly Jones, "Mary Church Terrell and the National Association of Colored Women, 1896–1901," *Journal of Negro History* 67 (Spring 1982): 20–33; Linda O. McMurry, *To Keep the Waters Troubled: The Life of Ida B. Wells* (New York: Oxford University Press, 1998), p. 282.

5. See language added to code in note 19, chapter seven.

6. U.S. Attorney, Southern District of Alabama, Alexander R. Pitts, February 28, 1916, to Attorney General Thomas Gregory,

7. Postmaster General Albert Sidney Burleson to Attorney General Gregory, March 30, 1916, Department of Justice, Record Group 60, file no. 1555690-8; Assistant Attorney General Charles Warren to postmaster general, April 6, 1916; Assistant Attorney General Charles Warren to Lee Douglas, April 6, 1916; Lee Douglas to attorney general, April 11, 1916, saying case will be tried at the September 1916 term and that the office has taken a "sworn statement from Callie House, which will prove very helpful."

8. U.S. District Court, Middle District of Tennessee, March term, 1916, Criminal Action nos. 520 and 521, Record Group 21, National Archives, Atlanta Region, box 17. The government materials cited below are in this collection unless otherwise noted. U.S. District Court, Middle District of Tennessee, March term 1916, Criminal Action Nos. 520 and 521. Thirteen other black alleged coconspirators, who held office in the organization, were charged in what would have been a conspiracy. The government hoped they would produce evidence against House. The others indicted included officers and board members William Atkins of Lynchburg, Virginia; Reverend Robert Page of Nashville, Tennessee; Matilda Hill of Johnston Station, Mississippi; and Millie Thompson of Vicksburg. They produced no evidence and were not prosecuted. Witnesses before the grand jury were George W. Stewart, W. R. King, Thomas W. Hardwick, J. L. Pemberton, Rick S. White, Doc Parchman, York Calloway, G. A. David, and A. J. Cole.

9. Douglas, requesting authority to pay from the attorney general, April 6, 1916; approved on April 10, 1916; Law Division to Robbins Company, Attleboro, Massachusetts, June 27, 1916.

10. "Slave Pension Scheme Exposed," *Tennessee American,* August 4, 1916. No mention has been found of Callie House or the association by Booker T. Washington, but he opposed any activity that differed from his advice to blacks. In September 1900, at a Tuskegee conference where he reiterated his "Stay in the South and cooperate with your former masters" admonition, he warned blacks against paying attention to ex-slave pension or emigration agents who would seduce them from these views; "Tuskegee Negro Conference Declarations Regarding the Best Interests of the Negro Race," *The Washington Post,* February 22, 1900.

11. On August 11, J. L. Pemberton reported to George Stewart at the Pension Bureau in Washington that "she is still in jail." On August 19, 1916, special examiner A. R. Smith reported to M. Whitehead, chief of the division, that she had made bond, no. 520. Thomas House and pawn-broker-bondsman Myer Morris had acted as sureties for her as principal, saying they were indebted to the United States for $3,000, to be levied on their "goods and chattels, lands and tenements" if she should not appear in court on the first day of the term, the fourth Monday of September 1916, Bond Form 94, August 14, 1916, National Archives and Record Administration, R.G. 21, Middle District of Tennessee,

Nashville Division, criminal file no. 520, Southeast Region, Atlanta, box no. 17; 1916 Nashville City Directory.

12. "Aunt Callie Was Whole Cheese in Ex-Slave Pension Body," *The Nashville Tennessean,* October 10, 1917, p. 5, identifies defense counsel; Nashville Colored Directory 1925, Biographical, Statistical, compiled by R. C. Grant names lawyers J. P. Rhines, Napier, and Burnely. U.S. District Court, Middle District of Tennessee, March term 1916, criminal action no. 521, Criminal Docket no. 520, Reports of Lee Douglas, Office of Postmaster General, Office of Solicitor, Fraud Order Case Files 1894–1951, case file no. 3839.

13. Aside from *The Nashville Tennessean's* reports, there is no trial transcript or other record in the files on the court proceedings.

14. Stanley A. Cook, "Path to the High Bench: The Pre–Supreme Court Career of Justice Edward Terry Sanford," Ph.D. dissertation, University of Tennessee, Knoxville, 1977, p. 1 and note 1, p. 83. During the Senate debate in the spring of 1970 on the failed confirmation of Judge G. Harold Carswell, nominated to serve on the U.S. Supreme Court, Senator Thomas Eagleton, Democrat of Missouri, cited Sanford as an example of mediocrity on the Court. "I realize that men of limited capacity have served on the court in the past," the future temporary 1972 Democratic vice presidential candidate told the Senate. "For every Oliver Wendell Holmes, we can dredge up an Edward T. Sanford." Senate minority leader Howard Baker of Tennessee replied that he found the statement "inappropriate," even though Sanford, a "competent jurist," of course suffered by comparison with the preeminence of Oliver Wendell Holmes, with whom he served on the Supreme Court.

15. Cook, "Path to the High Bench," pp. 14–17, 59–60.

16. Mark Curriden and Leroy Phillips, Jr., *Contempt of Court: The Turn of the Century Lynching That Launched 100 years of Federalism* (New York: Faber and Faber, 1999), pp. 199, 292–302, 340; Clark, "Path to the High Bench," pp. 66–67. Sanford resigned before the trial was over, became a federal judge, and later supervised the implementation of the Supreme Court order implementing the convictions in the case; J. S. Doherty, special examiner, to commissioner of pensions, October 6, 1916.

17. Clark, "Path to the High Bench," p. 83; Curriden and Phillips, *Contempt of Court,* p. 341.

18. Order of Judge Sanford, entered November 30, 1917, book 1, p. 616.

19. Special examiner Biller to commissioner of pensions, August 7, 1915.

20. *The Handbook of Texas on Line* from the *Dallas Morning News,* April 29, 1927, www.tsha.utexas.edu; E. W. Winkler, *Platforms of Political Parties in Texas* (Austin: University of Texas, 1916).

21. U.S. District Court, Eastern District of Texas, Docket no. 239, p. 177, filed November 1916, April 10, 1917, includes letter to Clark from House; Gordon James Russell, www.fjic.gov/servlet/GetInfo?jid=2075. Russell resigned from active duty on the Court in 1918 after contracting tuberculosis. He died on September 14, 1919. "Judge Russell Dies at Kerrville," *Houston Post,* September 16, 1919. Russell, a Republican, had been a county judge, district attorney, and member of Congress before President Taft nominated him to the district court. The government relied on the case of *United States v. Barnow,* which established that even if no office existed it was a crime to claim to be an official implementing such an office. *Lamar v. United States,* 240 U.S. 60, is also cited. The Beaumont newspaper reported the proceedings, for which no transcript has been found; "Ex-Slaves to Tell of Scheme That Defrauded Them; U.S. Grand Jury Gets Busy Today," *Beaumont Enterprise and Journal,* April 9, 1917; "Ex-Slave Pleads Case and Jury Acquits Him," *Beaumont Enterprise and Journal,* April 11, 1917.

22. "Ex-Slave Pleads Case and Jury Acquits Him," *Beaumont Enterprise and Journal,* April 11, 1917.

23. *Nashville Tennessean,* October 9, 1917, p. 4. According to federal prison records upon her incarceration two weeks later, House weighed 170 pounds and was 5 feet, 4½ inches tall; State of Missouri, Office of Secretary of State, Records Management and Archives Services, microfilm no. S232; Jefferson City Prison-Register of Inmates Received, Numerical Register no. 18593-20573, July 6, 1916, to March 18, 1918, p. 228, Register Number 20188, Callie D. House; one-year sentence from October 12, 1917, discharged August 1, 1918; pp. 654, 662.

24. "Aunt Callie Was the Whole Cheese in Ex-Slave Pension Body," *Nashville Tennessean,* October 10, 1917, p. 5.

25. Ibid.

26. "Aunt Callie Ruled with an Iron Hand," *Nashville Tennessean,* October 11, 1917, p. 8.

27. "Aunt Callie Was the Whole Cheese in Ex-Slave Pension Body."

28. The prosecution, to reduce any exculpatory effect of the handwritten letter presented in Clark's case, introduced several similar letters that seemed to indicate that House thought the bills had "passed." Unlike the other letters from House in the government's files, all of which were handwritten, these letters were typed. Even if one assumes they had been typed from her actual handwritten letters to present at the trial, there were no handwritten originals in the files. One typed letter, purportedly hers, said that an ex-slave bill had passed in 1913 but had not been signed into law and that she did not know "the Exact time when they would be paid" but she thought it "will not be long." Another typed letter, of August 1915, said that the Ex-Slave claim had been allowed in 1913 but that Taft had not signed it "because it was mixed up with other things he vetoed." The letters contradicted her handwritten letters if they were taken to mean she thought something had "passed." U.S. District Court, Middle District of Tennessee, March term 1916, Criminal Action no. 521, Criminal Docket no. 520, Copy Judgment, October 1917, U.S. District Court, Middle District of Tennessee, Criminal Docket Number 521, October 1920, nolle prossed. The letter to Clark is referred to several times in the government case; see letter from U. J. Biller after letter from commissioner of pensions to Douglas, August 11, 1916, identifying the letter to Clark and quoting the relevant language. Biller, special examiner for the Pension Bureau in Texas, to Lee Douglas, March 3, 1917. Biller, who was in New Orleans, said that he had received his subpoena and would be in Nashville in time with the papers from the trial of Clark. See also commissioner of pensions to Lee Douglas, February 27, 1917, which refers to the letter to Clark. The commissioner told Douglas that the Pension Bureau had certificates signed by House and "a letter in the hand writing of Callie D. House"; Douglas wrote the commissioner, on August 18, 1916, saying the letter to Clark "doubtless" would be valuable evidence; "Fraud Charges Are Sustained."

29. *Nashville Banner,* October 12, 1917.

30. The headlines on the day of her sentencing focused exclusively on war-related matters: "Negro Women Car Washers Take Men's Places in Chicago Plant." The only talk of civil rights was "Civil Rights Bill Hearings Closed," a story about efforts to pass a bill guaranteeing insurance for men who had paid no premiums during the war or up to

one year thereafter; *Chicago Daily Tribune,* October 27, 1917; *The Evening Star* (Kansas City), September 25, 1917.

31. "Callie House Gets One Year Sentence," *Nashville Tennessean,* October 13, 1917, p. 11.

32. Douglas to Gregory, November 12, 1917; Thomas Gregory, attorney general, to Lee Douglas, November 15, 1917; Order to Execute Judgement, U.S. District Court, Middle District of Tennessee, Edward Sanford, district judge, after a verdict of guilty by a jury on October 12, Callie D. House sentenced to one year and one day from October 12, 1917; judgment modified to change place of imprisonment from Atlanta to Jefferson City, Missouri; Record Group 15, Pension Bureau, Department of the Interior, Ex-Slave Pensions, National Archives (hereafter referred to as R.G. 15). State of Missouri, Office of Secretary of State, Records Management and Archives Services, microfilm no. S232; Jefferson City Prison-Register of Inmates Received, Numerical Register no. 18593-20573, July 6, 1916, to March 18, 1918, p. 228. Register no. 20188, Callie D. House; one-year sentence from October 12, 1917, discharged August 1, 1918; pp. 654, 662; Lawrence M. Friedman, *Crime and Punishment in American History* (New York: Basic Books, 1993), p. 269; Mary Ellen Curtin, *Black Prisoners and Their World: Alabama, 1865–1900* (Charlottesville: University Press of Virginia, 2000).

33. Emma Goldman, *Living My Life,* edited by Richard and Anna Maria Drinnon (New York: New American Library, 1977), pp. 625, 652.

34. Ibid., p. 653; Alice Wexler, *Emma Goldman: An Intimate Life* (New York: Pantheon Books, 1984), p. 248; The quotes are from Paul W. Garrett and Austin H. MacCormick, eds., *Handbook of American Prisons and Reformatories* (New York: National Society of Prisons and Reformatories, 1929), p. 539.

35. Goldman, *Living My Life,* p. 653.

36. Ibid., p. 653–654.

37. Ibid., pp. 658, 660.

38. Ibid.

39. Ibid., p. 653.

40. Ibid., Goldman refers to him as Captain Gilvan, but according to the *Official Manual of the State of Missouri,* published by the secretary of state, G. R. Gilvin was acting warden in 1917 and Porter Gilvin was

warden beginning in 1919. It's not clear whether they are the same person.

41. Ibid., pp. 654–655.

42. Ibid., pp. 660–661.

43. Ibid., pp. 662–663.

44. Ibid., p. 138.

45. State of Missouri, Office of Secretary of State, Records Management and Archives Services, microfilm no. S232; Jefferson City Prison-Register of Inmates Received, Numerical Register no. 18593-20573, July 6, 1916, to March 18, 1918, p. 228. Register no. 20188, Callie D. House; one-year sentence from October 12, 1917, discharged August 1, 1918; Goldman, *Living My Life,* pp. 654, 662. After Callie House left, Goldman remained in the prison until August 1919 with four months subtracted from her two-year sentence for good behavior.

46. Davidson County Deed Books, roll 181, vols. 388–389 (1909–10); roll 243, lots 518–519, 519 (1918–19), Tennessee State Library and Archives, Nashville, Tennessee.

9 *Passing the Torch*

1. For example, her son Thomas worked as a laborer, her son William as a porter and then a presser, and her daughter Annie took in washing at their Tenth Avenue home. The 1910 United States Manuscript Census ED 60, sheet 12, L 30, lists the house as owned but mortgaged, but there is no record of a deed to the Houses in the Tennessee State Library and Archives deed records.

2. Mary Frances Berry, *Black Resistance/White Law: A History of Constitutional Racism in America* (New York: Penguin, 1994), pp. 122–128.

3. Bobby L. Lovett, ed., *From Winter to Winter: The Afro-American History of Nashville, Tennessee, 1870–1930* (Nashville: Department of History and Geography, Tennessee State University, 1981), pp. 176–185.

4. Ibid., pp. 187–198.

5. Ibid., pp. 118–124.

6. Ibid., pp. 129–130.

7. State of Tennessee, Board of Vital Statistics, registration no. 21901, file no. 1391, death certificate no. 13311, Tennessee State Library and Archives, Nashville. The death certificates states her age as sixty-three,

but records made when she was alive indicate she was born in 1861 or 1862; 1928 Nashville City Directory.

8. Lovett, *Winter to Winter,* pp. 108–109.

9. Charles Guy was listed in Nashville city directories until his death as a laborer. On his death certificate his wife, Amanda, described him as a minister; Nashville city directories 1916–1934; death certificate, October 6, 1933, Nashville, State of Tennessee, Department of Health, Division of Vital Statistics.

10. Reavis L. Mitchell, "Zema W. Hill (1891–1970)," www.instate.edu/library/digital/hill.htm.

11. Zema Hill died on February 5, 1970, after a long illness and was buried in Mt. Ararat Cemetery; Reavis L. Mitchell, "Zema W. Hill (1891–1970)," www.instate.edu/library/digital/hill.htm.

12. Nashville city directories from 1928 to 1940; Delphia disappeared from the records; Thomas Ross and Annie later moved to Olympic Avenue in the same neighborhood. Mattie House, death certificate, March 7, 1971, Nashville, State of Tennessee, Department of Health, Division of Vital Statistics.

13. Hilary Howse's Confederate pension application no. 39815, Microfilm Division, National Archives.

14. "Movement Is Started to Care for Ex-Slaves," *Atlanta Constitution,* December 25, 1917; "Ex-Slaves Need Christmas Help from Atlantans," "Negro Mammies and Old Black Joes Object of Charity," *Atlanta Constitution,* December 19, 1922; "Funds Asked for Ex-Slaves *Atlanta Constitution,* December 15, 1918; "Will Help Ex-Slaves, Tag Day Is Now Planned by Negroes of Atlanta," *Atlanta Constitution,* November 20, 1920; "Churches Seek Funds for Former Slaves," *Atlanta Constitution* December 5, 1931; "Churches Individuals Aid Funds for Ex-slaves," Tuskegee Clippings file, Slaves. Brusey, Kizzie, and Savannah Holmes are listed in the Atlanta City Directory at the Holmes Institute, but I have not found them listed in the 1920 or 1910 Census, although the 1930 Soundex has a listing that appears to be "Nrunsey" misspelled. Atlanta City Directory, reel 11, 1921–1922, Microfilm Reading Room, Library of Congress.

15. Works Progress Administration Papers, Ex-Slave, box 83 (1934–37), Moorland-Spingarn Collection, Howard University Library.

16. Ibid.

17. Ibid.

18. Broxton to Department of Information, Department of the Interior, October 29, 1937; Joseph Greenberg, chief, Division of Bookkeeping and Warrants, Treasury Department, to Broxton, November 23, 1937; Brien McMahon, Assistant Attorney General, to Broxton, December 9, 1937; Division of Records, Department of Justice.

19. House to acting assistant attorney general Harrison Barrett, September 29, 1899.

20. See, e.g., Craig Jenkins and Charles Perrow, "Insurgency of the Powerless: Farm Worker Movements (1946–1972)," *American Sociological Review* 42, April 1977, pp. 249–268; David Blight, *Race and Reunion: The Civil War in American Memory* (Cambridge, Mass.: Harvard University Press, 2001), pp. 1–5.

21. Blight, *Race and Reunion,* pp. 1–5.

22. Ibid., p. 65; Mary Frances Berry, *Military Necessity and Civil Rights Policy: Black Citizenship and the Constitution, 1861–1868* (Port Washington, N.Y.: Kennikat Press, 1977), pp. 75–84.

23. Abraham Lincoln, Second Inaugural Address, March 4, 1865.

24. Nina Silber, *The Romance of Reconstruction: Northerners and the South, 1865–1900* (Chapel Hill: University of North Carolina Press, 1992); Blight, *Race and Reunion,* pp. 1–5.

25. Blight, *Race and Reunion,* p. 220.

26. Ibid., pp. 383, 387, 390.

27. Thomas Cripps, "The Reaction of the Negro to the Motion Picture *Birth of a Nation,*" *The Historian* 25 (May 1963): 344–362; Cripps, *Slow Fade to Black: The Negro in American Film, 1900–1942* (New York: Oxford University Press, 1977), pp. 41–69.

28. See, e.g., "Favor Ex-Slave Pensions," *The New York Times,* February 8, 1903; June O. Patton, J. S. Strickland, and E. J. Crawford, "Document, Moonlight and Magnolias in Southern Education: The Black Mammy Memorial Institute," *Journal of Negro History* 65 (1980): 149–155. Samuel Harris, principal of the Athens, Georgia, black high school, according to the tenets of Booker T. Washington, had whites charter a Mammy Memorial Institute for industrial education that would teach domestic chores.

29. Rayford Logan, *The Negro in American Life and Thought: The Nadir, 1877–1901* (New York: Dial Press, 1954).

Epilogue: The Reparations Movement Still Lives

1. Cathy Cohen and Michael Dawson, "Neighborhood Poverty and African American Politics," *American Political Science Review* 87 (June 1993): 286–302.

2. See, e.g., Randall Robinson, *The Debt: What America Owes to Blacks* (New York: Penguin, 2000); Raymond A. Winbush, ed., *Should America Pay? Slavery and the Raging Debate on Reparations* (New York: Amistad HarperCollins, 2003).

3. Mary Frances Berry and John W. Blassingame, *Long Memory: The Black Experience in America* (New York: Oxford University Press, 1982), pp. 409–411; E. David Cronon, *Black Moses: The Story of Marcus Garvey and the Universal Negro Improvement Association* (Madison: University of Wisconsin Press, 1955); Robert A. Hill, ed., *The Marcus Garvey and Universal Negro Improvement Association Papers,* vol. 1 (Berkeley: University of California Press, 1983), xxxv–cxvii; Tony Martin, *Race First: The Ideological and Organizational Struggles of Marcus Garvey and the Universal Negro Improvement Association* (Westport, Conn.: Greenwood Press, 1976).

4. Robert A. Hill, *The Marcus Garvey and Universal Negro Improvement Association Papers,* vol. 5 (Berkeley: University of California Press, 1983), pp. 182–187; quote from Randolph is on p. 183.

5. Berry and Blassingame, *Long Memory,* pp. 409–411.

6. Lawrence Levine, "Marcus Garvey and the Politics of Revitalization," in John Hope Franklin and August Meier, eds., *Black Leaders of the Twentieth Century* (Champaign-Urbana: University of Illinois Press, 1982), pp. 105–138; Berry and Blassingame, *Long Memory,* pp. 409–411.

7. Berry and Blassingame, *Long Memory,* p. 410.

8. Ibid, p. 411.

9. William Loren Katz, preface to *Philosophy and Opinions of Marcus Garvey,* edited by Amy Jacques-Garvey (New York: Arno Press, 1968), first published 1923–1925, p. xii.

10. Ibid.

11. E. Franklin Frazier, "The Garvey Movement," *Opportunity* 4 (Novem-

ber 1926): 346–348. Reprinted in Meier and Rudwick, eds., *The Making of Black America*, vol. 2 (New York: Atheneum, 1969), p. 204.

12. Compare the lists of delegates to UNIA conventions in Hill, ed., *The Marcus Garvey and Universal Negro Improvement Association Papers*, vols. 4 and 5, appendices, and list of state ex-slave pension agents filed May 13, 1902, with A. W. Roone, special examiner, Record Group 15, Pension Bureau, Department of the Interior, Ex-Slave Pensions, National Archives; Mary Gambrell Robinson, "The Garvey Movement in the Rural South, 1920–1927," Ph.D. dissertation, Georgia State University, 2002, p. 75.

13. Hill, *The Marcus Garvey and Universal Negro Improvement Association Papers*, vol. 1, p. 202; Mary Gambrell Rolinson, *The Garvey Movement in the Rural South, 1920–1927*, Ph.D. dissertation, Georgia State University, 2002, pp. 92–93; Bobby L. Lovett, ed., *From Winter to Winter: The Afro-American History of Nashville, Tennessee, 1870–1930* (Nashville: Department of History and Geography, Tennessee State University, 1981), p. 253. Carruthers lived with his wife, Louise, at 171 Fairfield Avenue; Nashville City Directory, 1924; in the 1930 directory the address is 116 Fairfield.

14. Berry and Blassingame, *Long Memory*, pp. 405–406.

15. Darlene Clark Hine, ed., *Black Women in America* (Brooklyn: Carlson Publishers, 1993), p. 812.

16. Queen Mother Moore formed the Reparations Committee of Descendants of United States Slaves, Inc., along with Daraubakari. In 1962, they presented a reparations petition to the United Nations; Winbush, *Should America Pay?*, p. 203.

17. William van der Burg, *New Day in Babylon: The Black Power Movement and American Culture, 1965–1975* (Chicago: University of Chicago Press: 1992), p. 8; James Baldwin, *No Name in the Street* (New York: Dial, 1972), pp. 119–120; the Malcolm X quote is from C. Eric Lincoln, *The Black Muslims in America* (Grand Rapids, Mich.: Eerdmann's Publishing Company, 1994; first published 1961), p. 92. Malcolm X did not repudiate reparations even after he left the Nation of Islam.

18. Martin Luther King, Jr., *Why We Can't Wait* (New York: Harper & Row, 1964), p. 134; James Bolner, "Toward a Theory of Racial Reparations," *Phylon* 29 (Spring 1968): 41–47; Kyle Haselden and Whitney M. Young, Jr., "Should There Be Compensation for Negroes?," *The New*

York Times Magazine, October 6, 1963, p. 43ff.; Graham Hughes, "Reparation for Blacks?," *New York University Law Review* 43 (December 1968): 1063–1074.

19. Berry and Blassingame, *Long Memory,* p. 406.
20. Ibid., pp. 218–221.
21. August Maier and Elliott Rudwick, *Black Detroit and the Rise of the UAW* (New York: Oxford University Press, 1979), pp. 162–174; Chris Jenkins and Hamil Harris, "Descendants of Slaves Rally for Reparations: Organizers Call Event Milestone in Movement," *The Washington Post,* August 18, 2002, p. 1.
22. John Conyers, Jr., with Jo Ann Nicholls Watson, "Reparations: An Idea Whose Time Has Come," in Winbush, *Should America Pay?,* pp. 14–21.
23. 50 U.S.C. Ann. Sec 1989; *Hohri v. United States,* 482 U.S. 64 (1987); 782 F2d 227 (1987); 842 F2d 779 (1988).
24. *Hohri v. United States,* 482 U.S. 64 (1987); 782 F2d 227 (1987); 842 F2d 779 (1988); Judge Skelly Wright's opinion; 586 F Supp. 769 (1984); Rhonda Magee, "The Master's Tools, from the Bottom Up: Responses to African American Reparations Theory in Mainstream and Outsider Remedies Discourse," *Virginia Law Review* 79, no. 863 (1993): 863–905.
25. Conyers with Watson, "Reparations," pp. 14–21.
26. Ibid. In 2000, Congressman Tony Hall of Ohio proposed a formal resolution to acknowledge and apologize for slavery. It, like Conyers's bill that he keeps reintroducing and the ex-slave pension legislation of Callie House, has never emerged from committee.
27. *Cato v. United States,* 70 F. 3d 1103 (9th Circuit, 1995) caused little stir, perhaps because it involved only three plaintiffs and commanded little media attention. It was dismissed for lack of standing, lack of jurisdiction, and the inability to overcome sovereign immunity. They proceeded pro se, but Eva Patterson and William McNeil of the Lawyers Committee for Civil Rights of San Francisco represented them pro bono on appeal. After District Judge Saundra Brown Armstrong dismissed the complaint, the court of appeals affirmed her order.
28. *Obadele v. United States,* 52 Fed. Cl. 432 (2002).
29. Ibid.
30. Daedria Farmer-Pallman describes her involvement in Winbush, *Should America Pay?,* pp. 22–31; Michael Orey, "Federal Suits Against Three U.S. Companies Seek Damages for Descendants of Slaves," *The*

New York Times, March 27, 2002, p. B10; Darryl Fears, "Aging Sons of Slaves Join Reparations Battle," *The Washington Post,* September 30, 2002, p. A3.

31. Tatsha Robertson, "Reparations for Slavery: An Old Idea Goes Mainstream," *The Boston Globe,* April 4, 2002, p. A1.

32. "Lawyers Hope Tulsa Case Can Lay Foundation for More Claims," *The Boston Globe,* February 26, 2003; Oklahoma Commission to Study the Tulsa Race Riot of 1921, Final Report (2001), available at www .ok-history.mus.ok.us/trrc/freport.pdf; Scott Ellsworth, *Death in a Promised Land: The Tulsa Race Riot of 1921* (Baton Rouge: Louisiana State University Press, 1982).

33. "Lawyers Hope Tulsa Case Can Lay Foundation for More Claims," *The Boston Globe,* February 26, 2003.

34. Jeremy Levitt, "Black African Reparations: Making a Claim for Enslavement and Systematic De Jure Segregation and Racial Discrimination Under American and International Law," *Southern University Law Review* 25, no. 1 (1997): 30–32.

35. Adjoa A. Aiyetoro, "Formulating Reparations Litigation Through the Eyes of the Movement," *New York University Annual Survey of American Law* 58 (2003): 457.

36. Levitt, "Black African Reparations," p. 32; William L. Patterson, ed., *We Charge Genocide: The Crime of the Government Against the Negro People* (New York: International Publishers, 1951).

37. Glenn Kessler, "IRS Paid $30 Million in Credits for Slavery," *The Washington Post,* April 13, 2002, p. 1; *United States v. Bridges,* 217 Fd. 3rd 841 2000 WL 931448 (4th Cir. Va.).

38. Chris Jenkins and Hamil Harris, "Descendants of Slaves Rally for Reparations: Organizer Calls Event Milestone in the Movement," *The Washington Post,* August 18, 2002, p. C1. In another new departure, Brown University president Ruth Simmons, the first black president in the Ivy League, established a committee to explore reparations in the context of a founders' involvement with the slave trade. Simmons noted that the building in which her office is located was built with the labor of slaves. *NBC Today,* March 30, 2004, WL56560808.

INDEX

Page numbers in *italics* refer to illustrations.

abolitionists, 12, 13, 255*n*

Abrams, G. T., 134

Adams, Henry, 29–30, 32

Addams, Jane, 147

Administrative Procedure Act
  (APA; 1946), 133, 248

Aetna Insurance Company, 245–6

affirmative action, 239, 242

Africa: black nationalism and, 231,
  233, 234–5, 237; emigration
  movement and, 28–30, 32, 33

African-American Repatriation
  League, 239

African Methodist Episcopal
  (A.M.E.) Church, 14, 19, 33, 72,
  264*n*; in Boone County, 104–7

African Methodist Episcopal
  Church Sunday School Union
  Publishers, 51

African Repository, 30

Afro-Creoles, 20–1, 118–19

agriculture, 18, 95–6, 102;
  depression in, 107, 108–9; land

distribution and, 11–13; radical
  organizations and, 26–7;
  sharecropping and, 13, 26, 102

Aiyetoro, Adjoa, 244

Akers, Gilbert, 102

Alger, Russel, 117

Allen, Richard, 64

Alston, Christopher, 241–2, *241,
  244, 249, 250*

American Colonization Society
  (ACS), 28–9, 30, 33

*American School of Magnetic
  Healing v. J. M. McAnnulty,*
  157–8

Ammond, Molly, *219,* 222

Amnesty Proclamation (1865), 12,
  178–9

antilynching efforts, 145, 147, 164,
  173, 189, 196, 213, 264*n*

Armstrong, Saundra Brown, 294*n*

Ash, Rebecca, 61

Atkins, William, 169, 201, 204,
  284*n*

Index

Atlanta, Ga., 11, 14, 66–7, 138; Association chapter in, 94, 137, 148, 218
Atlanta Constitution, 136–7, 218

Badger, Rainey, 91–2
Baird, William, 82
Baker, Howard, 285*n*
Banks, Nathaniel, 120
Baptists, 14, 19, 55, 104, 105–6, 213; Primitive, 55, 59, 69, 120, 216–17, 236
Barnes, Ervard (Edward), 119, 271*n*
Barrett, Harrison, 81–5, 88–90, 92, 123–8, 132, *160,* 265*n*; indictment of, 140, 274*n*
Bartlett, Charles, 75
Bashir, Chief Judge, 245
Beal, R. L., 107
beatings, 7, 8, 10, 97
Belknap v. Schild, 281*n*
Bell, Lillie J., 119, 271*n*
Belle Meade Plantation, *57*
Bendy, Edgar and Minerva, *219,* 220
Berry, Frances Southall, 217
Bilbo, Theodore, 237
Biller, U. A., 197
Bill of Rights, U.S., 195
Birth of a Nation (movie), 227–8
Bittker, Boris, 279*n*
Black, William, 269*n*
Blackburn, Edmond Spencer, 149, 156
"Black Capitalism" campaign, 240
Black Manifesto (Forman), 239–40
Black Muslims, 235, 237

black nationalism, 230–40; separatist state and, 236, 238–9; UNIA and, 231–7, *232,* 249, 251
Black Star Steamship Line, 233, 234–5
black women: in Civil War, 9, *9,* 10–11; education and, *16;* militant organizations of, 189; political role of, 22, 24, *25;* professional, 214
Blair, Henry, 42–3
Blight, David, 227
Blue Fox case, 280*n*
Bon Weir, Tex., Association chapter in, 197–8
Boone, John William "Blind," 104, 109
Boone County, Missouri, 93–117, *112, 113*
Botkin, Bill, 70, 72
Botkin, Jeremiah, 70
bounties, 34, 42, 75, 76, 202
Boyce, Cinthia, 102
Boyd, Hadley, 151
Boyd, Henry, 119, 271*n*
Boyd, Lottie L., 119
Boyd, Richard Henry, 70, 144, 214, 273*n*
Brandeis, Louis, 279*n*
Brashears, Amanda and Scott, 111, 114
Brewer, David, 158
Bridges, Gregory, 249
Briggs, Cyril, 234
Brooks, Walter, 72–3
Brooks-Higginbotham, Evelyn, 189
Brown, Elsa Barkley, 262*n*

Index

Brown, Henry, 158
Brown, John, 246
Brown, Lillie, 116
Brown, William D., 119, 271*n*
Broxton, Richard, 224
Bruton, Mrs. John, 97
Burleson, Albert Sidney, 191
Burroughs, Nannie Helen, 262*n*
Burton, Phillip S., 119, 271*n*
Butler, Peter, 28–9

Cailloux, André and Félicie, 48
Cannon, Joseph, 73–5
Canton, Miss., Jones in, 185–6
Carr, Benjamin, 169
Carruthers, James, 236
Carswell, G. Harold, 285*n*
Cavender, "Mistress" Lea, 119, 271*n*
cemeteries, 59, 64, 215–16, 290*n*
Centennial Exposition (1897), 66–9
Chase, Calvin, 72–3, 90, 174, *175*, 184, 266*n*
Chateauvert, Melinda, 189
Cheatham, Henry P., 39–40, *41*, 46
Childress, Wiley, 12
Christian Century, 239–40
Christian College, 102
Christiancy, George, 136
Christmas v. Russell, 280*n*
churches, black, 13, *13*, 14, 102, 104–5, 262*n*; civil rights and, 50; education and, 18–19; emigrationist idea and, 30, 33; mutual aid societies and, 64, 65; political role of, *13*, 22; reparations movement and, *13*, 50–1, 104, 169

churches, white, 8, 14
Civil Liberties Act (1988), 243
civil rights, 44, 65, 72, 143, 144, 179, 204, 287*n*-8*n*
Civil Rights Act (1866), 247–8
Civil Rights Congress, 248
civil rights movement (1960s), 50, 239
Civil War, U.S., 8–11, *9*, 42, 97; blacks in, 9–10, *9*, 20, 21, 24, 30, 47, 61, 72, 97–100, *99*, 109; in Boone County, 97–100; contraband camps in, 55, 56; cotton tax and, 176, 180; devastation of South in, 37; emigration and, 29; guerrillas in, 98–100, 268*n*; meaning of, 225–9; postmaster general in, 85–6; veterans' pensions and, 34, *35*, 44, 47–9, 61, 72–5, 109, 120–1, 149, 150, 225
Clansman, The (Dixon), 228
Clark, Augustus, 197–8, 287*n*
Clay, Henry and July, 111
Clift, J. W., 152, 202
clothes, 8, 96, 218
Cochran, Johnnie, 246–7
Cohen, Cathy, 230
colonization, in Africa, 28–30, 32
Colored American, 174
Colored Farmers' National Alliance and Cooperation Union, 26
Colored Methodist Episcopal Church, 14
Colored Relief Society, 65
"Colored Soldier, The" (Dunbar), 47

Columbia, Mo., 104, 107, 108, 115;
  Association chapter in, 93–6, 105;
  economic distress in, 109, 111
Commission on Wartime
  Relocation and Internment of
  Civilians, 242
Comstock, Anthony, 86
Comstock Law (1873), 86
Confederacy, 8–11, 37, 55, 150,
  225–8; black conventions in,
  20–2, 24; guerrillas in, 98–100,
  268*n*
Congress, U.S., *9*, 29, 39–43, 72–6,
  174, 186, 242–5; blacks in, 39–42,
  40, 41; cotton tax suit and, 176,
  178, 179–80; freedmen's pensions
  and, 34, 39–42, *40, 41*, 46, 60–1,
  62–3, 75–6, 79, 84, 91, 118, 125,
  128–32, *130*, 147, 148–9, 154, 167,
  170, 172, 191, 224; Japanese-
  American Redress and, 242–4;
  petitioning of, 6, 59, 60, *62–3*,
  79, 118, 125, 128, 131, 167, 170;
  post offices and mails regulated
  by, 85–7, 159–62, 182, 281*n*-2*n*;
  veterans' pensions and, 34, 47,
  73–5; *see also* House of
  Representatives, U.S.; Senate,
  U.S.
Connell, William J., 34, 271*n*
Connell pension bill, 34–5, 37,
  271*n*; lack of black congressional
  support for, 39–42, *40, 41*
Consolidated American Baptist
  Convention, 14
Constitution, U.S., 19, 85, 123, 128,
  172; *see also specific amendments*

constitutions, state, 21, 24–5, 27
contrabands, 8–10, *9*, 14, 55, 56, 98
Convention of Colored Men of
  Louisiana, 20, 21
Conyers, John, 244, 246, 249, 294*n*
Cooper, Edward, 131–2, 174
Cornish, Samuel, 59
Corps d'Afrique, 120
Cortelyou, George, 161
cotton tax suit, *175*, 176–83, *177*,
  186, 188, 244, 279*n*-82*n*
Covenant on Civil and Political
  Rights, 249
Crosby, B. F., 154, 155
Crumpacker, Edgar, 160–1
CSX Railroad, 245–6
Cuba, 117, 271*n*
Cuddy, H. V., 165
Cummings, Charles, 105–6
Cummings School (later Frederick
  Douglass Academy), 106

Daugherty, Harry M., 233
Davis, Nelson, 48
Dawson, Michael, 230
Debs, Eugene, 152
debts, 18, 24
Declaration of Independence, U.S.,
  89, 171
Democrats, Democratic Party, 27,
  33, 43, 70, 169, 173, 183, 212;
  freedmen pensions and, 34, *35*,
  128; Home for Ex-Slaves Bill
  and, 75; in Louisiana, 117, 119–20
Desdunes, Daniel, 118
desegregation, 242
Detroit, Mich., 239, 241–2

Index

Devans, G. R., 66

Diamond, Frederick S., 119, 271*n*

Dick, Robert Abraham Lincoln, 146–52, 154, 157, 202

Dickerson, Isaiah H., 44–6, *45,* 50–1, 59, 154–7, 162–5, 202, 277*n*; as Association general manager, 75, 82, 94–5, 125, 126, 135–9, 145, 148; Barrett's correspondence with, 82, 126; conviction overturned for, 137–8, 173; death of, 167; imposters and, 164–5; jailing of, 136, 138; Pension Bureau deposition of, 152, 154, 276*n*; press clippings about, 136–7; as Vaughan's agent, 44, *45,* 51, 152, 154

Dickson, Harris, 185

diet, 58, 65, 96, *103,* 208

Disciples of Christ, 69

District of Columbia Court of Appeals, 180, 243

Dixon, Thomas, 228

domestic workers, 52–4, 96

Douglas, Lee, 191–6, 202–3

Douglass, Frederick, 20, 38–9, *38,* 178, 179, 229

DuBois, W. E. B., 19, 190, 234

due process, 160–1, 247

Dunbar, Paul Laurence, 47

Dunn, Richard, 164–5

Eagleton, Thomas, 285*n*

Eaton, Lillie, 114

Eaton, Willie, 107

Edgehill contraband camp, 55, 260*n*

education, 14–19, *16, 23,* 24, 123, 231, 256*n*; Blair bill and, 42–3; in Boone County, 105–6; college, 18–19, 40, 41, 42, 51, 68, 144, 169; federal aid for, 39–43, *40,* 79; segregation and, 42, 106, 144, 186, 213; teachers and, 15, 17, *17,* 18–19, 106, 214; vocational, 90, 233, 291*n*; white fears about, 15, 17–18

elections: of 1860, 120; of 1864, 21; of 1868, 22, 24; of 1890, 41, 42, 43; of 1896, 174; of 1900, 85, 143; of 1904, 143, 161; of 1908, 143, 166, 169; of 1910, 169; of 1911, 68–9; of 1912, 169, 173, 183; of 1916, 197; federal supervision of, 43, 79

elite, black, 4, 6, 65–9, 72, 79, 90–1, 118–19, 131, 234, 240

Emancipation Proclamation, 21, 35

emigration, 28–33; African, 28–30, 32, 33; Kansas movement and, 30–3, *31,* 91, 95

Emigration Convention (1854), 29

employment, 26, 52–5, 117, 217, 231; in Boone County, 95–6, 101–2, 108–9, 111; pay disputes and, 94; segregation and, 173; *see also* domestic workers; washerwomen

equality, 37, 44, 67, 135, 229, 242

Essence, 249

Estes, Armstead, 104

Estes, Sanford, 105

Evans, H. Clay, 129, 138, 142, 150, *153*

Everleaner, Aunt, 4, 217

Exodus to Kansas Movement, 30–2
ex-slaves, *see* freedmen

family separations, 7, 8, 10, 97,
    268*n*
Farmer-Paellmann, Deadria, 245–6
Farrington v. Saunders, Collector,
    280*n*
Fields, Luvenia, 93, 95
Fields, Reuben, 93, 95
Fifteenth Amendment, 107, 174,
    226
Fifth Amendment, 243
First African Benevolent Society of
    Columbia, 105
First Amendment, 139, 195
Fisher, Hubert, 183, 184, 186
Fisk University, 19, 51, 215
Fleet Boston Financial, 245–6
Fleming, Walter, 267*n*
Ford, Gerald, 242
Forman, James, 239–40
Fortress Monroe, *9*
Fourteenth Amendment, 172, 174,
    179, 226, 247
fraud charges: Association accused
    of, 81–94, 122–41, 145–52, 154–69,
    172, 202–3; congressional
    modifications and, 182, 281*n*-2*n*;
    against Garvey, 235; history of
    regulation of mail use for, 85–7;
    against House, 190–204, 211;
    against Jones, 182–6, 190; lifting
    of, 149–50, 152; against local
    agents, 172; Mullins's
    appeasement and deference
    efforts and, 134–5; new officers'

strategy and, 152, 162, 163;
    publication of Barrett's notice
    about, 90–1, 127; second order
    of, 157; Supreme Court's
    strengthening of, 157–8
Frazier, E. Franklin, 22, 188, 235
Frazier, Garrison, 11
Free African Society, 64
free blacks, 14, 40–1, 98, 102, 116;
    emigration movement and,
    28–32; freedmen's relationship
    with, 20–1; political role of, 19,
    20–1, 24
freedmen: bushwackers vs., 100;
    education of, 14–19; emigration
    and, 29–30; land promised to,
    11–13, 20, 39, 72, 225; political
    activities of, 19–25, *23, 25*;
    poverty of, 11, 13, 14, 37, 49, 51,
    55–6, 60, 65, 66, 75, 79, 84, 88,
    100–1, 106–9, 111, 114–16, *115*, 159,
    173, 251; reparations cause of, *see*
    reparations
Freedmen's Bureau, 10–11, 22, 42,
    178, 247; education and, 15, 18,
    19, 43, 106
Freedmen's Bureau Act (1865), 12
Freedmen's Headlight, 154–5, 156
"Freedmen's Pension Bill"
    (Vaughan), 33–4, *36, 46*
Fugitive Slave Act (1850), 28

Gaines, James, 75
Gallinger, Jacob, 128, 129, *130*
Galveston, Tex., laundresses in, 189
Garth, Jefferson, 111
Garvey, Marcus Moziah, 231–7, *232*

Gary, Willie, 246–7

Georgia State Supreme Court, 137–8

Germany, 248

Gettysburg, fiftieth anniversary of, 227

Gettysburg Address, 226

Ghana, 237

Gibson v. Mississippi, 174

Gilchrist, Robert E., 152, 157, 162–3, 277*n*

Gilvin, G. R., 209, 288*n*-9*n*

Gitlow v. United States, 195

Gizzard, Eph, 65

Globe, 70, 144, 213

Goldman, Emma, 204, 206–10, *207,* 288*n*-9*n*

Goodwin, R. F., 162–3

Gosling, Joseph, 111

Gosling, Sylvester, 111

Gosling, W. H., 59

governmental (sovereign) immunity, 179–81, 243, 247, 248

Grand Army of the Republic, 150–1, *153*

"grandfather clauses," 27

grand juries, blacks excluded from, 174

Grant, Ulysses S., 24, 30

Graves, Sarah, *219*

Great Britain, 129, 147, 233, 234

great migration, 213–14, 224–5

Green, Constance, 266*n*

Green, George A., 119, 154–5, 271*n*

Greenaway, W. E., 166

Gregory, Thomas, 191, 204

Griffith, D. W., 227–8

Grimke, Francis, 72–3

Guy, Amanda "Mandy," 52, 125, 126, 167, 171, 290*n*

Guy, Ann, 27, 28, 33

Guy, Annie Mary, 52

Guy, Callie, *see* House, Callie Guy

Guy, Charles, 52, 54–5, 125, 126, 167, 171, 216, 217, 259*n*, 290*n*

Guy, Sarah, *see* House, Sarah Guy

Guy, Tom, 9–10

Hadan, Peter, 109

Hadley, John L., 169

Hair, W. R., 168–9

Hall, Tony, 294*n*

Hannon, Ellis Ken, 13

Harlem, 233, 237, 238

Harlem Renaissance, 213, 215

Harris, Samuel, 291*n*

Harris, Samuel P., 68–9

Harrison, Hubert, 234

Harrison, William Henry, 43

Hayes, Rutherford B., 30, 32, 140

Heflin, Thomas, 168

Henderson, C. C., 26

Hewlett, Emanuel D. Molyneaux, 174, 176, 184

Hill, Louis, 269*n*

Hill, P. F., 46, 70, 264*n*

Hill, Richard, 67–8

Hill, Zema W., 216–17, 290*n*

Hitchcock, Ethan A., 138, 168

Hoar, George, 129

Hohri v. United States, 243

Holmes, Brunsey R., 218, *223*

Holmes, Kizza, 218

Holmes, Oliver Wendell, 158, 285*n*

Holmes, Savannah, 218
Home for Ex-Slaves Bill, 72–5
Hooper, Ben W., 169
Hoover, Herbert, 224
House, Annie, 28, 125, 132, 167, 217, 257*n*, 290*n*; employment of, 126, 171, 194, 289*n*
House, Callie Guy: appearance of, 165, 194, 200, 204, 286*n*; arrest of, 191, 194; background of, 6, 8–10, 14–15, 27; death of, 4, 215–16, 236, 254*n*, 289*n*-90*n*; education of, 14–19, 27, 123, 189; federal officials' fear of, 4, 7, 85, 92, 124, 131, 138–9, 156–7; government charges against, 186–204, 224; imprisonment of, 7, 194, 204–11, *205*, 231, 235, 286*n*, 288*n*; indictment of, 191–2, 211; isolation of, 189–90; lack of respectability of, 186–7, 189; as laundress, 4, 6, 33, 52–4, 58, 125, 189, 212; libeling protested by, 127–8; marriage of, 28; as mother, 6, 28, 33, 125, 126, 132, 167, 171, 189, 194, 257*n*; Nashville residences of, 4–5, 52, 194, 212, 259*n*; photographs of, 76, *77, 78*; poor economic circumstances of, 6, 125–6, 194, 211; public speaking of, 94–5, 145, 152, 171; as racial outlaw, 3–4, 89; as seamstress, 52, 125, 189, 209, 212; as slave, 6, 8, 21; travels of, 81–2, 94–6, 104, 116–21, 122, 125, 132, 152, 167, 194; Vaughan's pension idea and, 34, 37–9, 42–6; *see also*

National Ex-Slave Mutual Relief, Bounty and Pension Association
House, Charles, 27, 28
House, Delphia, 28, 125, 132, 139, 167, 257*n*, 290*n*; employment of, 126, 171, 194
House, Mattie, 28, 125, 132, 167, 218, 257*n*, 290*n*; employment of, 126, 171, 194
House, Mrs. William, 217
House, Ross, 217
House, Sarah Guy, 27, 52
House, Thomas, 28, 125, 132, 167, 217, 257*n*, 290*n*; employment of, 126, 171, 194, 289*n*; letters to, 165–6; lot purchased and sold by, 211; mother's bond and, 194, 284*n*
House, William (father), 28, 33, 259*n*
House, William (son), 28, 125, 132, 167, 217, 257*n*; employment of, 126, 171, 194, 289*n*
House of Representatives, U.S., 41, 42, 43, 73, 149, 271*n*; Appropriations Committee of, 73–5
Howard, Oliver, 12
Howard University, 12, 42
Howse, Hilary, 218
Hudson, James, 104
Hulett, H. B., 97

Independent Order of St. Luke, 262*n*
Indian monies, 178, 280*n*

Industrial Council, 156–7, 276*n*, 277*n*
Ingraham, James, 20
Internal Revenue Service, 249
international law, 248–9
International Migration Society, 33

Jackson, Claiborne Fox, 98
Jackson, Jim, 100
Jackson, Miss., laundresses in, 189
Jackson, Samuel A., 119, 271*n*
Jackson, William Harding, Jr., 57
Jamaica, 233, 234
Japanese-American Redress, 242–5
Japanese-American Redress Law (1989), 243–4
Jefferson, Thomas, 28
Jefferson City, Mo., State Prison in, 204–11, *205*
Jenkins, "Reparations" Ray, 244, 249, *250*
Jewell, William, 97
Johnson, Andrew, 12, 178–9
Johnson, Charles S., 215
Johnson, J. Albert, 72–3
Johnson v. McAdoo, 183, 280*n*
Jones, Absalom, 64
Jones, Cornelius, 173–6, *175*, 178–87, 189, 230, 244; cotton tax suit and, 176–83, 186, 279*n*-82*n*; government attack on, 181–6
Jones, Elaine, 263*n*
Jones, James T., 119, 271*n*
Jones, Jennie, 119
Jones, Thomas (attorney), 162
Jones, Tom (father), 119, 120

Jones, Tom (Marcellin Zephilin; son), 119–21
Justice Department, U.S., 84, 127, 140, 148, 172, 191, 196, 198, 242; Office of Redress Administration in, 243; Pitts's correspondence with, 182–3

Kansas, 95, 99; emigration movement and, 30–3, *31*, 91, 95
Kansas City Association chapter, 94, 148
Keene, G. B., 159
Kendrick, George M., 215
Kentucky, 31, 98, 134
King, Martin Luther, 239
Ku Klux Klan, 25–6

Ladies' Relief Society, 65
Lamar v. United States, 286*n*
land, 19, *23*, 79, 101, 107, 178–9, 238, 255*n*, 269*n*; emigration and, 29, 31–2; fraudulent deals and, 182; promised to freedmen, 11–13, 20, 39, 72, 225
Lang, John, Jr., 104
Langston, John Mercer, 39, *40*, 41–2, 46, 70
Langston, Lucy, 41
Lawson, Edward, 111
Lawson, William C., 127, 145
Lawyers Committee for Civil Rights Under Law, 244
League of Nations, 234
Liberia, 28–30, 32, 33
Lincoln, Abraham, 12, 21, 35, 98, 147, 226

Index

Living My Life (Goldman), 206–11, *207*
Lodge, Henry, 43
Logan, Rayford, 7
lotteries, 86–7, 158
Louisiana, 20–1, 24, 30, 31, 116–21, 155, 197
lynching, 32, 65, 68, 84, 108, 143, 188, 196, 213, 237, 247; *see also* antilynching efforts

McAdoo, William G., 178, 180, 280*n*, 281*n*
McCall, John Ethridge, 183–4
McGee, Perry, 269*n*
Mack, Creasy, 114
McKinley, William, 68, 85, 88, 92, 117, 135, 161, 184
McKinley Tariff (1890), 43
McNairy, Dudley, *74, 75,* 76, 125, 127, 134, 135, 261*n*
McNeil, William, 294*n*
Malburn, William S., 178, 180
Malcolm X, 237–8
Malcolm X Society, 239
marriage, 102, 104, 158
Martin, Drucilla and Richard, *114*
Martinet, Louis, 118–19, 271*n*
Mason, Luke, 59, 261*n*
Mason, Squire, 59, 261*n*
Mason, William, 75, 76, 118, 128–9, 167, 271*n*
Mason Ex-Slave Pension Bill, 73, *74,* 75, 76, 79, 118, 125, 128, 167, 270*n*-1*n*
Masons, 105
Mathew, Phillip, 119, 271*n*

Mays, Benjamin, 89
medical services, 58, 115, 142, 147, 213
Meharry Medical College, 51, 144
Memphis, Tenn., 21, 44, 183–4, 262*n*
Memphis Commercial Appeal, 184–5
Merritt, Clarence, 197–200
Methodists, 14, 104
middle class: black, 51, 66, 144, 189–90, 230, 234; white, 61
Miller, Thomas E., 39, 40–1, *41,* 46
"Millions for Reparations Rally," 249
ministers, black, 14, 33, 72–3, 104, 273*n*; fraud complaints and, 82–3; political role of, 11, 21; Primitive Baptist, 55, 59, 120, 216–17, 236
Mississippi, *17,* 31, 37, 89
Missouri, 93–117
Missouri Compromise (1820), 97
Missouri State Prison, 204–11, *205*
Mitchell, Stanley P., 156, 276*n*, 277*n*
Moore, Audrey (Queen Mother), 237–8, *238,* 249
Morgan, John, 33
Morris, Alden, 50
Morris, Myer, 284*n*
Moten, Parker, 162
Mouton, Alexandre, 119–20
Mt. Ararat Cemetery, 215–16, 290*n*
Mueller v. Oregon, 279*n*
mulattoes, 11, 40–2
Mullins, J. B., 134–5

Murfreesboro, Tenn., 15, 26, 51, 52, 212

mutual assistance fraternities, 59, 60, 69, *76*, 105, 115, 143, 229, 262*n*, 263*n*, 271*n*; Association as, 61, 64–5, 122, 129, 131, 132, 135, 142, 147, 148, 155–6, 159, 163, *164*, 170, 172, 202, 218, 262*n*; in New Orleans, 64, 117–18; women's, 262*n*

NAACP (National Association for the Advancement of Colored People), 143, 164, 189–90, 213, 215, 228, 234, 244

NAACP-LDF, 263

Napier, James C., 67, 69, 70, 169, 214

Nashville, Tenn., 10, 52–60, 66–70, 132, 137, 169, 212–18; author's first homes in, 4; benevolent institutions in, 65; "Black Bottom" in, 55, 260*n*; black nationalists in, 236; black professional class in, 23, 144, 214–15; Centennial Exposition in, 66–9; city directories of, 54, 126, 166, 217–18, 236, 259*n*, 261*n*, 267*n*, 290*n*; commercial laundries in, 53–4; contraband camps in, 55, 56, 260*n*; education in, 19, 144, 169, 213; emigration movement and, 29, 33; Hadley Park in, 169, 213; House's residences in, 4–5, 52, 194, 212, 259*n*; lynching in, 65; Mt. Ararat Cemetery in, 215–16, 290*n*;

Nineteenth Annual Convention in, 169–70; political activism in, 21–2; postmaster in, 85, 124, 125, 133–6, 138, 154, 165–6, 170; reparations movement in, 50–1, 69–70, 144; segregation in, 58–9, 213, 215; smallpox in, 58, 65; streetcar boycott in (1905), 144, 158–9; Vaughan's visit to, 46; white neighborhoods in, 3, 56

Nashville *Colored Tennessean*, 21–2

Nashville Provident Association, 65

Nashville Tenn Daily News, 154, 155–6

National Baptist Convention, 14, 262*n*

National Baptist Publishing Board, 51, 70, 144

National Black United Front, 249

National Coalition of Blacks for Reparations in America (N'COBRA), 244, *250*

National Convention of Colored Citizens of the United States (1864), 19–20

National Equal Rights League, 20

National Ex-Slave Mutual Relief, Bounty and Pension Association: agents of, 94, 125, 127, 135, 145, 154, 167, 197–8, 203, 236; Alston's knowledge about, 241, *241*; black nationalism compared with, 231, 235–6; chapters of, *13*, 93–121, 137, 139, 145, 148, 149–50, 155, 157, 159, 167, 170, 171, 172, 181, 186, 202, 212, 218, 231; chartering of, 59, 64, 69, 79, 83; demise of,

212, 225; dual mission of, 61, 64, 69, 122, 201; ex-slaves as victims of, 190, 191–2, 198–9; federal attack on, *see* fraud charges; fees and dues collected by, 79–80, 82, 94, 139, 145, 146, 191, 198, 201; financial problems of, 159; first convention of (1898), 60, 70–80, *71, 74, 77,* 81, 83; formula used by, 34, 75; Grand Army of the Republic vs., 150–1, *153;* House as leader of, 6, 152, 154, 156–70, 189, 262*n;* House as officer of, 6–7, 60, 69, 70, *71,* 73, 75, 81–5, 88–92, 94–6, 104, 106, 116, 122–8, 131–52, 155; House's stepping down in, 152, 156–7, 163, 202; membership and size of, 7, 60, 82–3, 85, 88, 94, 114–16, 135, 136, 137, 139, 145, 171, 186, 201; membership badge of, 192–4, *193,* 198; new officers selected by (1902), 152, 162, 163; Nineteenth Annual Convention of (1914), 169–70; organizing of, 50–2, 59–61, 69–80, *71, 74, 76-78,* 82, 122–5, 145, 157, 166, 172; original certificate of, 76, *76,* 79; as poor people's movement, 4, 6, 51–2, 90; self-help emphasis of, 61; Washington conventions of, 149, 166

National Industrial Advocate, 94, 134

National Urban League, 143

Nation of Islam, *see* Black Muslims

Negro World, 234, 236

New Orleans, La., 20, 64, 124, 237; Association chapter in, 93, 94, 116–21, 148, 155

New Orleans *Tribune,* 20

New York Times, 240

Nixon, Richard, 240

Nkrumah, Kwame, 237

Nuremberg trials, 248

Obadele, Imari, 239, 244–5

obscenity, 86

Ogletree, Charles, 244, 246–7

Oklahoma, 95, 186

Ovington, Mary White, 190

Packard foundry, 241–2

Page, R., 169, 284*n*

Parchment, Doc, 201

Parrish, Henry, 168

Patterson, Delicia, 269*n*

Patterson, Eva, 294*n*

Payne, Postmaster General, 140

Peace Movement of Ethiopia, 237

Peckham, Rufus, 158–9

pension act (1890), 47

Pension Bureau, U.S., 48, 88, 121, 127, 181, 202, 264*n*-5*n;* Association targeted by, 4, 82–4, 133, 140–1, 152, 163, 165, 166–7, 172, 198, 282*n*-3*n;* Dickerson's deposition at, 152, 154, 276*n;* Dick's letter sent to, 151; Pension Committee consultation with, 129; Vaughan's relations with, 46, 82, 92

pensions, 4, 19, *23,* 33–49, *35, 62-3;* black nationalism and, 235–6; as compensation for slavery, 4, 19, 23, 33–49, *35, 50–2, 60–1, 62–3,* 69, 70, 75–6, 79; *see also* National Ex-Slave Mutual Relief, Bounty and Pension Association; number eligible for, 148–9; summary of continuing belief in, 218–25, *219–23;* for Union army veterans, 34, *35,* 44, 47–9, 61, 72–5, 109, 120–1; Vaughan as advocate of, 33–9, *35*

Perkins, George, 72

Pettus, Edmund, 128

Philadelphia, Pa., mutual aid society in, 64

Pinchback, Pinckney Benton Stewart, 20

Pitts, Alexander R., 182–3, 191

Plessy, Homer, 118, 173

Plessy v. Ferguson, 116, 119

political activism, 19–27, *23;* church role in, *13,* 22; conventions and, 19–22, 24; Washington's discouragement of, 7

"Political Discussion, A," 25

Pollock v. Farmer's Loan and Trust Co., 281*n*

Populist Party, 27, 152

Post Office Department, U.S., 265*n;* Association problems with, 4, 81–90, 92, 122–41, 145–52, 154–69, 198; Dick's meeting with officials of, 147–9; Jones attacked by, 181–6; Lawson's correspondence with, 127; lotteries and, 86–7, 158; obscenity and, 86; Stephens's

appeal rejected by, 133; Supreme Court's strengthening of, 157–8; Vaughan's relations with, 92, 146; *see also* fraud charges

poverty, the poor, 29–34, *57;* black nationalism and, 230, 231, 240; emigration movement and, 29–32; of freedmen, *see* freedmen, poverty of; mutual aid societies and, 117–18; in Nashville, 55–6, 58; of slaves, 96–7; white, 26–7, *53, 65*

Powell, P., 236

Price, Sterling, 98, 99

Primitive Baptists, 55, 59, 69, 120, 216–17, 236

Providence Bank, 245–6

Public Clearing House case, 158

Pullman Porters Benevolent Association, 263*n*

Quarles, Ralph, 41–2

Queen Mother Moore Reparations Resolution for Descendants of Enslaved Africans, 246

Randolph, Asa Philip, 233, 234

Reconstruction, 11–18, 21–8, 116, 147, 225; in *Birth of a Nation,* 227–8; Civil Rights Acts and, 247–8; cotton tax suit and, 178–9; education and, 14–18; end of, 25–8, *31,* 39, 44; land distribution and, 11–13; political activism and, 21–6, *23, 25,* 30–1; state constitutions and, 21, 24–5

Reconstruction Act (1867), 21, 22

Reid, W. L., 81, 83

religion, 8; black nationalism and, 239–40; freedom and, *13,* 14, 19, *23,* 96, 97

reparations, 230–51; black nationalism and, 231, *232,* 235–40, *238*; Douglass's support for, *38,* 39; emigration and, 29; federal education aid as, 39–43, *40,* 79; Japanese-American Redress and, 242–5; land distribution and, 11–13; opponents of, 4, *38,* 39–44, *40, 41,* 70, 79, 143–4, 172, 190, 284*n*; petitioning for, 4, 6, 7, 59, 60, *62–3,* 69, 79, 94, 115, 116, 122, 125, 128, 131, 142, 145, 167, 170, 173, 186; Vaughan's pension advocacy and, 33–9, *35, 36,* 267*n*; *see also* National Ex-Slave Mutual Relief, Bounty and Pension Association

reparations lawsuit, 172–83; lawyers selected for, 173–6, *175*; *see also* cotton tax suit

Republican Banner, 55

Republicans, Republican Party, 22, 24, 26, 27, 39–43, 68, 143, 176, 212, 240; freedmen's pensions and, 70, 85, 128–9, 149; Home for Ex-Slaves Bill and, 72, 73

Republic of New Africa (RNA), 238–9, 244–5

respectability, 186–7, 189–90, 283*n*

Reunionists, 37, 150, 225–7

riots, 213, 234, 246–7

Roberts, Ernest, 73, 75

Rogers, A. W., 152, 162, 166

Roosevelt, Franklin D., 224, 237

Roosevelt, Theodore, 85, 140, 155, 161, 176, 184, 196; Washington's dinner with, 145, 152

Rosser, L. E. B., 166

runaway slaves, *31,* 98, 99, *99,* 100

Russell, Gordon James, 198, 286*n*

Russwurm, John, 59

Rutherford County, Tenn., 8, 14, 27–8, 33, 51, 58; black population of, 8, 27; black schools in, 14, 15, 18, 19, 123, 256*n*; in Civil War, 10

St. Paul's African Methodist Episcopal Church, 104, 105

Sanford, Edward T., 194–7, 199, 203, 285*n*

Savary, John, 13

Scott, Armond, 166

Scott, John, 236

seamstresses, 52, 108, 125, 126, 189, 209, 212

segregation, 28, 32, 65–8, 108, 131, 144–5, 179, 248; Centennial Exposition and, 66, 67–8; in education, 42, 106, 144, 186, 213; in Nashville, 58–9, 213, 215; in New Orleans, 116, 118–19; streetcar boycott and, 144, 158–9, 228–9; Wilson and, 169, 173, 228

self-help, 61, 229, 231, 236

Senate, U.S., 32, 43, 72, 149, 161, 167, 271*n,* 285*n*; Pensions Committee in, 128, 129, 131, 267*n*

Settlement House movement, 147

Shaw, Tiney, *219,* 221

Sherley, Swagar, 168

Sherman, William Tecumseh, 11, 12
shotgun houses, 52, 55
Silber, Nina, 227
Simmons, Ruth, 295*n*
Sims, Carlton, 26
Singleton, Benjamin "Pap," 30–2, 51
Sixteenth Amendment, 281*n*
slave owners, *110*; abuses by, 7, 8, 10, 89, 96, 97; compensation for, 98, 147; former, disenfranchisement and, 26; slaves taken south by, 98, *99*
slavery, slaves, 27, 39–40, 89, *110*, 225–7, 231, 237, 239, 245–6; abolition of, 10, 11, 19, 20, 21, 24, 37, 55, 98, 100, 226, 227; in Boone County, 95–100; contrabands, 8–10, *9*, 14, 55, 56, 98; emigration and, 28; pensions as compensation for, *see* National Ex-Slave Mutual Relief, Bounty and Pension Association; reparations; taken South, 98, *99*; Vaughan's views on, 37, 46
slave trade, 28, 245–6, 268*n*
smallpox epidemic (1895), 58, 65
Smith, A. R., 284*n*
Smith, Charles Emory, 89
Smith, H., 124
Smith, Nathan, 59
Smith, Squire, 111, *112*
Smith, W. B., 156
Smith, Wilford, 174
Society for the Suppression of Vice, 86

South, the: great migration and, 213–14, 224–5; pension plan as remedy for, *36*, 37, 42, 166; reconciliation and reunion and, 37, 150, 225–7
Southall, James M., 194
South Carolina State College for Negroes, 41
Southern Farmers' Alliance, 26
Southern Methodists, 14
Spanish-American War, 117
Stanton, Edwin, 11
State of Louisiana v. W. G. McAdoo, Secretary of Treasury, 281*n*
Stephens, H. Perry, 132–3, 194–7, 203
Stones River, Battle of (1862–63), 10
Straight University Law School, 118
Straun, Jake, 114
streetcar boycott (1905), 144, 158–9, 228–9
Student Nonviolent Coordinating Committee (SNCC), 239–40
Supreme Court, District of Columbia, 176
Supreme Court, Georgia State, 137–8
Supreme Court, U.S., 119, 174, 243, 280*n*, 281*n*, 285*n*; cotton tax suit and, 180, 182, 183, 186
Syracuse, N.Y., black convention in (1864), 19–20

Taft, William Howard, 166–7, 169, 286*n*
tariffs, 43

taxes, 18, 109, 159, 240, 249, 281*n*; cotton, *see* cotton tax suit; income, 84; poll, 26, 58, 109
Taylor, J. A., 72–3
Taylor, Preston, 69, 70, 158–9, 214–15
teachers: black, 15, *17*, 18–19, 106, 126, 214; white, 15, 17, *17*, 106
Tennessean, 200, 201, 202
Tennessee, 12–15, 20, 236; abolition in, 21, 55; Civil War in, 8–10, 21; education in, 14–15, 17–19, 144, 169, 213; emigration movement in, 29, 30–1, 33; end of Reconstruction in, 26; segregation in, 28, 58–9, 65, 66, 213, 215; *see also* Rutherford County, Tenn.; *specific cities and towns*
Tennessee Agricultural and Industrial (A&I) College, 144, 169, 213
Tennessee American, 194
Thirteenth Amendment, 174
Thurston, John, 129, 271*n*
Tillman, Dorothy, 246
Torrance, Eliakam "Ell," 150–1, *153*
Tourgee, Albion, 43–4, 118, 227
Treasury, U.S., 43, 72, 169, 224, 280*n*; cotton tax suit and, 176, 178, 179–80
Trieber, Jacob, 265*n*
Tubman, Harriet, 48–9
Tulsa, Okla., 1921 riot in, 246–7
Turner, Harriet, 111
Turner, Henry McNeal, 33, 264*n*

Turner, Phoebe, 111
Turner, Sandy, 111
Tuskegee Syphilis Study, 263*n*
Tuttle, John, 97
29th Colored Infantry Regiment, 9–10
Tyner, James, 89, 133, 159–60, *160,* 161, 265*n*; indictment of, 140, 274*n*

Union Army, 8–10, 44, 55, 100, 120; blacks in, 9–10, *9,* 20, 21, 24, 30, 47, 72, 98, 109, 119–21, 226; pensions for veterans of, 34, *35,* 44, 47–9, 61, 72–5, 109, 120–1, 149, 150, 225
United Brothers of Friendship, 105
United Nations, 248
United States v. Barnow, 286*n*
United Trans-Atlantic Society, 32
Universal Negro Improvement Association (UNIA), 231–7, *232,* 249, 251

vagrancy law, 108
Vaughan, Walter, 33–9, *35,* 44–6, 59, 60, 70, 92, 94, 137, 146, 151, 277*n*; Dickerson as agent for, 44, *45,* 51, 152, 154; motives of, 37, 46, 92, 166; Pension Bureau investigation of, 82, 267*n*; pension pamphlet of, 33–4, *36,* 46; "testimonial" letters sought by, 38–9
Vaughan's Justice Party, 151–2, 276*n*

Vicksburg, Miss., Association
    chapter in, 94, 148
Virginia, *9, 13,* 327
"Voices from the Tomb of the
    Slaves" (pamphlet), 185–6
voting rights, 7, 19–27, *23,* 58, 143,
    231; property qualifications and,
    24, 27; protection of, 39–42, *40*

Walker, Maggie Lena, 262*n*
Walters, Alexander, 72–3
Walton, Isaac, 265*n,* 276*n*
Warfield, Henry, 104
Warren, M. A., 168
washerwomen, 96, 108, 125, 126,
    189, 212; in Civil War, 9, *9,* 61;
    work of, 52–4, *53*
Washington, A. W., 139
Washington, Booker T., 4, 7, 32–3,
    66–9, 135, 190, 194, 233, 284*n,*
    291*n;* accommodationist speech
    of (1895), 66–7; at Centennial
    Exposition, 68, 69; Roosevelt's
    dinner with, 145, 152
Washington, D.C., 165, 262*n;*
    Association conventions in, 149,
    166; Association mass meeting in
    (1903), 156; ex-slave old age
    home proposed for, 72–5, 186;
    lobbyists in, 94, 127; reparations
    rally in, 249; segregation in, 173
Washington, D.C. *Colored
    American,* 131
Washington Bee, 72, 90, 174, *175,*
    181, 184, 186
Washington Evening Star, 91

Washington Post, 156, 162
Watson, J. D., 182–3
Watson, Tom, 26–7
Wells-Barnett, Ida B., 147, 189–90
Wheeler, H., 97
Whipper, William, 24
White, Edward, 158
White, Linda, 155
White, Thomas J., 107
Whitehead, M., 284*n*
whites, 24, 68, 169, 215, 236, 273*n;*
    black education limited by, 15,
    17–18; black nationalism and,
    234, 239, 240; in Boone County,
    98–102; class divisions of, 26;
    emigration movement and, 32,
    33; freedmen's emulating of, 108;
    in Kansas, 32; poor, 26–7, *53,* 65;
    reparations cause ridiculed by, 4,
    79, 88, 91; as teachers, 15, 17, *17,*
    106; Vaughan's pension plan and,
    37, 82, 91; as veterans, 47–8;
    violence used by, 7, 25–7, 30
white supremacy, 17–18, 25, 116, 131,
    227
Williams, Alice, 192
Williams, Dorcas, 109
Wills, Auderine, 111
Wills, A. W., 85, 124, 125, 133–6, 138,
    154, 155, 170, 272*n;* Thomas
    House letters and, 165–6
Wills, W. H., 276*n*
Wilson, J. H., 156
Wilson, Woodrow, 169, 173, 183,
    191, 197, 228
Woods, Allen, 111

Woods, Oliver, 114
World War I, 188, 213
World War II, 241, 242–3, 248
Worrill, Conrad, 249
Wright, J. Skelly, 243
Wright v. Ellison, 280*n*

Young, Whitney, 239
Young Men's Christian Association
  (YMCA), 86, 213

Zephilin, Marcellin (Tom Jones),
  119–21, 271*n*

A NOTE ON THE TYPE

This book was set in Adobe Garamond. Designed for the Adobe Corporation by Robert Slimbach, the fonts are based on types first cut by Claude Garamond (c. 1480-1561). Garamond was a pupil of Geoffroy Tory and is believed to have followed the Venetian models, although he introduced a number of important differences, and it is to him that we owe the letter we now know as "old style." He gave to his letters a certain elegance and feeling of movement that won their creator an immediate reputation and the patronage of Francis I of France.

Composed by North Market Street Graphics,
Lancaster, Pennsylvania
Printed and bound by R. R. Donnelley,
Harrisonburg, Virginia
Designed by Virginia Tan